Corporate Governance in Japan

Historical Roots from the Yamato to the Tokugawa Eras

Magdalena Jerzemowska

Routledge
Taylor & Francis Group
NEW YORK AND LONDON

First published 2025
by Routledge
605 Third Avenue, New York, NY 10158

and by Routledge
4 Park Square, Milton Park, Abingdon, Oxon, OX14 4RN

Routledge is an imprint of the Taylor & Francis Group, an informa business

ISBN: 978-1-032-80550-4 (hbk)
ISBN: 978-1-032-80651-8 (pbk)
ISBN: 978-1-003-49793-6 (ebk)

DOI: 10.4324/9781003497936

Typeset in Times New Roman
by Apex CoVantage, LLC

Contents

1 Japanese corporate governance

An introduction

To understand the contemporary economic, political, and strategic positions of countries, and the roots of important differences between their developmental experiences, it is necessary to place recent developments in their historical context.[1] There is no doubt that the distant past has had a significant impact not only on the shape of modern societies and states but also on their corporate governance systems.[2] Despite this, insufficient attention has been devoted to how the historical development of countries has influenced the relationship between economic actors and their ownership, and to placing the establishment of decision-making processes and controls to balance the interests of all stakeholders in their historic perspective. Rarely are the roots of corporate governance looked for in the ancient history of countries. This confirmed Aguilera and Jackson writing that the conceptualization of corporate governance in terms of its roots in social relations remains an unfulfilled challenge. Economic activity occurs within the context of social relations, and it is social action to the extent that it is oriented towards others.[3] The social dimension will be explored when tracing the roots of Japanese corporate governance.

Japan is of particular interest because it developed a unique model of corporate governance. Despite a general fascination with Japan and its history, the history of its corporate governance is not commonly known. It should be remembered that the term *corporate governance* was used for the first time in the mid-1970s, in the United States, and so only in the latter stages of the 20th century did it become the subject of worldwide debate by academics, regulators, executives, and investors.[4] However, many of the issues falling within the field of interest of contemporary corporate governance were developed in antiquity. Over the centuries, these problems were reflected in works such as Homer's *The Odyssey*, Shakespeare's *The Merchant of Venice*, and Adam Smith's *The Wealth of Nations*. Economic activity was carried out by people and various forms of organizations. These forms of business organization evolved over time, culminating in the establishment of joint-stock companies in 16th century (the first joint-stock company was created in Britain in 1553).[5] Walker argues that many characteristics of a joint-stock company (such as perpetual succession, the use of

DOI: 10.4324/9781003497936-1

a common seal, and management by a Committee or Board) appeared earlier in guilds, which in the 14th century began to be replaced by corporations.[6] Hence, enterprises (corporations) existed well before they were defined in law.

The use of the term *corporate governance* in reference to ancient times may be controversial. But its analysis, when a historical perspective is adopted, must take account of differences in the development of civilizations. Problems related to property ownership and its protection, the separation of ownership and control, embezzlement, fraud and even takeovers or bankruptcies were not uncommon in all ancient civilizations.[7] Corporations can be defined in several aspects. Hein cites the following early (1819) definition of a corporation – *an artificial being that is invisible, intangible, and existing only in contemplation of law*.[8] Corporations had such attributes as the right of formation by registration, limited liability, perpetual succession, the right to sue and be sued, to purchase and hold real property, to have a common seal, and to govern by enacting private by-laws and statutes. Its most important characteristics, being the essence of corporateness, were immortality (a perpetual succession of many persons) meaning that its interests or shares must be transferable, and individuality (acting as a single individual).[9] The definitions of corporation provided by Jensen and Meckling (1976) may be historically appropriate. They defined corporation as *a nexus of contracts* or *a compromise of interests*.[10] These definitions fully correspond to the characteristics of Japanese corporations developing during the period analysed in this book, especially from the 3rd century to 1600. The research presented here should be treated as a historical journey to find the roots of the current Japanese model of corporate governance.

It is possible to identify similarities or differences between the nature of corporate governance in given historical periods and indicate the consequences of the specific features of the particular systems. The level of development of ancient governance mechanisms, and methods of control, and their sophistication and complexity, are surprising. Some methods and tools developed in antiquity are still used today, for example, contracts written by scribes were used in ancient Babylon, accounts may be traced back to ancient Egypt, and property rights were recognized in ancient Greece. Governance systems and mechanisms changed frequently over time, so their detailed examination could be performed over short, specific periods. An analysis spanning many centuries can only be done in a general way; otherwise, it would be very extensive. Therefore, this study does not treat corporate governance as a rigid paradigm but rather considers its most important specific aspects, in particular, identified eras, due to the length of the historical period considered and the number of important events that took place in it. In each analysed era, an attempt is made to consider corporate governance, as K. Rost suggests,[11] in the context of social, regulatory, and market changes.

Corporate governance has gained increasing attention in recent years with many publications concerned with both national and international aspects. In a broader context, corporate governance is considered as *the system of laws, rules, and factors that control operations at a company*.[12] This view emphasizes the role of the state in corporate governance.[13] According to Baker and Quéré, the various state interventions in corporate governance, dating back well before the 20th century, were intended to facilitate revenue generation, contribute to military defense, and improve the administration of organizations.[14] Aguilera and Jackson draw attention to a growing literature illustrating the importance of politics in shaping corporate governance. They argue that political outcomes affect the distribution of power between social groups and that the institutionalization of ideas determined the nature of the firm. They define corporate governance as the *patterns of decision-making and control within corporations*.[15] At the organizational level, corporate governance reflects the control exercised by capital, labour, and management, resulting in diverse coalitions in which management is often at the centre of these interactions.[16] Political approaches regard institutions as the result of rules or constraints on behaviour, imposed by powerful groups.[17] These *rules of the game* include both formal rules (e.g. law and contracts) and informal rules (e.g. norms and customs).[18] Such rules characterize the structure of incentives and opportunities available to economic actors, so institutions influence economic performance. They are *humanly* devised constraints that structure political, economic, and social interaction.[19] Tricker writes that *whenever a principal has to rely on agents to handle his or her business, governance issues arise*.[20] Corporate governance also explores how culture (through religion or morals) affects the design of control mechanisms in organizations, by showing how governance mechanisms in organizations can be modified to address questions about norms, values, and social capital, or by generating information about governance mechanisms in *nonmarket* organizations.[21] In this book, it is understood, after Adrian Cadbury, as the way in which *ownership is directed and controlled*,[22] in the light of *the community in which firms operate, the political conditions, laws and regulations*, thus the environment in which entities operate.[23]

McCahery and Vermeulen propose a model of corporate governance that revolves around six key components which provide a link between the investor community, the business units, and the customers or society, depending on communication and conversation. The group (subsidiary)-level coordination is supported by connection, collaboration, and co-creation. They find that companies that embrace the six components are usually wealthier, healthier, and more competitive, and will encounter difficulties if they deviate from good corporate governance, a key source of a company's culture and competitiveness.[24] According to Larcker et al., structural measures of corporate governance, such as *board characteristics, stock ownership, institutional ownership, activist stock ownership, existence of debt-holders, mix of executive compensation, and antitakeover variables, may be divided into 14 governance constructs*. These may be called the parts of the jigsaw (some are smaller than others) creating corporate governance. Particular pieces of this puzzle relate to centuries (epochs) of the analysis of Japanese corporate governance and will be noted in the relevant chapters.[25]

Max Weber defined the state as *an entity which possesses a monopoly on the legitimate use of physical force in a particular territory*.[26] Baker and Quéré write that states have always existed in one form or another through the *arts of government* and that the state has governed and controlled corporate enterprises throughout history.[27] It should be stressed that although business enterprises have existed throughout history, the concept of the corporation as a primary organizational form for business enterprise is of more recent origin. The word *corporation* is derived from *corpus*, the Latin word for body, or a *body of people*. In Ancient Rome, corporate entities were created by law, and they were often associated with guilds or social clubs. In medieval Europe, churches were incorporated, as well as local governments. From the 15th century onwards, many European nations used joint-stock companies (i.e. corporations) to engage in colonial ventures, such as the Dutch East India Company or the British East India Company. Operating procedures and internal control practices of medieval merchant guilds were often set forth in the charters and by-laws of those entities. Thus, a corporation does not just involve a business enterprise but also a *body of people*.[28] In this book, the primary role of the state in corporate governance is considered in the period from 250 to the end of 16th century (Yamato (250–710), Nara (710–794), Heian (794–1185), Kamakura (1185–1336), Ashikaga (1336–1567), and the Azuchi–Momoyama Period (1568–1600)). The use of laws, rules, and regulations to control the operations of the state, and its provinces, villages, towns, families, and *shōen*, is highlighted. In other words, the governance and control of state-owned and privately owned lands and enterprises are characterized. In this research, Japan is compared to a business group or a large family, consisting of subordinated firms (corporations) more or less closely connected with the centre of power (or families with degrees of kinship and diverse personal relationships).

In the earliest periods of Japanese history, land was the most important and desired, but limited, property. The development and control of land ownership over 15 centuries is central to the formation of the governance system of the country. The functioning of clans and the creation of entities to protect and extend land ownership, and to make it less risky and more profitable, suggest that corporate governance mechanisms were present already at the dawn of Japanese history.

As noted earlier, many countries, even today, follow centuries-old traditions and customs, and this is especially true of Japan, which developed a unique model of corporate governance. This book analyses the key events of Japanese history from the beginning of the Yamato era to the creation of the Tokugawa *Shōgunate*, that is, from around the 3rd century to the 17th century, and it demonstrates how historical events affected corporate governance. It traces the reasons for the uniqueness of Japanese corporate governance, starting from the federation of the *uji* and the creation of the Yamato kingdom up to the Tokugawa *Shōgunate*. A general examination of Japanese history reveals the factors influencing stages of economic development, and culture, as well as the reasons (social, political, or economic) for the emergence of specific mechanisms and features of corporate governance. This study attempts to identify the roots of the main factors responsible for shaping the foundations of the current Japanese model of corporate governance. According to Morck and Steier, *the history of corporate governance in Japan is more complicated and variegated than in any other major country.*[29]

As the analysis concerns a country, governance is analysed in selected historical periods at two levels – macroeconomic and microeconomic. The macroeconomic level is concerned with the organization of the state, while the microeconomic level deals with the individual units within the state, such as *uji*, provinces, districts, villages, townships, and also *be* corporations, *shōen*, and *za* corporations. It should be noted that the changes took place mainly at the macro level, which focused on the interests of the ruling aristocracy, to which the micro level had to adapt. However, the individual units of the state were adapted in an innovative way to the requirements coming from above, focusing on maximizing their own interests. Changes were made to the distribution of decision rights, the responsibilities of organizations and their rules, the instruments for the selection of leaders, the monitoring of their actions, and the effectiveness of these mechanisms in the context of social, regulatory, and market changes.

The book comprises four chapters, which characterize the development of Japanese corporate governance up until the 17th century. After an introduction chapter, Chapter 1 characterizes the period of Japanese history from its dawn to 645 AD, the emergence of the Yamato state, and the main social, economic, and political issues taking place in this era. Special attention is paid to the reasons for state centralization efforts and issues concerning the creation of the resultant governance system in the emerging state. The Yamato state is characterized as the cradle of Japanese corporate governance. The then-existing Clan Federation is compared to today's enterprises competing to maintain or increase their position in a competitive market. The centralization of power led to the creation of Japan, which can be treated as a business group, or a large family, consisting of subordinated subgroups more or less closely connected with the centre of power. The role of the *uji–kabane* system in the centralization of Japan and in creating unity is underlined, as well as influences stemming from the contacts with China and Korea, referred to as a process of hybridization, also called the *transplant effect*,[30] *in which forms become separated from existing practices and recombine with new forms in new practices*.[31] The hybridization process involves organizational practices developed in one country being transferred to another, thereby undergoing adaptation.[32]

The governance systems in the discussed eras are considered in the light of selected corporate governance theories, and the most important factors that shaped the specificity of contemporary Japanese corporate governance are highlighted. The governance system is considered at a macro scale and at a micro scale. Prince Shōtoku's reforms are presented as forming the basis for the creation of the *Ritsuryō* State, and the implementation of Buddhism, which had a huge impact on the formation of Japanese corporate governance and its specific characteristics. The content of legal documents issued by Prince Shōtoku indicates that he could be regarded as the father of Japanese social responsibility and good governance. The characteristics of the *be* corporations, discussed at the end of the first chapter, suggest that the term *corporate governance* can be used in relation to the initial stage of the development of the Yamato State.

Chapter 2 presents the foundations of the corporate governance system that emerged in the *Ritsuryō* State. The creation of the *Ritsuryō* State and the causes of its fall are discussed, along with the effect of the Taika reforms on some aspects of corporate governance. A new bureaucratic order was followed by amendments introduced by successive emperors. The advantages and weaknesses of the state legal system are acknowledged. The shortcomings of the *Ritsuryō* State, principally the egotism of the aristocracy and high officials who had the power to legislate and grant themselves privileges, led to its slow decline. Emperors at that time reigned but did not govern effectively, and therefore to strengthen their power and abilities the position of a cloistered emperor was added to the governance system. An emperor abdicated and usually joined a Buddhist monastery but retained power and influence. This position was created because weak emperors, without political power, were subject to manipulation at court by powerful families exerting indirect control over them. The reigning titular emperor, the former emperor's chosen successor, was largely treated as a figurehead, responsible for fulfilling all the ceremonial roles and formal duties of the emperor. But the retired emperor was able to counterbalance the influence of Fujiwara (a powerful family of imperial regents, dominating the imperial court until the Meiji Restoration in 1868) and the warrior class. It is known as *cloistered rule* (*insei*) or *monastery administration* and was a form of government during the Heian era. Through the cloistered emperors, control of the monarch's position was to return to the imperial family, allowing it to successfully compete for the perks of power.

Although the Heian period was very civilized and peaceful in nature, it was not free of conflicts. The culmination of a decades-long struggle for power and dominance of the Imperial court and for control of Japan, between the Taira and Minamoto clans, known as the Genpei War (1180–1185), was played out. The notable consequences of the struggle were the rise of the *bushi* class, the fall of the Taira clan, and the establishment of the Kamakura *Shōgunate* under Minamoto no Yoritomo in 1192.

The *Ritsuryō* state may be viewed as a hybrid of the Japanese *uji* (stratified clan) society and the historic Chinese civilization. It is an excellent example of hybridization, as Chinese legal codes were revised, modified, and adapted to allow for Japanese conditions, and the heritage of *uji* society. Hybridization points to a further consequence, namely growing complexity of organizational practices within national systems. Institutions (and corporations) chose their corporate governance practices within the boundaries of prevailing institutional constraints and past coalitions.[33] Religion was an important factor in political consolidation. The system of governance in the macro (state) and micro (local and family) scales is described, and particular attention is devoted to the formation, characteristics, and significance of *shōen* and the consequences of their creation for politics, the economy, and corporate governance. Important changes in agriculture are also discussed, along with the role of taxation policy in establishing revenues for the elites.

Chapter 3 is devoted to the Kamakura *Shōgunate* (1185–1333). The rise, development, and fall of the Warrior State are presented, and its corporate governance system is described. The ancient monarchical court and aristocratic system ended when Yoritomo established a military government called *shōgunate*, or *bakufu*, in his home city Kamakura in 1192. The emperor and his weak government remained in Heian. The implementation of the main tasks of the *shōgunate*, such as restoring order and creating a new balance between central and local authority after the period of instability and war, is discussed. The formation by the *shōgunate* of a well-established system of loyalty to the leader, modelled on family clans, is described, as well as the reciprocal obligation (loyalty/benevolence), underpinned by Confucianism, as an established pattern of vassalage and the hallmark of Japanese feudalism. The governance structure of the *shōgunate* is presented along with the economic situation of the country, its provinces, and social groups. The Mongol invasions and their political, social, and financial consequences for the country and society are also discussed. Financial difficulties and the impoverishment of the *samurai* are cited as the main reasons for the push to abolish the *shōgunate* and restore the power of the emperor. These conflicts led to a 56-year (1336 to 1392) period called the *Wars Between the Courts* (the Southern Court at Yoshino and the Northern Court at Kyōto) when two emperors reigned simultaneously, each claiming legitimacy. This tumultuous period ended with the overthrow of the Kamakura *Shōgunate* and the rise of the Ashikaga *Shōgunate*.

Good administration and governance under the *jitō–shugo* system in the Kamakura era improved the country's economic situation, and a steady rise in agricultural productivity increased the prosperity of the traders who distributed rice and other commodities across Japan. Craftsmen gradually became more specialized to meet the growing demands of consumers. Merchants and artisans started to form strong guilds, known as *za*, which were organized under the auspices of temples, shrines, or civil aristocrats, from whom they gained special monopoly privileges and exemptions from customs duties. The process of shaping corporate governance in the Kamakura *Bakufu* is summarized in the context of the corporate governance theories applicable to this era. Some factors responsible for the specific features of the current Japanese corporate governance are also traced and characterized.

Chapter 4 presents two stages of the development of the state and corporate governance, the first of which covers the period of the Muromachi *Shōgunate* (1336–1573) and the second one is related to the period of the Azuchi–Momoyama *Shōgunate* (1573–1603). There was relative peace in the country during the Muromachi *Shōgunate*, and a smooth-running economy, until the beginning of the 15th century. The reasons for the decline and fall of the Muromachi *Shōgunate*, also called Ashikaga *Shōgunate*, are described. The inconclusive Onin Civil War of 1467–1477, which devastated Japan and started the darkest age in Japan's history, is mentioned. Then, attempts were made to present the process of centralization of the country in the Azuchi–Momoyama era (1573–1603), carried out successively by three great unifiers – Oda Nobunoga, Hideyoshi Toyotomi, and Tokugawa Ieyasu. They were able to win power and provide stability and order in the country, based on the implementation of a very restrictive governance system and strict adherence to its rules. Any insubordination or breach of law met with severe punishment. The fourth chapter concludes with the characteristics of the governance system and an overview of its control tools, as well as the selected corporate governance theories that are applicable to this period. The advantages and disadvantages of the *za* corporations are also described in Chapter 4.

This book provides a historical perspective, extending from the beginnings of Japan to the 17th century, on the main events that shaped corporate governance, and attempts to identify the emergence or reinforcement of unique features that characterize contemporary Japanese corporate governance. The analysis is based on a critical analysis of the literature on Japanese history, and its economy, social ideas, and governance. The period of the study covers more than 15 centuries, which are documented with varying degree of accuracy, and sometimes evaluation, by various authors. Due to this multiplicity and diversity of historical events, views, and judgments, as well as the length of the analysed period, this book should be treated only as one of the first contributions to the study of the early historical determinants of Japanese corporate governance.

I would like to thank professor Emeritus Yoji Koyama from Niigata University for his help in introducing Japan to me.

Notes

1 M. Beeson, The Weight of History. In: Regionalism and Globalization in East Asia, reprinted in S. Breslin, R. Higgott (eds.), The International Relations of the Asia-Pacific. Vol. III. The International Political Economy of Development in East Asia. *Sage*, London 2010, p. 3.

2 C. R. Baker, B. P. Quéré, The Role of the State in Corporate Governance. *Accounting History* 2014, Vol. 19, No. 3, pp. 291–307.

3 R. Aguilera, G. Jackson, Hybridization and Heterogeneity across National Models of Corporate Governance. *Economic Sociology: European Electronic Newsletter, ISSN: 1871-3351, Max Planck Institute for the Study of Societies (MPIfG), Cologne* 2002, Vol. 3, No. 2, pp. 17–25.
4 B. R. Cheffins, The History of Corporate Governance. *Law Working Paper N°. 184/2012*. January 2012, https://papers.ssrn.com/sol3/papers.cfm?abstract_id=1975404.
5 L. W. Hein, The British Business Company: Its Origins and Its Control. *The University of Toronto Law Journal* 1963, Vol. 15, No. 1, pp. 134–154.
6 C. E. Walker, The History of the Joint Stock Company. *The Accounting Review* 1931, Vol. 6, No. 2, pp. 97–105.
7 E. Honjo, The Economic Development of Japan. *Kyoto University Economic Review* 1931, Vol. 6, No. 1, pp. 14–28.
8 L. W. Hein, The British Business Company . . . op. cit., pp. 134–154.
9 Ibidem.
10 M. C. Jensen, W. H. Meckling, Theory of the Firm: Managerial Behavior, Agency Costs and Ownership Structure. *Journal of Financial Economics* 1976, Vol. 3, No. 4, pp. 305–360.
11 K. Rost, Introduction to the Corporate Governance of Religion. The Zurich Open Repository and Archive, *University of Zurich*, 2017.
12 S. Gillan, Recent Developments in Corporate Governance: An Overview. *Journal of Corporate Finance* 2006, Vol. 12, No. 3, pp. 381–402.
13 S. Gillan, L. Starks, Corporate Governance, Corporate Ownership, and the Role of Institutional Investors: A Global Perspective. *Journal of Applied Finance* 2003, Vol. 13, No. 2, pp. 4–22.
14 C. R. Baker, B. P. Quéré, The Role of the State in Corporate Governance. *Accounting History*, 2014, Vol. 19, No. 3, pp. 291–307.
15 R. Aguilera, G. Jackson, Hybridization and Heterogeneity . . . op. cit.
16 M. Aoki, The Co-operative Game Theory of the Firm. *Clarendon Press,* Oxford 1986.
17 P. A. Hall, R. M. Taylor, Political Science and the Three New Institutionalisms. *Political Studies* 1996, No. 44, pp. 936–957.
18 D. North, Institutions, Institutional Change, and Economic Performance. *Cambridge University Press*, Cambridge 1990, p. 4.
19 D. North, Institutions. *Journal of Economic* 1991, Vol. 5, No. 1, pp. 97–112.
20 B. Tricker, Corporate Governance. Principles, Policies, and Practices. *Oxford University Press*, Oxford 2015, p. 4.
21 K. Rost, Introduction to the Corporate Governance . . . op. cit.
22 A. Cadbury, Cadbury Report. Report of the Committee on the Financial Aspects of Corporate Governance. *Gee and Co. Ltd*., London 1992.
23 S. Gillan, Recent Developments in Corporate Governance . . . op. cit.
24 J. A. Mc Cahery, E. P. M. Vermeulen, Six Components of Corporate Governance That Cannot Be Ignored. Lex Research Topics in Corporate Law & Economics Working Paper No. 2014–2, European Corporate Governance Institute (ECGI) – *Law Working Paper No. 248/2014*, Tilburg Law School Research Paper No. 08/2014. March 9, 2014.
25 D. F. Larcker, S. A. Richardson, A. I. Tuna, How Important Is Corporate Governance? May 2005, SSRN: https://ssrn.com/abstract=595821 or http://dx.doi.org/10.2139/ssrn.595821.
26 M. Weber, Politics as a Vocation. *Lecture to Free Students Society of Munich University*, 1919, www.ne.jp/asahi/moriyuki/abukuma/weber/lecture/politics_vocation.html.
27 C. R. Baker, B. P. Quéré, The Role of the State in Corporate Governance . . . op. cit.

28 Ibidem.
29 R. K. Morck, L. Steier, The Global History of Corporate Governance: An Introduction. In: R. K. Morck (ed.), A History of Corporate Governance around the World: Family Business Groups to Professional Managers. *University of Chicago Press*, Chicago and London 2005, p. 19.
30 R. K. Morck, L. Steier, A History of Corporate Governance around the World . . . op. cit., p. 48.
31 J. N. Pieterse, Globalization as Hybridization. *International Sociology* 1994, No. 9. pp. 161–184.
32 R. Aguilera, G. Jackson, Hybridization and Heterogeneity . . . op. cit.
33 Ibidem.

Bibliography

A History of Corporate Governance around the World: Family Business Groups to Professional Managers. R. K. Morck (ed.). *University of Chicago Press*, Chicago and London 2005.

Aguilera, R., G. Jackson, G., Hybridization and Heterogeneity across National Models of Corporate Governance. *Economic Sociology: European Electronic Newsletter, ISSN: 1871-3351, Max Planck Institute for the Study of Societies (MPIfG), Cologne* 2002, Vol. 3, No. 2, pp. 17–25.

Aoki, M., The Co-operative Game Theory of the Firm. *Clarendon Press*, Oxford 1986.

Baker, C. R., Quéré, B. P., The Role of the State in Corporate Governance. *Accounting History* 2014, Vol. 19, No. 3, pp. 291–307. https://doi.org/10.1177/1032373214533175.

Cadbury, A., Cadbury Report. Report of the Committee on the Financial Aspects of Corporate Governance. *Gee and Co. Ltd.*, London 1992.

Cheffins, B. R., The History of Corporate Governance. *Law Working Paper N°. 184/2012*. January 2012. https://papers.ssrn.com/sol3/papers.cfm?abstract_id=1975404.

Gillan, S. L., Recent Developments in Corporate Governance: An Overview. *Journal of Corporate Finance* 2006, Vol. 12, No. 3, pp. 381–402. https://doi.org/10.1016/j.jcorpfin.2005.11.002.

Gillan, S., L. Starks, L., Corporate Governance, Corporate Ownership, and the Role of Institutional Investors: A Global Perspective. *Journal of Applied Finance* 2003, Vol. 13, No. 2, pp. 4–22. https://doi.org/10.2139/ssrn.439500.

Hall, P., A., Taylor, R. M., Political Science and the Three New Institutionalisms. *Political Studies* 1996, No. 44, pp. 936–957. https://doi.org/10.1111/j.1467-9248.1996.tb00343.x.

Hein, L. W., The British Business Company: Its Origins and Its Control. *The University of Toronto Law Journal* 1963, Vol. 15, No. 1, pp. 134–54. *JSTOR*. https://doi.org/10.2307/824910.

Honjo, E., The Economic Development of Japan. *Kyoto University Economic Review* 1931, Vol. 6, No. 1, pp. 14–28. https://repository.kulib.kyoto-u.ac.jp/dspace/bitstream/2433/125201/1/ecb0061_014.pdf

Jensen, M. C., Meckling, W. H., Theory of the Firm: Managerial Behavior, Agency Costs and Ownership Structure. *Journal of Financial Economics* 1976, Vol. 3, No. 4, pp. 305–360.

Larcker, D. F., Richardson, S. A., Tuna, A. I., How Important Is Corporate Governance? May 2005. SSRN: https://ssrn.com/abstract=595821 or http://dx.doi.org/10.2139/ssrn.595821.

Mc Cahery, J. A., Vermeulen, E. P. M., Six Components of Corporate Governance That Cannot Be Ignored. Lex Research Topics in Corporate Law & Economics Working

Paper No. 2014–2. European Corporate Governance Institute (ECGI) – *Law Working Paper No. 248/2014*. Tilburg Law School Research Paper No. 08/2014. March 9, 2014.
North, D., Institutions, Institutional Change, and Economic Performance. *Cambridge University Press*, Cambridge 1990.
North, D., Institutions. *Journal of Economic* 1991, Vol. 5, No. 1, pp. 97–112.
Pieterse, J. N. Globalization as Hybridization. *International Sociology* 1994, No. 9, pp. 161–184.
Regionalism and Globalization in East Asia. Reprinted in: S. Breslin, R. Higgott (eds.), The International Relations of the Asia-Pacific. Vol. III. *The International Political Economy of Development in East Asia. Sage*, London 2010.
Rost, K., Introduction to the Corporate Governance of Religion. *The Zurich Open Repository and Archive, University of Zurich* 2017. www.researchgate.net/deref/https%3A%2F%2Fdoi.org%2F10.5167%2Fuzh-133251?_tp=eyJjb250ZXh0Ijp7ImZpcnN0UGFnZSI6InB1YmxpY2F0aW9uIiwicGFnZSI6InB1YmxpY2F0aW9uIiwicG9zaXRpb24iOiJwYWdlQ29udGVudCJ9fQ.
Tricker, B., Corporate Governance. Principles, Policies, and Practices. *Oxford University Press*, Oxford 2015.
Walker, C. E., The History of the Joint Stock Company. *The Accounting Review* 1931, Vol. 6, No. 2, pp. 97–105.
Weber, M., Politics as a Vocation. *Lecture to Free Students Society of Munich University* 1919. www.ne.jp/asahi/moriyuki/abukuma/weber/lecture/politics_vocation.html

Part 1

The period of state centralization and its consequences for corporate governance

2 The genesis and development of the Yamato State

The history of Japan may be traced back to at least 1,300 BC. Its early period lasted till 710 CE consisting of three epochs – *Jomon* (10,000 BC–300 BC) named after cord markings on early pottery; the *Yayoi* Period lasting from 300 BC to 250 CE (named after a site in Tokyo where a new type of pottery was first found in 1884), and the *Yamato* Period (250–710), which is commonly broken into the Kofun (*Tumulus*) Era (250–538) and the *Asuka* Era (538–710).

Japan, called the *ever-fruitful land of reed-covered moors, and luxuriant rice fields*,[1] was first mentioned in Chinese chronicles in 82 CE under the name of *Wa* (land of dwarfs) and summarized as a country *that had reached a high degree of civilization*.[2] According to recorded texts, the *dwarfs* were calm and long-lived, they did not have animals, and they covered themselves with one piece of material with little sewing involved and did not use footwear. The men wore a band of cloth around their heads, exposing the tops. The *Jomon* people used stone weapons and lived in primitive thatched-roofed pits. They had bows, arrows, and javelins with stone and iron blades.[3] In *Yayoi* Period, the *Wa* made their living by foraging, fishing, and hunting; they produced wheel-turned pots and practised weaving, spinning, and advanced agriculture.[4] The *divine-given rice* was first (about 1,000 BC) grown in dry fields and marshy areas but around 500–300 BC emigres from Korea and China introduced the advanced techniques of making and maintaining paddy fields. The *wet* cultivation of rice (using irrigation channels with dams and drains) as well as planting and harvesting required collective (communal) effort.[5] It not only encouraged but also required a denser population to live in one place, thereby forcing effective cooperation. This resulted in the unification of communities under the rule of powerful landowners and the formation of social classes.[6] Chinese Chronicles in 297 record that the *Wa* cultivated grains, rice, hemp, and mulberry trees and did spin, weave, and produce fine linen and silk fabrics. They served meat on wooden trays and ate with their fingers.[7] Women were noted for their chastity; elders were respected, and often lived to over a hundred years of age, they believed in augury and paid tribute in kind. Raised-floor buildings were constructed, and various provinces held fairs where goods were bartered.[8]

DOI: 10.4324/9781003497936-3

Ancient Japan was a tribal society, divided into clans called *uji*, united under the leadership of a chieftain, claiming descent from a common ancestor and worshipping the group's ancestral deity (*kami*), each having its own territory and governed by a form of tribal government. The chieftain, a direct descendant of the clan's deity (*ujigami*), was the link between the group and its deity.[9] He was the master of the household, the family, and controlled the entire property of the *uji*. The principle of primogeniture was very important in the *uji*. If a great *uji* had no heir, the proper *kami* of a small *uji* succeeded to the vacant position of leader. Clans (*uji*) were bound together by loyalty and intermarriages with the main families.[10]

According to Yamamura and Murakami, in the early history of Japan, two cycles of development may be distinguished – the cycle of the *uji* society (the evolution of a stratified clan society) and the cycle of the *ie* society (the evolution of a secondary civilization). The *uji* (clan) had two forms, an earlier stratified and simpler federation called proto-*uji* and the later more developed form, the meta-*uji*, which was a more tightly organized hierarchal form of the proto-*uji*. Thus, the cycle of the *uji* society is divided into the proto-*uji* (from the 3rd century BC to the 1st century CE) and the proto-*uji* federation period (from the 1st century to the middle of the 4th century). The period of *meta-uji* or the Kofun (Old Tumuli) era lasted from the late 4th century to the middle of the 7th century. The meta-*uji* was no longer a federation but rather a more tightly organized hierarchy of previous proto-*uji*, created by leading proto-*uji* members and characterized by more advanced agricultural (e.g. large-scale irrigation) and military technologies.[11]

The *uji* which accepted the Chinese and Korean immigrants acquired important skills, such as smelting, producing weapons, armour, and agricultural tools gaining competitive advantage, power, and wealth.[12] Henshall writes that the combination of inter-tribal warfare, emergence of elites, and competition for control of resources led to increasing politicization.[13]

Around the 3rd century, the Yamato clan (based in Nara) became leader of a federation and formed the Yamato kingdom, a political union of the *uji* of favoured lineages, having *Kofun* culture as its base.[14] Yamato was a complex of the *uji* and *be* corporations (occupational groups), headed by the Daio *uji* (the imperial clan), descendants of the Sun Goddess Amaterasu-no-Omikami, deity of the Yamato clan.[15] According to the Chronicles of Japan (*Nihon Shoki and Kojiki*), the history of Japan began on 11 February 660 BC, when Jimmu Tenno, descendant of this Goddess became the first emperor (Chinese model) creating a dynasty that prevails to this day, and laying the foundation for modern Japan.[16] At the basis of the social structure stood the trinity of Kami, mythologically called the Central Master (Naka-Nushi), who was the progenitor of the imperial family and the two Constructive Chiefs (Musubi no Kami) who were the nobility, the official class. The descendants of Amaterasu, herself a descendant of the Central Master, occupied the throne in unbroken succession, and the descendants of the two Constructive Chiefs served as councillors, ministers, and generals.

The conception of official functions, Amaterasu, the Sun Goddess, attached to the person of her grandson four chiefs and one chieftainess who were given certain functions and offices. These offices were hereditary for all time, and the families of their holders constitute the aristocracy of the nation, marrying among themselves and filling the highest offices from generation to generation. Their members bore the title of *hiko* (son of the Sun) and *hime* (daughter of the Sun). There is no evidence concerning ancestors of the middle and lower classes which accepted a subordinate position without active protest.[17]

The Yamato *uji* gradually developed great political power and authority relying on diplomacy, persuasion, threats, and coercion rather than military confrontation. It incorporated local chiefdoms and gave them places within the Yamato hierarchy. Around 318, the head of the Yamato court came to be called the *great king*.[18] As the general head of all the *uji*, he worshiped the national deities, established or abolished *uji*, nominated chieftains (*uji no kami*), and settled disputes between them.[19] These functions of the monarch have not changed much for nearly 2,000 years.[20] These prerogatives are important with respect to governance. They gave the king power over the clans and forced their chieftains to seek appointments and avoid the loss of the sovereign's support.

The refugees who came to Wa in 475, because of the civil war in Paekche and the retreat of Japanese troops from there, brought new technologies, knowledge, and religious systems. The newcomers not only taught the *uji* to construct irrigation systems, open new lands, and produce new, attractive crafts. Korean officials provided the Wa with knowledge concerning government organization and operation, land control, tribute collection, and culture (written scripts).[21] Hane and Perez write that Yamato owed its primacy *to its success in mobilizing groups of skilled immigrants and supervising the distribution of foreign prestige goods*.[22] The implementation of innovations helped the Yamato to build a strong and wealthy clan, gain hegemony, and become a government accepted by continental rulers.[23] Its kings were in frequent contact with Chinese rulers.[24]

By the 5th century, the *uji* united with the Yamato in economic, military, religious, and family ties. The *uji* became semi-independent, political, administrative units, approved, and controlled by the Yamato ruler, forming the basic, decentralized management and supervisory structures until their abolition in 604.[25] The cooperation was based on mutual benefits, fear, ideological commitment, and personal participation in the emerging imperial system. The significant economic benefits of working together, as members of a federal organization, included the right of the federal government to maintain control of trade (exports and imports), remove barriers to trade between its members, coordinate, and enforce common defense and security obligations, all of which promoted solidarity and peace among members.[26]

The Yamato established an unprecedented level of central control over the *uji*.[27] According to Henshall, this way of operating is widely accepted to this day, and the Yamato's highly hierarchical administrative system is a hallmark of Japanese business practices.[28] By the 6th century, the Yamato king was transformed into an emperor (*tennō*[29]) residing in the capital, which was customarily changed with each new emperor.[30]

The inhabitants of early Japan were divided into three classes of different statuses – the *kwobetsu* (imperial class), the *shimbetsu* (*kami* class), and the *bambetsu* class (local origin and immigrants from Korea and China) further divided into sub-classes.[31] Only members of the first two classes, the major landowners, could create *uji*, occupy important positions, and receive the titles assigned to a given class. The distinction between *kwobetsu* and *shimbetsu* was the beginning of the Japanese state. Although it existed at an earlier date, it was not formally recognized until the 4th century.

The belief that the imperial dynasty was founded by the descendants of the Sun Goddess was used by the Yamato clan to gain political hegemony. It was supported by Shinto, *an animistic folk religion acknowledging the presence in nature of sacred beings as gods and spirits, which became the state religion in the 5th century and since then has been used by the leaders of Japan to unify the people under the imperial family*.[32]

Confucian philosophy of moral behaviour and social stability was absorbed by the Yamato elites, although with slight modifications, in the middle of the 6th century.[33] Confucianism strengthened the power of central government and stabilized the Japanese society.[34] It assumed that everything that happens must be in accordance with the order of heaven, promoting the two principles of *ren* (humanity) and *junzi* (nobleman). *Ren* is the main virtue and primary duty of the nobleman. It is based on kindness and love for people and includes good conduct, compassion, and benevolence. These principles should limit the absolute power of the emperor, heads of the families, commanders, and officials. For the sake of the well-being of their subordinates, they should not give orders incompatible with their welfare. The *junzi* principle applied to the nobleman, that is, the one who adheres to Confucian virtues.[35]

Confucianism focused on duties of care, obedience, and respect between ruler and subject, father and son, and husband and wife, requiring care in return for obedience.[36] It was valued for its practical utility, stressing the need for good government and ethics, social hierarchy, harmony, duty, and respect for authority.[37] Care, respect, and loyalty to superiors had become the overriding priorities and important factors determining the specificity of Yamato corporate governance understood as the way *the ownership is directed and controlled*. These values were important in Yamato, considered as a specific entity, and are still respected in Japanese corporations.[38]

As noted earlier, the Yamato monarchs, seeking to increase their power, began conferring hereditary ranks (*kurai*) and titles (*kabane*), which denoted position, official status, and relationship with the ruler.[39] It became a formally recognized political structure in the 5th and 6th centuries, called the *uji–kabane* system,[40] aimed at strengthening the control and power of the emperor and the emergence of new clan alliances.[41] Without the titles, no one could occupy a high governmental position.[42]

The process of unification of the clans resulted in the development of a vertical relationship between the clans, their chieftains, and the heads of the communities. The chieftain of the *uji* (*uji no kami*) governed all its households, while the head of the great *uji* (*o-uji no kami*) controlled all the *uji* of which the *o-uji* was composed. They were absolute masters of their land, exercised absolute power over their families, and dependants – domestics (*kakibe*), serfs (*tomobe*), and slaves.[43] People living on private land were owned by a landowner. The *uji no kami* dealt with all the problems in his *uji*, only in complex cases consulted the *kami* of *o-uji* or the imperial court. This structure of solving problems may be viewed as the *internalization*, which is practised by Japanese corporations till today.

Kami claiming direct descent from the first emperor (*kwobetsu-uji*) were awarded title of *omi;* the descendants of founding gods (*shimbetsu-uji*) received the title of *muraji*, in the case of *o-uji, o-muraji*, and *ō-omi*, respectively. The former supervised all members of the *kwobetsu-uji*, while the latter governed all members of the *shimbetsu-uji*. They were the highest officers in government before 645, but *omi* was higher title than *muraji*.[44] Beneath them were aristocrats (*maetsukimi*) who functioned as counsellors. Local affairs were administered by *kuni-no-miyatsuko* or *tomo-no-miyatsuko*. The word *miyatsuko* means honourable (*mi*) servant (*yatsuko* or *yakko*). The heads of *kwobetsu-uji* predominated among the former, while the latter were among the *shimbetsu-uji*. They received also various other titles, *sukune* (noble), *ason* or *asmi* (court noble), *kimi* (duke), and *wake* (lord).[45] Lower-ranking titles were awarded to leaders of smaller, distant *uji* who had to swear allegiance. Day-to-day affairs of government were supervised by representatives of the *be* corporations, who carried out their functions hereditarily.[46] The *uji no kami* discharged all offices in his *uji*, leased a part of his land to its members, collected a percentage of the produce, and presented a portion of it to the court.[47] He was named *kabane* after the system.

The Yamato had a well-organized system of administration. The most important unit of local administration was *kuni*, with subdistricts called *agata.*[48] *Kuni* was ruled by a country lord (clan chief) appointed *kuni-no-miyatsuko* by the Yamato Emperor while submitting the clan to the empire and was granted one of the official family titles in the *uji–kabane* system. The *kabane* appointments were intended to strengthen the emperor's control.[49]

Brinkley and Kikuchi write that at that time, the lands of the Yamato, though governed by the emperor, were not owned by him. He possessed the imperial household's estates (*mi-agata*), those belonging to members of the imperial family, and the confiscated lands. The *mi-agata* produce met the requirements of the court; they were managed by the headmen of districts (*agata no nushi*). The private estates belonging to non-royal aristocrats called *tadokoro* existed in association with the *be* corporations.[50]

In the 3rd century BC, by order of the court, *miyake* lands, cultivated for purposes of state revenue, were established in several provinces. Scholars generally agree that a royal estate was a piece of land whose inhabitants, buildings, and produce were possessed by a Yamato king as a hereditary right and, at first, managed directly by the court. *Miyake* signified a public estate or the storehouses for keeping the produce and offices for administering agricultural affairs. They were sources of income and instruments of military and political control.[51] Later, Crown-owned estates and hereditary corporations *be* and rustic corporations (*tabe*) of rice field cultivators, were managed by special chiefs who were responsible for their efficient administration and production.[52] Their overseers were termed *tazukasa*, and the officials in charge of the stores were called *mi-agata no obita*. Thus, rice for public use was grown and stored in the *miyake* districts and intended for the needs of the region's administration and the support of the court. There was a custom that newly acquired land became a *miyake*, increasing the emperor's power. The royal estates were placed in regions of special economic and strategic importance to the Yamato court. In the past, the hereditary chiefs of local clans, whom the king appointed governors of the provinces, owned their own estates as their main source of income. They were rulers of the country, owners of provincial domains, and governors who could not be removed at the request of the empire and who held office for an indefinite period.[53]

From around 374, most governors who administered their own estates as *kuni-no-miyatsuko* offered them to the king and then administered them to the court. They became appointees of the court administering the affairs of the *kuni*, functioning mainly as bureaucratic tribute collectors.[54] *Miyake*, as well as *be* corporations,[55] were divided into those managed directly by the court and those managed indirectly through provincial governors (*kuni-no-miyatsuko*) also called *kokuso*.[56] With the growth of imperial power, the number of *kuni-no-miyatsuko* was increasing (120 officials before 645).[57] Those governing towns and villages were called *tomo-no-miyatsuko*.[58] These offices were hereditary, and the families of their holders constituted the aristocracy of the nation, marrying among themselves and filling the highest offices from generation to generation.

The extensions of court control produced a new two-layered system of local government (districts below provinces), and this dual form of administration was preserved until the middle of the 7th century. The appointment of provincial governors was designed to extend the prestige of the Court rather than to facilitate the administration of provincial affairs, especially to strengthen the throne's authority when the hereditary *miyatsuko* was too powerful. Often the blood relatives of sovereign, who did not participate in the administration of state affairs, but had distinguished themselves by ability or courage, went to the provinces as governors.[59] When a monarch wanted to gain control of an area, a district (agata, arable land) was established and divided into the *inaki* (granary) and the *mura* (village). They were under officials called *nushi*. In early times, in distant regions, such appointments were nominal, but in central Japan, district supervisors became local agents under court control even though they were usually the hereditary heads of old clans. They were responsible (like royal estate managers) to provincial governors.

The administration of royal estates and districts created a great demand for scribes familiar with foreign management techniques.[60] It is presumed that the art of writing came to Japan around 140 BC from Korea and China, but the knowledge concerning ideographs was very limited till the 6th century. In the 3rd century, members of the imperial family and the aristocracy began to read Chinese works, but the use of the characters was limited to recording the family chronicles or business transactions. These who could read and write were enlisted into the imperial service. As an occupation, writing was entrusted to members of the penman's craft group (*be*), monopolizing positions and professions related to writing, as secretaries, councillors, notaries, ambassadors abroad, etc.[61]

At that time there was no annual tax regularly imposed on the people, except occasional universal requisitions for public works, festivals, or military operations. The emperor could decide only on the taxes paid by the *be* corporations and *tomobe* belonging to the Crown. In cases when the monarch wanted funds from the entire nation, the order had to be given to *o-omi* and *o-muraji*, who passed it to the *omi* and *muraji* who in turn gave orders to the *uji no kami* who passed it to the *kami* of the *ko-uji*, who finally gave it to every household.[62] The chain of responsibility was well defined. About the end of the 6th century, the court got so powerful that the *uji* chiefs did not interfere with the sovereign's rights, because to refuse a requisition or failure in complying with the throne's request was liable to punishment.

In early Yamato, religious rites, political and administrative functions were not differentiated, so articles needed for both were kept in the same store (*imi-kura*), under the charge of the *Imibe-uji*. In 405, as the Court grew richer, a separate institution called a domestic store or treasury (*uchi-kura*) was established for storing gold, silver, jewels, precious utensils, brocade, satin, etc. Two Koreans were appointed to keep its accounts. Later, due to a significant increase in the production of textiles and other goods, a third treasury was added, called *okura*, a name still used for the imperial treasury. In this way, a national treasury was created.[63] A member of Soga family (Soga no Machi) was made responsible for all three of them, which expanded enormously the power of that clan.

Governmental functions were called *matsuri* – *worship of* or *service to the gods*. Thus, laws (*nori*) were divine decrees, and religion served as an instrument of political control.[64] There was no written law in the Yamato era although the ideographic scripts became known before the 5th century. According to the Yamato law, *the king can do no wrong* and this rule was extended to crown princes. Everyone else was held liable for breaches of the law.

Crimes in ancient Japan were divided into two classes: sins against heaven and sins against the state.[65] The sins against heaven included injuries to agricultural works, such as breaking down the ridges of rice fields, filling up drains, destroying aqueducts, sowing seeds twice in the same place, spitting in rice fields, flaying an animal alive, etc. The crimes against the state were cutting and wounding (the living or the dead), defilements caused by diseases associated with leprosy, unnatural offences, evil acts of children towards parents or of parents towards children, etc. Custom-prescribed punishments (death, exile, degradation, assignment to a life of slavery, tattooing on the face, confiscation of wives and children), and the only form of the lawsuit was based on tortures (boiling water test, cutting the sinews, extracting the nails and the hair, burying alive, roasting), the death penalty might be inflicted on ex-parte evidence, and the whole family had to suffer the penalty of the crime committed by its member.[66] However, high-ranking persons were allowed to make amends for their wrongdoing by performing a religious purification (*harai*) ritual, with the perpetrator paying all expenses.[67] The offences might be expiated by presenting lands or other valuables to the Throne.

The duty of executing sentences, as well as the military duties, was entrusted to the *mononobe*, the military corporation by the ancestors of the Otomo, the Mononobe, and the Kume families. Chen Shou in 289 wrote in his book titled *The Three Kingdoms* (*San-kuo-chih*) that Japanese respected the law and recognized social differences, they were not litigious, and thieves were rare. Totman argues that these qualities persisted in Japanese society up to the present.[68]

In the 6th century, the kings of Yamato suffered military failures in Korea, challenges to their authority in the provinces and succession disputes at court. These problems made them aware that Japan must be unified to strengthen its position to face internal and external threats. Therefore, they decided to use Chinese achievements and experience for the purposes of stabilization and development of the country. The ubiquitous influence of Chinese culture began as a result of the establishment of regular exchanges between Japan and China. (In her letters, Empress Suiko called the Chinese emperor the ruler of the nation where the sun sets, signing herself as the ruler of the nation where the sun rises.)[69] The leaders undertook such reforms as the growth of power centres outside the Nara plain, improvements in Yamato's control system, support of the spread of Chinese culture, and appointments to high offices of able leaders, familiar with Chinese technology and learning. Chinese institutions, arts, sciences, and ways of daily life were brought to Japan by many official emissaries and students and faithfully copied with some modifications.[70] For centuries, the Chinese high civilization flowed widely into Japan inducing great changes in the social and political life of the country.[71] But the ancient Japanese selectively imported Chinese achievements, implementing only those, which suited their needs and preferences.[72] Thus, they used hybridization.

Chinese civilization influenced social, political, and legal institutions, as well as history, culture, especially literature (poetry), which included the writing system, philosophical schools (Chinese religious beliefs and teachings of ethics), arts and crafts (painting, sculpture, architecture).[73] The Buddhist religion, Confucian ethics, Chinese culture, and administrative system started to be absorbed. Three doctrines were functioning in Japan in the 6th and 7th centuries, Shinto teaching about the origin of the country, a nature cult, animism, and ancestor worship but not dealing with the present or the future, Confucianism discussing the present but not concerned with the past or the future, and Buddhism preaching about the future. Buddhism was officially recognized as a religion in 552, because it was considered important for the protection of the state. It was promoted by the ruling class, especially the Soga clan. Most of the Chinese ideas entered Japan via Korea and underwent some national Japanese modifications,[74] and over time, native Japanese features became increasingly popular.

An important date in Japanese history was the year 593, when Empress Suiko appointed regent Prince Shōtoku, who, inspired by Buddhism, began to implement reforms modelled on Chinese achievements.[75] He understood well that to develop as an independent nation, Yamato must learn and adopt Chinese advanced technologies, political structures,[76] and urgently strengthen imperial control over the state's sacred and secular affairs.[77] To limit the power of clans and build the strong position of the imperial family, Chinese laws were used. The *uji–kabane* system did not encourage diligence in the performance of duties.

In 603, Regent Shōtoku Taishi, established, according to the Chinese pattern, the Twelve Level Cap and Rank System (*kan'i*), which awarded court ranks to individuals for their lifetime. The court officials had to wear silk caps of various colours, symbolizing their rank.[78] Twelve of such grades were instituted, named after Confucian six moral qualities – virtue, humanity, decorum, faith, righteousness, and knowledge, each comprising two degrees, greater and lesser.[79] The caps were made of silk in a distinctive colour for each grade, gold and silver for the highest grades, silver for the medium grades, and copper for the low grades. The caps indicated official status without any reference to hereditary titles. Hair ornaments became also a mark of rank.[80] Mason and Caiger remind that this system was in force until the mid-20th century as the final and very important measure of the relative status of the empire's subjects, as well as the names of offices and all the ramifications of perennial bureaucracy.[81]

Prince Shōtoku initiated a system of promotion based on merit and individual achievements by appointing talented people to government positions, regardless of their clan or title. He encouraged the appointment of men of ability; therefore, the Chinese pattern of entry by examination (inaugurated by Liu Fang, founder of the Chinese Han dynasty in 202 BC) began to be used.[82] It was to replace the old native Japanese system of inheritance of office.[83] The highest qualifications and skills (quality) were guaranteed by systems of rigorous state examinations and apprenticeships, modelled on China, which candidates for government positions had to complete. Thus, social responsibility was promoted, encouraging the development of humanistic values, respect for the rights of individual members of society and its institutions, as well as fairness compatible with existing laws and education.

Prince Shōtoku also proclaimed a Seventeen-article Constitution (604), embracing moral and political principles, treated as the first written laws of Japan.[84] Wren writes that these articles were a set of moral instructions addressed to all clans, referred to the sanctions of conscience, were written in the style of Chinese classics, and constituted a codification of Confucian ethics.[85] This Constitution established the ideals of the state and the principles of human conduct. It formulated moral and political imperatives reflecting social responsibility. Its first three recommendations provided ideological support for the remaining 14. Precept 1 affirms the primacy of the Confucian principle of harmony at the top and benevolence at the bottom, according to which officials are obliged to obey the emperor and their parents. Precept 2 postulates conversion to Buddhism, as this will enable the official to transform evil into good, follow established teachings, and straighten out anything distorted. Precept 3 prescribes obedience to the commands of one's ruler (heaven (emperor)–earth relations), providing support for imperial power. Precepts 4 to 17 show officials how they should serve the emperor in accordance with the teachings of Confucius and the Buddha: do the right thing (4), administer punishments carefully and impartially (5 and 6), fill offices with the able (7), get up early and work late (8), act in good faith (9), do not despise others (10), recognize merit in service (11), rulers must not oppress the people (12), treat subordinates fairly (13), banish jealousy (14), do not put personal considerations above the public good (15), do not disturb farmers in planting and harvesting (16), and consult with others and reach consensus on important issues (17).[86] Brinkley and Kikuchi argue that, with the exception of precept 10, the Shōtoku, Code can be a guide for any community of any age.[87]

The constitution distinguished the ruler, government ministers, and the people as the three human elements making up the state, and indicated the duties and rights of each of them.[88] It introduced the idea of a centralized state governed by a single ruler and provided a kind of fundamental law of the nation. The document was strongly influenced by Buddhism (prince Shōtoku was its first major propagator in Japan) which aided the centralization of political authority. It also implemented many of the ethical and political doctrines of Confucian Chinese government and promoted all things Chinese.[89] The central government used ideas and vocabulary of Chinese government to gain control over the country.[90] They helped the Imperial House to regain a legitimacy, which had been diminished by the great clans. Although Chinese culture, Confucian ethics, and Buddhist religion were quickly absorbed, imperial hold over the *uji* remained weak until the mid-7th century, when centralized government was adopted.[91]

Japanese historians speak of Regent Shōtoku as the father of Japanese civilization.[92] He succeeded in introducing a centralized government and managed to implement the complex Chinese bureaucratic system to strengthen the centre of power. Chinese laws were used to limit the power of the clans and build the strong position of the imperial family. The Court was given a proper organization and its own etiquette. Regent Shōtoku issued a law that was formally in effect (disused) until 1600, allowing people to petition for redress of grievances.[93] He also introduced the Chinese-style calendar and was supposed to have invented kana, the Japanese syllabary of simplified Chinese characters, used for phonetic purposes only.[94] According to Henshall, Japan wished to achieve the best and to become a strong nation, and therefore adopted a series of Chinese practices. It was an early example of *the incorporation of the strengths of others, combined with a willingness to learn and emulate.*[95] Thus, already in antiquity, Japan used hybridization to improve its political system, governance, and economy, successfully repeating this process often in the following centuries, including the 21st century. The death of Prince Shōtoku in 622 halted the reforms for over two decades.

Notes

1 F. Brinkley, D. Kikuchi, A History of the Japanese People from the Earliest Times to the End of the Meiji Era. *The Encyclopaedia Britannica Co,* New York, London 1912, p. 16.
2 C. Andressen, A Short History of Japan. From Samurai to Sony. *Allen & Unwin*, Canberra 2002, p. 25.
3 A. Zischa, Japonia. *Trzaska, Evert i Michalski S.A.*, Warszawa, 1936, p. 4.
4 W. S. Morton, J. K. Olenik, Japan. Its History and Culture. *McGraw-Hill Companies Inc*, New York 2005, p. 7.
5 C. Andressen, *A Short History of Japan* . . . op. cit., p. 23.
6 Britannica, www.britannica.com/place/Japan/Rise-and-expansion-of-Yamato#ref276125
7 R. H. P. Mason, J. G. Caiger, A History of Japan. *TUTTLE Publishing*, Tokyo, Rutland, Vermont, Singapore 1997, p. 23.
8 K. Hara, An Introduction to the History of Japan. *Yamato Society Publication, G. P. Putnam's & Sons. The Knickerbocker Press*, New York, London, 1920, p. 65.
9 Britannica, www.britannica.com/place/Japan/Rise-and-expansion-of-Yamato#ref 276125;
10 C. Andressen, A Short History of Japan . . . op. cit., p. 28.
11 K. Yamamura, Y. Murakami, Ie Society as a Pattern of Civilization: Introduction. *Journal of Japanese Studies* 1984, Vol. 10, No. 2, The Society for Japanese Studies, pp. 279–363.
12 R. H. P. Mason, J. G. Caiger. A History of Japan, op. cit., p. 21.
13 K. G. Henshall, A History of Japan: From Stone Age to Superpower. *Palgrave Macmillan,* London 2012, p. 13.
14 C. D. Totman, A History of Japan. *Blackwell Publishing,* Malden; Oxford; Carlton 2005, pp. 52–53.
15 K. G. Henshall, A History of Japan . . . op. cit., p. 31.
16 K. Hara, An Introduction to the History of Japan . . . op. cit., p. 54; A. Zischa, Japonia, op. cit., pp. 3–7.
17 F. Brinkley, D. Kikuchi, A History of the Japanese People . . . op. cit., p. 61.
18 H. G. Wren, The Legal System of Pre-Western Japan. *Hastings Law Journal* 1968, Vol. 20, No. 1, pp. 217–244.
19 J. E. Kidder, The Earliest Societies in Japan. In: D. M. Brown (ed.), The Cambridge History of Japan. Vol. 1, Ancient Japan. Cambridge University Press, Cambridge 1993, p. 93.
20 F. Brinkley, D. Kikuchi, A History of the Japanese People . . . op. cit., p. 96.

21 C. D. Totman, A History of Japan . . . , op. cit., p. 53.
22 M. Hane, G. Perez, Premodern Japan. A Historical Survey. *Routledge Taylor & Francis Group*, New York, London 2018, pp. 14–15.
23 C. D. Totman, A History of Japan . . . op. cit., p. 53.
24 C. J. Kiley, State and Dynasty in Archaic Yamato. *The Journal of Asian Studies* November 1973, Vol. 33, No. 1, pp. 25–49.
25 Britannica, www.britannica.com/place/Japan/Rise-and-expansion-of-Yamato#ref276125.
26 S. Pistone, Raison d'Etat, Peace and the Federalist Strategy. *The Federalist Political Revue Essays Year XLIII* 2001, No. 1, p. 10.
27 C. D. Totman, A History of Japan . . . op. cit., p. 53.
28 K. G. Henshall, A History of Japan . . . op. cit., p. 16.
29 www.britannica.com/place/Japan/Yamato-decline-and-the-introduction-of-Buddhism
30 C. Andressen, A Short History of Japan . . . op. cit., p. 28.
31 F. Brinkley, D. Kikuchi, A History of the Japanese People . . . op. cit., pp. 27, 93.
32 M. Hane, G. Perez, Premodern Japan . . . op. cit., pp. XIV and 15.
33 R. H. P. Mason, J. G. Craige, A History of Japan . . . op. cit., pp. 39–42.
34 K. Hara, An Introduction to the History of Japan . . . op. cit., p. 42.
35 P. Klitinska, Myśl Konfucjusza. *ACTA ERASMIANA* 2016, No. XIII, Uniwersytet Wrocławski, pp. 1–13.
36 H. G. Wren, The Legal System of Pre-Western Japan . . . op. cit., pp. 217–244.
37 L. Ellington, Japan. A Global Studies Handbook. *ABC-CLIO Inc*, Santa Barbara, Denver, Oxford 2002, p. 23.
38 C. Andressen, A Short History of Japan . . . ., pp. 32–33.
39 D. M. Brown, Introduction. In: The Cambridge History of Japan. Vol. 1. Ancient Japan . . . op. cit., p. 28.
40 B. L. Batten, Foreign Threat, and Domestic Reform: The Emergence of the Ritsuryō State. *Monumenta Nipponica* 1986, Vol. 41, No. 2, pp. 199–219.
41 D. M. Brown, The Yamato Kingdom. In: The Cambridge History of Japan. Vol. 1. Ancient Japan . . . op. cit., p. 137.
42 B. L. Batten, Foreign Threat, and Domestic Reform . . . op. cit.
43 J. E. Kidder, The Earliest Societies in Japan. In: The Cambridge History of Japan. Vol. 1. Ancient Japan . . . op. cit., p. 96.
44 J. E. Kidder, The Earliest Societies in Japan. In: The Cambridge History of Japan. Vol. 1. Ancient Japan . . . op. cit., p. 95.
45 F. Brinkley, D. Kikuchi, A History of the Japanese People . . . op. cit., p. 99.
46 B. L. Batten, Foreign Threat, and Domestic Reform . . . op. cit., pp. 199–219.
47 F. Brinkley, D. Kikuchi, A History of the Japanese People . . . op. cit., p. 95.
48 B. L. Batten, Foreign Threat, and Domestic Reform . . . op. cit.
49 D. M. Brown, The Yamato Kingdom. In: The Cambridge History of Japan. Vol. 1. Ancient Japan . . . op. cit., p. 137.
50 F. Brinkley, D. Kikuchi, A History of the Japanese People . . . op. cit., pp. 95–96.
51 D. M. Brown, The Yamato Kingdom. In: The Cambridge History of Japan. Vol. 1. Ancient Japan . . . op. cit., pp. 139–152.
52 F. Brinkley, D. Kikuchi, A History of the Japanese People . . . op. cit., pp. 71–95.
53 J. E. Kidder, The earliest societies in Japan. In: The Cambridge History of Japan. Vol. 1. Ancient Japan . . . op. cit., p. 97.
54 C. D. Totman, A History of Japan . . . op. cit., p. 53.
55 B. L. Batten, Foreign Threat, and Domestic Reform . . . op. cit.
56 Online dictionary of history and traditions in Japan: Kuni no miyatsuko, www.docoja.com:8443/jisho/mainword?dbname=histg&mainword=Kuni_no_miyatsuko.
57 M. Hane, G. Perez, Premodern Japan . . . op. cit., p. 15.
58 F. Brinkley, D. Kikuchi, A History of the Japanese People . . . op. cit., pp. 62, 95.
59 Ibidem, p. 87.

60 D. M. Brown, The Yamato Kingdom. In: The Cambridge History of Japan. Vol. 1. Ancient Japan . . . op. cit., p. 158.
61 K. Hara, An Introduction.to the History of Japan . . . op. cit., pp. 60–62.
62 F. Brinkley, D. Kikuchi, A History of the Japanese People . . . op. cit., pp. 95, 124, 125.
63 Ibidem, p. 114.
64 M. Hane, G. Perez, Premodern Japan . . . op. cit., p. 13.
65 F. Brinkley, D. Kikuchi, A History of the Japanese People . . . op. cit., p. 95.
66 C. D. Totman, A History of Japan . . . op. cit., p. 44.
67 F. Brinkley, D. Kikuchi, A History of the Japanese People . . . op. cit., pp. 95, 125, 126.
68 C. D. Totman, A History of Japan . . . op. cit., p. 43.
69 The Empress H. B. Montgomery, The Empire of the East. *METHUEN & CO*, London 1908, p. 34
70 R. H. P. Mason, J. G. Caiger. A History of Japan . . . op. cit., pp. 39–42.
71 L. Ellington, Japan: A Global Studies Handbook . . . op. cit., p. 23.
72 K. Yamamura, Y. Murakami, Ie Society as a Pattern of Civilization . . ., op. cit.
73 D. M. Brown, Introduction. In: The Cambridge History of Japan. Vol. 1. Ancient Japan . . . op. cit., p. 30.
74 R. H. P. Mason, J. G. Caiger. A History of Japan . . . op. cit., pp. 39–42.
75 H. B. Montgomery, The Empire of the East . . . op. cit., p. 34.
76 W. S. Morton, J. K. Olenik, Japan. Its History and Culture . . . op. cit., pp. 18–20.
77 D. M. Brown, Introduction. in: The Cambridge History of Japan. Vol. 1. Ancient Japan . . . op. cit., p. 32.
78 B. L. Batten, Foreign Threat, and Domestic Reform . . . op. cit.
79 M. W. Meyer, Japan A Concise History. *Rowman & Littlefield Publishers Inc*, Plymouth 2009, p. 38.
80 F. Brinkley, D. Kikuchi, A History of the Japanese People . . . op. cit., p. 164.
81 R. H. P. Mason, J. G. Caiger. A History of Japan . . . op. cit., p. 75.
82 C. Andressen, A Short History of Japan . . . op. cit., p. 33.
83 K. G. Henshall, A History of Japan . . . op. cit., p. 18.
84 V. M. Carkeek, The Taihō Code, the First Code of Japan. *Washington Law Review* 1926, Vol. 1, No. 3, pp. 181–194.
85 H. G. Wren, The Legal System of Pre-Western Japan . . . op. cit.
86 I. Mitsusada, D. M. Brown, The Century of Reform. In: The Cambridge History of Japan. Vol. 1. Ancient Japan . . . op. cit., pp. 180, 181.
87 F. Brinkley, D. Kikuchi, A History of the Japanese People . . . op. cit., p. 141.
88 www.britannica.com/place/Japan/Yamato-decline-and-the-introduction-of-Buddhism
89 R. H. P. Mason, J. G. Caiger, A History of Japan . . . op. cit., p. 39.
90 H. G. Wren, The Legal System of Pre-Western Japan . . . op. cit.
91 Britannica, www.britannica.com/place/Japan/Rise-and-expansion-of-Yamato#ref 276125.
92 F. Brinkley, D. Kikuchi, A History of the Japanese People . . . op. cit., pp. 95 and 143.
93 V. M. Carkeek, The Taihō Code, the First Code of Japan . . . op. cit.
94 C. Andressen, A Short History of Japan . . . op. cit., p. 35.
95 K. G. Henshall, A History of Japan . . . op. cit., p. 17.

Bibliography

Andressen, C., A Short History of Japan. From Samurai to Sony. *Allen & Unwin*, Canberra 2002.

Batten, B. L., Foreign Threat and Domestic Reform: The Emergence of the *Ritsuryō* State. *Monumenta Nipponica* 1986, Vol. 41, No. 2, pp. 199–219. www.jstor.org/stable/2384665.

Brinkley, F., Kikuchi, D., A History of the Japanese People from the Earliest Times to the End of the Meiji Era. *The Encyclopaedia Britannica Co*, New York, London 1912. https://archive.org/details/historyofjapanes00briniala/page/n5/mode/2up.

Britannica. www.britannica.com/place/Japan/Yamato-decline-and-the-introduction-of-Buddhism

Britannica. www.britannica.com/place/Japan/Rise-and-expansion-of-Yamato#ref276125

Carkeek, V. M., The Taiho Code, the First Code of Japan. *Washington Law Review* 1926, Vol. 1 No. 3, pp. 181–194.

Ellington, L., Japan. A Global Studies Handbook. *ABC-CLIO Inc*, Santa Barbara, Denver, Oxford 2002.

Hane, M., Perez, G., Premodern Japan. A Historical Survey. *Routledge Taylor & Francis Group*, New York, London 2018. file:///D:/Users/wzr/Downloads/9780429494819_previewpdf.pdf.

Hara, K., An Introduction to the History of Japan. *Yamato Society Publication, G. P. Putnam's &Sons. The Knickerbocker Press*, New York, London 1920.

Henshall, K. G., A History of Japan: From Stone Age to Superpower. *Palgrave Macmillan*, London 2012. www.gutenberg.org/files/37186/37186-h/37186-h.htm.

Kiley, C. J., State and Dynasty in Archaic Yamato. *The Journal of Asian Studies*, Vol. 33, No. 1, [Cambridge University Press, Association for Asian Studies], 1973, pp. 25–49. www.jstor.org/stable/2052884.

Klityńska, P., Myśl Konfucjusza, Uniwersytet Wrocławski. *ACTA ERASMIANA* 2016, No. XIII, pp. 1–13.

Mason, R. H. P., Caiger, J. G., A History of Japan. *TUTTLE Publishing*, Tokyo; Rutland, VT; Singapore 1997. file:///D:/Users/wzr/Downloads/A_History_of_Japan_Mason_Caiger%20(5).pdf.

Meyer, M. W., Japan: A Concise History. *Rowman & Littlefield Publishers Inc*, Plymouth 2009. file:///D:/Users/wzr/Downloads/epdf.pub_japan-a-concise-history-4th-edition.pdf.

Montgomery, H. B., The Empire of the East. *METHUEN & CO*, London 1908. www.gutenberg.org/cache/epub/28690/pg28690-images.html.

Morton, W. S., Olenik, J. K., Japan. Its History and Culture. *McGraw-Hill Companies Inc*, New York 2005. https://vdocuments.mx/japan-its-history-and-culture-56811b380a71d.html.

Pistone, S., Raison d'Etat, Peace and the Federalist Strategy. *The Federalist Political Revue Essays Year XLIII* 2001, No. 1. www.thefederalist.eu/site/*index.php/en/essays/2021-raison-detat-peace-and-the-federalist-strategy*.

Rost, K., Introduction to the Corporate Governance of Religion. *The Zurich Open Repository and Archive, University of Zurich*, 2017. www.researchgate.net/deref/https%3A%2F%2Fdoi.org%2F10.5167%2Fuzh-133251?_tp=eyJjb250ZXh0Ijp7ImZpcnN0UGFnZSI6InB1YmxpY2F0aW9uIiwicGFnZSI6InB1YmxpY2F0aW9uIiwicG9zaXRpb24iOiJwYWdlQ29udGVudCJ9fQ

The Cambridge History of Japan. Vol. 1. Ancient Japan. D. M. Brown (ed.). *Cambridge University Press*, Cambridge 1993.

Totman, C. D., A History of Japan. *Blackwell Publishing*, Malden; Oxford; Carlton 2005. www.perlego.com/book/1006239/a-history-of-japan-pdf.

Wren, H. G., The Legal System of Pre-Western Japan. *Hastings Law Journal* 1968, Vol. 20, No. 1, pp. 217–244. https://repository.uchastings.edu/hastings_law_journal/vol20/iss1/5.

Yamamura, K., Murakami, Y., *Ie* Society as a Pattern of Civilization: Introduction. *Journal of Japanese Studies* 1984, Vol. 10, No. 2, The Society for Japanese Studies, pp. 279–363. www.jstor.org/stable/132142.

Zischa, A., Japonia. *Trzaska, Evert i Michalski S.A.* Warszawa 1936.

3 Yamato as the cradle of Japanese corporate governance

Creation of the foundations of the Japanese corporate governance system

Analysis of the Yamato corporate governance has turned out to be a difficult task because of the length of the evaluation period and the number of fundamental changes taking place during it. Therefore, the research is only a part contribution to the knowledge of its corporate governance. But even such an introductory examination shows the sophistication of the way in which ownership *was directed and controlled* in ancient Japan. Its governance stems much from pre-history beliefs and religious attitudes forming the foundations of such concepts as the belief in Imperial Line divinity, the enduring political and military family hierarchies, and the awareness of a unique, self-directed, and autonomous national identity.[1]

The analysis of Yamato governance given here is carried out on both the macroeconomic and microeconomic levels. The first aspect is concerned with the state organization and governance, the latter with relations between and within the *uji* and the *be* corporations. In the period under consideration, the macroeconomic order of the state organization and governance had changed more in comparison to the microeconomic level. An attempt was made to explain corporate governance in the context of social, regulatory, and market changes.[2]

The struggles for land ownership and power have determined Japanese history. The first stage of the process of creating Yamato corporate governance is concerned with the *uji*, the autonomous, self-governing organizations, struggling to continue their existence and to gain wealth and power. According to Honjo, the *uji* greatly contributed towards the development of agriculture and of other industrial arts by employing the members of a family, especially the people of the *be* corporations. It was the family that formed the foundations of an economy based on land and clan (family) relations. It was an economy of self-sufficiency, with the family as the economic unit and the association of the *be* corporations as the centre of the labour system.[3]

DOI: 10.4324/9781003497936-4

After strengthening their position, the *uji* had begun to compete for hegemony which was finally gained by the Yamato clan. Its king, striving to create a centralized state, managed to transform the *uji* federation into a hierarchical structure, later into a state. Initially, in Yamato, the relationship between the monarch and the clan chieftains was not dependent on land donations, as land was only under the monarch's governance after the second half of the 7th century.

The competitive advantages of the clan system resulted not only from ambition and military strength but also from clever diplomacy, the ability to learn and adopt new ideas and technologies from highly developed civilizations. These efforts were then supported by the *uji–kabane* system, a governance model based on the symmetry of interests between the ruler and the *uji's* chieftains and conflicts of interest between individual *uji* (corporations). It ensured obedience and motivated leaders of the *uji* to seek the king's favours and subordinate to him. The Yamato kings created a relationship structure obliging magnates to provide certain services in exchange for the right to administer their own territories and obtain certain titles.[4] In this way, the chieftains were made agents of the monarch, creating the governance system because *whenever a principal has to rely on agents to handle his or her business, governance issues arise*.[5] A nationwide, formal, multi-level system of governance and private control, overseen by the Yamato ruler, was thereby established. Hybridization and foreigners played an important role in its creation, both, on the macro and micro levels. It propagated the values that, throughout Japanese history, well into modern times, shaped the specificity (character) of Japanese society.[6] Dollinger writes that there is plenty of evidence that the ethos of the Confucian tradition continues to contribute to interpersonal and organizational practices in contemporary Japanese companies that have consciously chosen to diverge and maintain their traditions in social and interpersonal matters. In terms of technology, they embraced Western science and practice because it was, and still is, in their best interests. When the issue was the adoption or design of a socio-technical system, the Japanese chose the harmony of the system over the rights of the individual.[7]

Analysis of the literature enables to consider clans (*uji*) as enterprises with a specific hierarchy, pursuing their own objectives, competing for resources and dominance. Significant characteristics of corporation (corporateness) included a perpetual succession of many persons acting as a single individual, individuality, right to sue and be sued, to gain and hold real property, to have a common seal, and to govern by making by-laws and private statutes. Also Japan, which emerged as a state as a result of the centralization of the *uji*, can be compared to a corporation (business group), pursuing specific objectives, managing, and coordinating its constituent enterprises (*uji*). This business group subjected multiple firms (clans) to one ultimate authority. This forced entities that were members of the group to act honestly towards each other, and enabled specialized companies to create links in interconnected production chains, and let each raise risk-tolerant equity financing. Business groups acquired reputations for fair dealing.[8]

This approach may be traced back to Confucianism, which was introduced to Japan in the 5th century and advocated the transfer of the principles and patterns of the family to the structure of the state. The state was to function in accordance with the Order of Heaven. The family was a state in miniature, and the politics of the state were an extension of the family ethic.[9] Thus, Japan may be treated as a monopolistic *multidivisional* corporation. This type of firm is characterized by a central office that not only controls the most relevant financial allocations and has the last word on strategic planning but also allows its divisions a high degree of autonomy in matters of operation.[10] It can be compared to a group in which appropriate relations are created between the owners, managers, and the entities (enterprises) that make up this group.[11] If the federation of *uji* is treated as a federation of corporations (macroeconomic aspect), the vertical relations between the Yamato and the *uji* may be viewed in the light of the Resource Dependency Theory, the Social Networks Theory, and the Managerial and Class Hegemony Theory.

The following three core ideas of the Resource Dependency Theory (RDT) explain the internal and external actions of organizations – social context matters, strategies to enhance organizational autonomy and pursuit of interests, and power (not just rationality or efficiency). The emphasis on the strength and tactics available to organizations distinguishes the RDT[12] from other approaches.[13] It regards an organization as a member of a relatively stable alliance which *involves agreements between two or more organizations to pursue joint objectives through a coordination of activities or sharing of knowledge or resources*.[14] In the RDT aspect, clans built inter-clan networks due to the interlocking of resources between them. As open systems, they were limited by their own resources, abilities, and the external social, institutional, or industrial environment.[15] Thus, clan resources influenced the behaviour of the entire organization – the state ruled by the king. Organizations need resources to exist, and they adopt various strategies to obtain them. What mattered in Yamato was military, economic, and organizational resources, the intellectual potential of individual clans, access to sources of wealth, the scope of know-how and technology, and the ability to cooperate with other clans. In addition, important features include the ability to create relationships with other clans, *be* corporations and their elites, as well as political and social networks. The *assets* at the monarch's command included military leadership, ritual or magical powers, judicial authority, so the cornerstones of legitimacy.[16]

The leader of the emerging state created related alliances (coalitions), made conquests in order to gain power, improved the organizational structure, and increased legitimacy.[17] State synergy effects influenced solidarity, relationships, integrity of clans, and limited their use of force.[18] Organizational aims result from coalitions of many actors whose goals may be contradictory or complementary. The state may or may not be directly involved but plays a critical role in defining and institutionalizing coalitions.[19] They are shaped by the reciprocal relationships and resource dependencies between their members.[20] Coalitions themselves define what resources are important in relation to their goals. Coalitions, organizational goals, and resources condition each other. The unequal exchanges generate differences in power, authority, and access to further resources.[21] If power plays a role in conducting organizational life, then RDT is applicable.[22]

According to the Theory of Social Networks (TSN), those involved in corporate governance processes are linked through networks.[23] The focus is on the role of social relationships in transmitting information, channelling personal influence, and enabling changes in attitudes or behaviour.[24] Applying this to the *uji*, it can be said that their owner-managers already had some common characteristics, such as social standing (they were all chieftains of clans), class (belonged to *highest* class), income (they were rich), education (differentiated by innovations and their adoption), institutional or corporate links (the *uji* and *be* corporations), and the background and lifestyle of key players (social order, wealth, and the same values). Social networks can enhance or disrupt independent and objective governance activities, so identifying and monitoring them provide insight into governance processes and rights.[25] Chiefs played a key role in the networks because they connected the *uji* with their strategic surroundings, the Yamato kingdom. Royal and aristocratic power was exercised through a multitude of personal networks.[26]

The Managerial and Class Hegemony Theory (MCHT)[27] perspective on governance of *uji* (corporations) focused on how chief executives (CEOs) perceived themselves and what subsequent impact this had on their behaviour and corporate governance. They perceived themselves as an elite group and behaved as such, dominating both the *uji* and *be* (corporation) organizations and their external linkages.[28] Appointments to top management positions had to be tailored to this elite and uphold its image. A hegemon (monarch) had to strengthen his position (power) by implementing an effective system of motivation and supervision – the *uji–kabane* system. Such efforts were undertaken by the rulers of Yamato amid high-intensity power struggles between elite members. The Managerial and Class Hegemony Theory sees corporate governance as an interpersonal, political process.[29] The monarch's self-esteem affected the court (board of directors) behaviour and performance. In Yamato, clan chiefs, with their own self-awareness and knowledge of ongoing operations and decision-making power, dominated the Court (board) decisions.

An important factor in gaining hegemony and political consolidation was religion. Monarchs conducted the worship of the national deities, using sacred symbols and ceremonies, reinforced with secular rituals of respect and reward. The new order unified and supported the emerging imperial regime.[30] The rulers built vertical and horizontal dependency structures in which the whole *uji* association functioned as a corporation. A formal, effective system of corporate governance was established in the form of a nationwide, multi-level system of private control headed by the Yamato king. The hegemony of aristocrats was confirmed by the Confucian heavenly order.

The land was administered and controlled by appointed officials with a specific hierarchy. The vertical governance relations were clear, and the chain of responsibility was defined. This system was supported by clan laws and harsh punishments for breaking it. A very important step in the development of governance was the Seventeen-article constitution (604) which distinguished between the ruler, the government, and the people making up the state and demarcated the duties and rights of each. The unity of the *uji* in making the state depended on ability to conclude and fulfil contracts by the leaders of the clans making up the *uji* association and on the way of resolving conflicts of interest. This leads to the Agency Theory, which can be applied at the macro and micro levels in the Yamato period.

At the micro level, in accordance with the justification presented earlier, *uji* operating under the supervision of a sovereign can be compared to current corporations competing on the market. They were governed by owners approved and supervised by the monarch, so there was no separation of ownership and control within them. The aim of the *uji* was to maximize the interests (growth of personal possession, power, and position) of principals who were masters of their lands, tribesmen, and dischargers of all offices. The chieftains (top managers) exercised the power of life and death over their clansmen. At the *uji* level, the Agency Theory defined the relations between the *uji* chiefs, the leaders of *be corporations*, and appointed officials. However, the internal governance of the *uji* did not foster many agency conflicts. Perhaps those appearing between the chiefs and the aristocratic heads of the *be* corporations, who were high-level professional managers responsible for the production process, were the most frequent. The *be* corporations were created to organize, protect, and extend highly specialized production and ownership, and increase its efficiency and profitability. They confirmed the existence of corporate governance in early Japan. If *uji* were corporations, they had to pursue common goals and maintain the previously mentioned features typical of this form of business organization. Clan leaders (principals) applied the principle of internalizing problems in their *uji*. However, they were aware that internal conflicts were dangerous and could threaten independence or even existence of the *uji*. For these reasons, Agency Theory is not among those most relevant to the early Yamato period.

To sum up, the analysis of the literature allows us to trace some of the factors responsible for the specificity of the current Japanese corporate governance. These features include a strong group identity – with the family (clan), corporation (*be*), and community. Such factors as the ability to cooperate, organize teamwork, and self-sacrifice, stemmed from the agriculture and legal requirements. The suppression of individual interests for the good of the group was reinforced by Confucianism, which had been influencing the social system since the dawn of the state. It can be concluded that its principles are followed to this day by the

Japanese and their corporations.[31] Confucianism promotes the importance of loyalty which has been the distinguishing feature of Japanese culture for a very long time.[32] It focuses on the duty of care, submissiveness, responsibility, obedience, and respect in relations between superiors and inferiors. This reciprocal obligation has become an established pattern, promoting the values of morality and discipline since Prince Shōtoku rule. These Confucian values are still respected and belong to the most important features of Japanese corporate governance. Other characteristics of it are internalization of problems, unity against outsiders, respect for law and recognition of social differences, stemming from a highly developed sense of responsibility in the Japanese character, or conversely, the old practice of severe punishment of offenders and their families. The emphasis on diligence was manifested in directing corporate governance (supervision) in the state, the *uji* and *be* corporations, towards stimulating efficiency, competitiveness, and development by relying on records of business transactions, controls, and penalties. The respect for superiors, knowledge, and education is another feature of Japanese corporate governance coming from ancient times.

For centuries, a very important characteristic and a hallmark of Japanese society, culture, politics, economy, and corporate governance has been hybridization reinventing Japanese civilization. Despite having exceptional respect for their own traditions, the Japanese have shown a great ability to implement the highest and best achievements of other nations and to adapt them to their own circumstances and needs. The centuries-old ability to adopt innovations, legal principles and procedures, and apply them in unique ways,[33] continues to play a very important role in shaping Japanese corporate governance.

Based on the facts described in the literature regarding the organization and functioning of clans in ancient Japan, it can be assumed that everything that contributed to gaining competitive advantage was important for their chieftains and carefully cultivated. The dissatisfaction of clan members could result in a reduction in the clan's defensive strength, which could lead to its annihilation (bankruptcy), hostile takeover, or the need to pay tribute (financial losses). The condition for the unity, strength, and development of the clan was the acceptance of the rule of the chiefs, who were obliged to take care of the welfare and safety of their subordinates, and therefore had to take socially responsible decisions and actions.

Be corporations and their characteristics

In Yamato, there were two interwoven social organizations – the *uji* system and the *be* corporation system. Both worked in clearly defined areas and were ruled by hereditary heads holding *kabane* titles.[34] *Uji* was a lineage group defined by blood, not by common occupation. The chief was the owner of the *uji* who controlled the land and all members of his clan.[35] Those that could not trace their genealogy to the divine ancestor were attached to the *uji* as subordinates. Some clan chieftains were also heads of the *be* corporations but usually the heads of the latter were their rival aristocracy.[36] The conduct of warfare and the distribution of economic goods were exclusive functions of the *uji*.

The *be* corporations (the term is of Korean origin and means attendants) developed within certain *uji* as hereditary in families, but their members were not related by blood. Their other names are *mure* (the heard) and *kakibe* (domestics). The *be* corporations were subordinated and controlled by the *uji*.[37]

This extensive and complex occupational-group system had evolved at the same time as the *kabane* system to provide continuous revenue to the *uji* they were attached to. The *be* corporations served the court or powerful *uji* (which militarily protected them) providing revenues, independently pursuing some branch of industry, or rendering fixed services from generation to generation at the local or the national level.[38] Most of the *be* corporations were agricultural units, producing rice for themselves and their superiors. But there were also *tomobe*, a group of households associated not only by common ancestry but usually by a common occupation.[39] These institutions comprised groups of men providing specialized services or non-agricultural products to the imperial government or to the court nobles. They were engaged in crafts, fishing, or specific court functions, consisting of artisans of the same occupation, such as weavers, potters, armourers, builders, and temple servants.[40] Thus, the *be* existed for every category of occupation and were used to denote family names.[41] They were structured like clans, specialized corporate associations of artisans of the same occupation, aimed at securing efficiency by specialization.[42] There were three social groups in the *uji* and *be* – the hereditary heads appointed by the emperor or *uji* chieftains, the members – peasants or artisans attached to the *uji* and *be* corporations as subordinate, manual labourers, and the household slaves being at the bottom of the social hierarchy.[43] There were local *be* and *be* operating over greater part of the empire. They were managed by an officially appointed chief who had workers (*kakibe*) under his authority.[44] The *be* and *tomobe* corporations did not exist to capture economic gains for their members as membership was not voluntary.[45] The principles of clearly defined responsibilities and segregation of duties were well ingrained in them. Their transactions were recorded and authorized, and independent performance checks were performed.[46] Honjo argues, given the *be* corporations' involvement in a variety of manual labour, that in ancient times there was a systematic division of labour among their residents.[47] The existence of the *be* corporations makes it possible to talk about *corporate* governance even at the dawn of Japan.[48] The *be* corporations, because of their specialized craft functions and serf like organization, played an important role in economic development and political integration of the Yamato State.[49] The attachment of either an agricultural or an artisan *be* corporation was of great importance and benefit to the *uji*, and to its chieftain.[50] The power, income, and prestige of the monarchs and clan heads were related to the number and strength of the *be* belonging to them.[51] *Be* corporations were so important because there was more land than labour in early Japan, making skilled workers highly sought after. Another reason was that their attachment to the court or clans created the military and economic power of these clans and the Yamato State.

Some imperial *be* ran the growing royal estates, handing a large portion of their produce to the monarch, to provinces (*kuni*) and districts (*agata*) that served as arms of Yamato control.[52] As noted earlier, the cultivators of *miyake* were called rustic corporation (*ta-be*), they had overseers (*tazukasa*), and officials in charge of the stores (*mi-agata no obita*). In ancient Japan, officials and their offices had the same names. *Miyake* also signified a public estate or the store for keeping the produce, *tsukasa* was applied alike to an overseer and to his place of transacting business. The chiefs of the *be* corporations, officially designated managers *(tomo-no-miyatsuko)* to control their activities, were aristocrats (*omi* class) or the royal family members.[53] They exercised the power of life and death over the *be* corporation members, and it was only after the reform of 645 that the corporations were allowed to appeal the decisions of their chiefs to the (newly established) central government.[54]

All the *be* corporations discharging functions for the court were attached to the imperial *uji*.[55] Some early *be* (*nashiro* and *koshiro* abandoned by 531) assisted the court in the *kami* ceremonies as the *be* corporation of Palace Attendants, or Palace Stewards, or Palace Archers. The military duties were entrusted to the Otomo, the Mononobe, and the Kume families who formed the military *be*. They were the hereditary military authority (Mikoto deity descendants) who wore armour, carried swords, spears and bows, guarded the palace, and asserted the imperial authority throughout the provinces.

Foreigners having technical skills or literary attainments were formed into corporations of people (*tamibe*). They had personal freedom and were directly dependent on the court and devoted to manufacturing articles for the use of the imperial household, producing valued articles (iron swords, bronze mirrors), performing crucial services and tasks associated with the construction of huge burial mounds and complex irrigation systems.[56] The skilled foreigners such as brocade weavers or scribes were welcomed in Japan, and their leaders, along with refugee aristocrats, were accepted into the ranks of Japanese nobility (over 33% of 1,182 families of the Yamato nobility were Korean).[57]

At the beginning of the 6th century, the military failure in Korea, preceded by a serious rebellion in Kyushu, shattered the foundations of the Yamato Kingdom. Therefore, after 540, the ministers decided that Yamato should concentrate on maximizing its wealth and control. Steps were taken not only to manage the royal estates more efficiently, by utilizing imported managerial techniques, but also to increase control over them, and the income they generated. But the communication difficulties caused that the central government had some problems with exercising its power in the more distant provinces. The local officials administrating the royal estates on the court's behalf were made responsible for improving that. In 540, they started to register farmers of the *miyake*, because the monarch attempting to increase his income from and control over distant regions needed accurate records. Efforts to register all residents and keep written records of business activities were accompanied by strengthening ancient self-government as a means of tightening Yamato control. The first office to receive attention was that of district supervisor (*agata nushi*).[58] Any gaps in the supplies provided by the sovereign's own people were to be compensated by the *tomo-no-miyatsuko*.

According to Batten, the *be* corporations system was thought to be the primary means of population control before 645 (in the pre-Taika period). The decentralized community was brought under the control of the chiefs of clans, aristocrats, or the royal family – owners of the *uji* and *be*, which served these courts in a variety of hereditary functions. The result was a nationwide, multi-level system of private control under the overall authority of the Yamato king.[59]

Notes

1 M. W. Meyer, Japan: A Concise History. *Rowman & Littlefield Publishers Inc*, Plymouth 2009, pp. 6, 7, 9.
2 K. Rost, Introduction to the Corporate Governance of Religion. The Zurich Open Repository and Archive, University of Zurich, 2017.
3 E. Honjo, The Economic Development of Japan. *Kyoto University Economic Review* 1931, Vol. 6, No. 1, pp. 14–28.
4 C. D. Totman, A History of Japan. *Blackwell Publishing,* Malden; Oxford; Carlton 2005, pp. 52, 53.
5 B. Tricker, Corporate Governance. Principles, policies, and Practices. *Oxford University Press*, Oxford 2015, p. 4.
6 C. Andressen, *A Short History of Japan. From Samurai to Sony. Allen & Unwin*, Canberra 2002, p. 33.
7 M. J. Dollinger, Confucian Ethics and Japanese Management Practices. *Journal of Business Ethics* 1988, Vol. 7, No. 8, pp. 575–584.
8 L. Dau, R. K. Morck, B. Yeung, Corporate Governance, Business Group Governance and Economic Development Traps. *NBER Working Paper* November 2020, No. w28069.
9 P. Klityńska, Myśl Konfucjusza, Uniwersytet Wrocławski, *ACTA ERASMIANA* 2016, No. XIII, pp. 1–13.
10 K. Rost, Introduction to the Corporate Governance . . . op. cit.
11 R. Aguilera, G. Jackson, Hybridization and Heterogeneity across National Models of Corporate Governance. *Economic Sociology: European Electronic Newsletter, ISSN: 1871-3351, Max Planck Institute for the Study of Societies (MPIfG), Cologne* 2002, Vol. 3, No. 2, pp. 17–25.
12 J. Pfeffer, G. R. Salancik, The External Control of Organizations: A Resource Dependence Perspective. *University of Illinois at Urbana-Champaign's Academy for Entrepreneurial Leadership Historical Research Reference in Entrepreneurship,* 1978. SSRN: https://ssrn.com/abstract=1496213.
13 G. F. Davis, J. A. Cobb, Resource Dependence Theory: Past and Future. *Research in the Sociology of Organizations* 2010, Vol. 28, pp. 21–42.
14 W. R. Scott, G. F. Davis, Organizations and Organizing: Rational, Natural, and Open System Perspectives. *Pearson Prentice Hall,* Upper Saddle River NJ 2007, pp. 206–207.

15 Z. Q. Zhan, X. J. Deng, Why They Connected: A Theoretical Analysis on the Cause of Interfirm Network Formation. *Open Journal of Social Sciences* 2014, No. 2, pp. 232–237.
16 C. J. Kiley, State and Dynasty in Archaic Yamato. *The Journal of Asian Studies* 1973, Vol. 33, No. 1, Cambridge University Press, Association for Asian Studies, pp. 25–49.
17 Based on G. F. Davis, J. A. Cobb, Resource Dependence Theory: Past and Future. *Research in the Sociology of Organizations* 2010, No. 28, pp. 21–42.
18 M. Zehir, A. Findikli, K. Çeltekligil, Resource Dependence Theory, Firm Performance and Producers-Suppliers Relationships. 14th ISMC and 8th ICLTIBM-2018, *The European Proceedings of Social & Behavioural Sciences* 2018, pp. 162–172.
19 J. W. Cioffi, S. S. Cohen, The State, the Law and Corporate Governance: The Advantage of Forwardness. In: S. S. Cohen, G. Boyd (eds.), Corporate Governance and Globalization. *Edward Elgar*, Northampton 2000, pp. 307–349.
20 J. Pfeffer, G. Salancik, The External Control of Organizations: A Resource Dependence Approach. *Harper & Row,* New York 1978.
21 T. Mendis, Analysis of Corporate Governance. Theories and their Implications for Sri Lankan Companies. *Journal of the Faculty of Graduate Studies* 2012, University of Kelaniya, Vol. 1, pp. 29–46.
22 G. F. Davis, J. A. Cobb, Resource Dependence Theory . . . op. cit., pp. 21–42.
23 B. Tricker, Corporate Governance. Principles, *Policies* . . . op. cit., p. 68.
24 W. Liu, A. Sidhu, A. M. Beacom, T. W. Valente, Social Network Theory. In: P. Rossler, C. A. Hoffner, L. van Zoonen (eds.), The International Encyclopaedia of Media Effects. *Wiley*, New York 2017, p. 1.
25 B. Tricker, Corporate Governance. Principles, Policies . . . op. cit., p. 68.
26 M. J. Jones, Internal Control, Accountability and Corporate Governance. Medieval and Modern Britain Compared. *Accounting, Auditing & Accountability Journal* 2008, Vol. 21 No. 7, pp. 1052–1075.
27 A. Gramsci, T. R. Bates, Gramsci and the Theory of Hegemony. *Journal of the History of Ideas* April– June 1975, Vol. 36, No. 2, pp. 351–366.
28 T. Mendis, Analysis of Corporate Governance Theories and Their Implications for Sri Lankan Companies. *Journal of the Faculty of Graduate Studies, University of Kelaniya* 2012, Vol. 1.
29 B. Tricker, Corporate Governance. Principles, Policies . . . op. cit., pp. 68–69.
30 C. D. Totman, A History of Japan . . . op. cit., p. 54.
31 C. Andressen, A Short History of Japan . . . . op. cit., p. 33.
32 K. Hara, An Introduction to the History of Japan. *Yamato Society Publication, G. P. Putnam's & Sons. The Knickerbocker Press*, New York, London 1920, p. 65.
33 J. McEldowney, Hybridization: A Study in Comparative Constitutional Law. *Penn State International Law Review* 2010, Vol. 28: No. 3, Article 5, pp. 355–376.
34 J. E. Kidder, The Earliest Societies in Japan. In: D. M. Brown (ed.), The Cambridge History of Japan. Vol. 1. Ancient Japan. *Cambridge University Press,* Cambridge 2008, p. 101.
35 R. H. P. Mason, J. G. Caiger. A History of Japan . . . op. cit., p. 31. D. M. Brown, The Yamato Kingdom. In: The Cambridge History of Japan. Vol. 1, Ancient Japan, op. cit., p. 138.
36 J. E. Kidder, The Earliest Societies in Japan. In: The Cambridge History of Japan. Vol. 1, Ancient Japan . . . op. cit., p. 101.
37 D. M. Brown, The Yamato Kingdom. In: The Cambridge History of Japan. Vol. 1. Ancient Japan . . . op. cit., p. 138.
38 M. Hane, G. Perez, Premodern Japan. A Historical Survey. *Routledge Taylor & Francis Group*, New York, London 2018, p. 15.

39 T. Toyoda, Japanese Guilds. *The Annals of the Hitotsubashi Academy* 1954, Vol. 5, No. 1, pp. 72–85.
40 C. Andressen, A Short History of Japan . . . op. cit., p. 28.
41 M. Hane, G. Perez, Premodern Japan . . . op. cit., p. 15. D. M. Brown, The Yamato Kingdom. In: The Cambridge History of Japan. Vol. 1. Ancient Japan . . . pp. 139–140.
42 F. Brinkley, D. Kikuchi, A History of the Japanese People . . . op. cit., pp. 71 and 95.
43 C. Andressen, A Short History of Japan . . . op. cit., p. 28.
44 R. H. P. Mason, J. G. Caiger. A History of Japan. *TUTTLE Publishing,* Tokyo; Rutland, VT; Singapore 1997, p. 31. D. M. Brown, The Yamato Kingdom. In: The Cambridge History of Japan. Vol. 1. Ancient Japan . . . op. cit., p. 138.
45 K. Yamamura, The Development of Za in Medieval Japan. *The Business History Review* Winter 1973, Vol. 47, No. 4, pp. 438–465.
46 M. J. Jones, Internal Control, Accountability and Corporate Governance: Medieval and Modern Britain Compared. *Accounting, Auditing & Accountability Journal* 2008, Vol. 21, No. 7, pp. 1052–1075.
47 E. Honjo, The Economic Development of Japan. *Kyoto University Economic Review* 1931, Vol. 6, No. 1, pp. 14–28.
48 D. M. Brown, The Yamato Kingdom. In: The Cambridge History of Japan. Vol. 1. Ancient Japan . . . op. cit., p. 139.
49 R. H. P. Mason, J. G. Caiger, A History of Japan . . . op. cit., p. 30.
50 C. J. Kiley, State and Dynasty in Archaic Yamato . . . op. cit.
51 R. H. P. Mason, J. G. Caiger, A History of Japan . . . p. 30.
52 www.britannica.com/topic/be.
53 D. M. Brown, The Yamato Kingdom. In: The Cambridge History of Japan. Vol. 1. Ancient Japan . . . op. cit., p. 138.
54 J. E. Kidder, The Earliest Societies in Japan. In: The Cambridge History of Japan. Vol. 1. Ancient Japan . . . op. cit., p. 100.
55 Ibidem, p. 99.
56 D. M. Brown, The Yamato Kingdom. In: The Cambridge History of Japan. Vol. 1. Ancient Japan . . . op. cit., pp. 139, 140.
57 W. S. Morton, J. K. Olenik, Japan. Its History and Culture . . . op. cit., p. 14.
58 D. M. Brown, The Yamato Kingdom. In: The Cambridge History of Japan. Vol. 1. Ancient Japan . . . op. cit., pp. 156, 157.
59 B. L. Batten, Foreign Threat, and Domestic Reform . . . op. cit.

Bibliography

Aguilera, R., Jackson, G., Hybridization and Heterogeneity across National Models of Corporate Governance. *Economic Sociology: European Electronic Newsletter, ISSN: 1871-3351, Max Planck Institute for the Study of Societies (MPIfG), Cologne* 2002, Vol. 3, No. 2, pp. 17–25.

Andressen, C., A Short History of Japan. From Samurai to Sony. *Allen & Unwin*, Canberra 2002.

Batten, B. L., Foreign Threat and Domestic Reform: The Emergence of the *Ritsuryō* State. *Monumenta Nipponica* 1986, Vol. 41, No. 2, pp. 199–219. www.jstor.org/stable/2384665.

Brinkley, F., Kikuchi, D., A History of the Japanese People from the Earliest Times to the End of the Meiji Era. *The Encyclopaedia Britannica Co*, New York, London 1912. https://archive.org/details/historyofjapanes00briniala/page/n5/mode/2up.

Cioffi, J. W., Cohen, S. S., The State, the Law and Corporate Governance: The Advantage of Forwardness. In: S. S. Cohen, G. Boyd (eds.), Corporate Governance and Globalization. *Edward Elgar*, Northampton 2000, pp. 307–349.

Dau, L., Morck, R. K., Yeung, B., Corporate Governance, Business Group Governance and Economic Development Traps. *NBER Working Paper No. w28069*. November 2020 SSRN: https://ssrn.com/abstract=3727144.

Davis, G. F., Cobb, J. A., Resource Dependence Theory: Past and Future. *Research in the Sociology of Organizations* 2010, No. 28, pp. 21–42. http://dx.doi.org/10.1108/S0733-558X(2010)0000028006G.

Dollinger, M. J., Confucian Ethics and Japanese Management Practices. *Journal of Business Ethics* 1988, Vol. 7, No. 8, pp. 575–584. www.jstor.org/stable/25071802www.jstor.org/stable/25071802.

Gramsci, A., Bates, T. R., Gramsci and the Theory of Hegemony. *Journal of the History of Ideas* April–June 1975, Vol. 36, No. 2, pp. 351–366.

Hane, M., Perez, G., Premodern Japan. A Historical Survey. *Routledge Taylor & Francis Group*, New York, London 2018. file:///D:/Users/wzr/Downloads/9780429494819_previewpdf.pdf.

Hara, K., An Introduction to the History of Japan. *Yamato Society Publication, G. P. Putnam's &Sons. The Knickerbocker Press*, New York, London 1920. www.gutenberg.org/files/37186/37186-h/37186-h.htm

Honjo, E., The Economic Development of Japan. *Kyoto University Economic Review* 1931, Vol. 6, No. 1, pp. 14–28.

Jones, M. J., Internal Control, Accountability and Corporate Governance: Medieval and Modern Britain Compared. *Accounting, Auditing & Accountability Journal* 2008, Vol. 21, No. 7, pp. 1052–1075. https://repository.kulib.kyoto-u.ac.jp/dspace/bitstream/2433/125201/1/ecb0061_014.pdf.

Kiley, C. J., State and Dynasty in Archaic Yamato. *The Journal of Asian Studies* 1973, Vol. 33, No. 1, Cambridge University Press, Association for Asian Studies, pp. 25–49. www.jstor.org/stable/2052884.

Klityńska, P., Myśl Konfucjusza, Uniwersytet Wrocławski, *ACTA ERASMIANA* 2016, No. XIII, pp. 1–13.

Liu, W., Sidhu, A., M. Beacom, Valente. T. W., Social Network Theory. In: P. Rossler, C. A. Hoffner, L. van Zoonen (eds.), The International Encyclopedia of Media Effects. *Wiley*, New York 2017.

Mason, R. H. P., Caiger, J. G., A History of Japan. *TUTTLE Publishing*, Tokyo; Rutland, VT; Singapore 1997. file:///D:/Users/wzr/Downloads/A_History_of_Japan_Mason_Caiger%20(5).pdf

McEldowney, J., Hybridization: A Study in Comparative Constitutional Law. *Penn State International Law Review* 2010, Vol. 28, No. 3, Article 5, pp. 355–376. http://elibrary.law.psu.edu/psilr/vol28/iss3/5.

Mendis, T., Analysis of Corporate Governance Theories and Their Implications for Sri Lankan Companies. *Journal of the Faculty of Graduate Studies, University of Kelaniya* 2012, Vol. 1. www.researchgate.net/publication/338357928_Analysis_of_Corporate_Governance_Theories_and_their_Implications_for_Sri_Lankan_Companies.

Meyer, M. W., Japan: A Concise History. *Rowman & Littlefield Publishers Inc*, Plymouth 2009. file:///D:/Users/wzr/Downloads/epdf.pub_japan-a-concise-history-4th-edition.pdf.

Morton, W. S., Olenik, J. K., Japan. Its History and Culture. *McGraw-Hill Companies Inc*, New York 2005. https://vdocuments.mx/japan-its-history-and-culture-56811b380a71d.html.

Murdoch, J., History of Japan, From the Origins to the Arrival of the Portuguese in 1542 A.D. Vol. I. *The Asiatic Society of Japan*, London 1910. file:///D:/Users/wzr/Documents/Japonia%20Ks1/Ksi%C4%85%C5%BCki%20Hist/A%20history%20of%20Japan%20Volume%201%20(1903).pdf.

Pfeffer, J., Salancik, G. R., The External Control of Organizations: A Resource Dependence Perspective. *University of Illinois at Urbana-Champaign's Academy for Entrepreneurial Leadership Historical Research Reference in Entrepreneurship*, 1978. SSRN: https://ssrn.com/abstract=1496213

Rost, K., Introduction to the Corporate Governance of Religion. *The Zurich Open Repository and Archive, University of Zurich*, 2017. www.researchgate.net/deref/https%3A%2F%2Fdoi.org%2F10.5167%2Fuzh-133251?_tp=eyJjb250ZXh0Ijp7ImZpcnN0UGFnZSI6InB1YmxpY2F0aW9uIiwicGFnZSI6InB1YmxpY2F0aW9uIiwicG9zaXRpb24iOiJwYWdlQ29udGVudCJ9fQ.

Scott, W. R., Davis, G. F., Organizations and Organizing: Rational, Natural, and Open System Perspectives. *Pearson Prentice Hall*, Upper Saddle River, NJ 2007.

The Cambridge History of Japan. Vol. 1. Ancient Japan. D. M. Brown (ed.). *Cambridge University Press, Cambridge* 2008.

Totman, C. D., A History of Japan. *Blackwell Publishing,* Malden; Oxford; Carlton 2005. www.perlego.com/book/1006239/a-history-of-japan-pdf.

Toyoda, T., Japanese Guilds. *The Annals of the Hitotsubashi Academy* 1954, Vol. 5, No. 1, pp. 72–85. *JSTOR*. www.jstor.org/stable/43751448.

Tricker, B., Corporate Governance. Principles, Policies, and Practices. *Oxford University Press*, Oxford 2015.

Yamamura, K., The Development of Za in Medieval Japan. *Business History Review* December 1973, Vol. 47, No. 4, pp. 438–465. www.jstor.org/stable/3113366?seq=1&cid=pdf-reference#references_tab_contents.

Zehir, M., Findikli, A., Çeltekligil, K., Resource Dependence Theory, Firm Performance and Producers-Suppliers Relationships. 14th ISMC and 8th ICLTIBM-2018, *The European Proceedings of Social & Behavioural Sciences 2018*, pp. 162–172. www.europeanproceedings.com/files/data/article/107/4360/article_107_4360_pdf_100.pdf.

Zhan, Z. Q., Deng, X. J., Why They Connected: A Theoretical Analysis on the Cause of Interfirm Network Formation. *Open Journal of Social Sciences* 2014, No. 2, pp. 232–237. http://dx.doi.org/10.4236/jss.2014.29039www.scirp.org/pdf/JSS_2014082711424950.pdf. www.britannica.com/topic/be.

Part 2

Introduction to the *Ritsuryō* State and its corporate governance system

4 The rise and fall of the *Ritsuryō* State

The death of Prince Shōtoku in 622 and the opposition by the great *uji* delayed the reforms aimed at empowering the emperor for almost a quarter of a century. But the enlightened elites understood well that magnates could not continue to do what they wanted, because the nation would remain incapable of any collective effort or enterprise.[1] Such aims as achieving political integration of Yamato, strengthening the power of the state, and reforming the government to prepare against any pressures, especially from the expanding Tang dynasty in China, had to be achieved.[2] Kiley writes that if the royal prerogatives are mainly ritualistic and the political administration is in the hands of several autonomous associations, it cannot be said that a state exists.[3] The systematic implementation of the *ritsuryō* population and land policy began after the Japan's defeat in Korea (Paekche) in 663 and the resulting stagnation, which caused the upheaval needed to convince the Japanese ruling class to reform.[4] In 645, the ruling Soga clan was overthrown by the prince, later Emperor Tenchi (661–71) with the help of Fujiwara no Kamatari (614–69), who initiated the rule of the Fujiwara family lasting until the 11th century. This perpetuated the earlier trend of influential individuals or families wielding power while emperors remained figureheads.[5] Then, the Taika reform was introduced, a new government and administrative system based on the Chinese model. The name Taika (great change) stemmed from the *year's name* which was given to an era for the first time in Japanese history. The Japanese were adopting the year period, or reign names (*nengo*), of the Chinese (a practice there dating back to 140 BCE), wherein the rulers characterized all or part of their reigns by descriptive terms.[6] The Taika reform was possible, thanks to the change of power at court and the initially limited scale and nominal character it had. Its purpose was to create a fully centralized imperial state out of the loosely associated *uji*. It was to be ruled by the emperor in accordance with a system of written laws and with the help of bureaucratic officials appointed to office and dismissed by the emperor (the right to hire and fire). The aims of the Taika reform were to abolish the system of hereditary office holders, to differentiate aristocratic titles from official ranks, to make all the people direct subjects of the emperor, and to establish the imperial ownership of all the land in the empire.[7]

DOI: 10.4324/9781003497936-6

The Yamato *uji* (the Throne) adopted the *ritsuryō* system to retain its hegemony in the emerging nation state. *Ritsuryō* is the historical legal system based on Confucianism and Chinese law. The written legal codes were called *ritsuryō*, and a state that was governed by these legal codes was called a *Ritsuryō* State (the state of codified law). It promoted the concept of a centralized political order (the *ritsuryō* system) referring to the governmental structure as defined by *ritsu* – the criminal code, and *ryō* – meaning administrative law on government structure and procedures.[8] Its architects Prince Nakano Ōe (planner) and Prince Kamatari (executor) were determined to transform Yamato economically and politically[9] and hoped that a strong centralized government would enable Japan to resume and bring to a success its activities in the Korean peninsula.[10] According to Holcombe, the *ritsuryō* system created in the 7th and 8th centuries was a hybrid Confucian-Legalist system, in which Confucian motives were predominant.[11] Thus, the *Ritsuryō* State may be viewed as a hybrid of the two organizational principles, the Japanese *uji* (stratified clan) society and the Chinese historic civilization.[12] The periods of development of Japanese law can be classified in various ways. One of them divides the period 702 to 1868 into two subperiods – the period of Chinese reception, from the Taihō Code (702) to the Kamakura period (1185) and the period of harmonization of these Chinese importations with indigenous law (1186–1868). This latter period is further divided into the Shikimoku period including the Kamakura and Muromachi regimes (1185–1467), Kokuho period when law was decentralized and provided by local lords for their own domains (1467–1603), and the Tokugawa period of centralized codified law (1603–1868). All of these are basically feudal, though the character of Kamakura feudalism was different from Tokugawa feudalism.[13]

The *Ritsuryō* State was an organized structure linking the emperor with the ordinary people through a hierarchy of central, provincial, district, and local governmental organs staffed by proper aristocrats. Their duties included ensuring that the peace was maintained and that the producers sent the agreed tribute to the government.[14] In the absence of absolute political and military power, the throne could maintain its hegemony only by gaining the support of potential competitors in exchange for economic and political benefits. Therefore, to gain support of the upper class, in 645, reformers introduced a system of compensation for those who lost their privileges.[15] According to Yamamura, *ritsuryō*'s economic system was the result of the leaders' desire to maintain political balance and ensure that their economic base was expanded or maintained. It had economic advantages such as the disappearance of slaves and semi-slave skilled labour, the adoption of contractual arrangements between landowners and cultivators, rational methods of taxation.[16] Slaves amounted to about 5% of the subjects of the emperor and were divided into private and public. On their account, the owner of the household owning slaves received a land allocation (one-third of the part granted to a free-born subject) to cover his taxes. The public slaves were in a much more favoured position. They received as much land as a freeman, although they could not 'deal with it freely', and they were exempt from all forced labour apart from their specific tasks.

Batten distinguishes three stages of the *ritsuryō* institutional reforms. The first stage was the emergence of *Ritsuryō* State in the Taika period (645–654), the second (664–671) concerned the expansion of a provincial and district system of central bureaucracy, having the structural features of the mature *Ritsuryō* State, and the reorganization of *be* communities into households and townships, leading to the completion of The first *ritsuryō* code in 668 (the Ōmi Code). The third stage of reform began in 672, allowing the *Ritsuryō* State to move closer to its final form by the 690s and continue to reform. Initially, the *ritsuryō* system seemed to work well, but soon it began to break down.[17]

The first stage of the reform began on the New Year's Day in 646, with promulgation of the Taika Reform Edict of four articles strengthening the political power of the emperor.[18] Article I declared that land and people controlled by the *uji* were to be placed under imperial administration. It also abolished *miyake* (royal rice-growing estates) together with *kakibe* (privately held *be*), *koshiro* (*be* established for memorial of the royal family), and *tadokoro* (estates belonging to non-royal aristocrats) owned by the central and local elites (*omi, muraji, tomo-no-miyatsuko, kuni-no-miyatsuko*, and *mura-no-obito*). In this way, private holdings of land and *be* corporations of agricultural workers were abolished. The land was parcelled out and controlled by the government, and farmers were to work for the state, not individuals, as free subjects and leaseholders from the state.[19] Prince Nakano was the first who surrendered formally and voluntarily his estates and subjects to the emperor. Some nobles followed his example but those who did not were forced to do so, by an edict making it obligatory and universal.[20]

Article II defined the provinces or metropolitan regions, with the appointment of the necessary officials, and provided for the improvement of the communication system, roads, and bridges, for connections to the external provinces. It decreed that a capital city must be established as the centre of the governance system.

Article III ordered the compilation of population, taxation registers, and the formalization of the land laws. Censuses (first was taken in 670) were to register the population for the allocation of rice land (*kabunden*) to farmers at so much land *per mouth* in the family, for assessment of taxes, and for the appointment of local headmen. The peasants could use the land granted but could not dispose of it privately, because it belonged to the emperor. Officials at the provincial and district levels, as agents of the central government, were obliged to control the population of the country through regular censuses and paddy surveys conducted, at first, every four, and later, every six years. The governors were to prepare registers of population, books of accounts, and a system of the receipt and re-granting of distribution land as a basis for the systematic allocation of paddy land to keep it in the hands of free farmers.[21] The land taken over by the state was redistributed among all who had achieved a certain age with the right to cultivate it in exchange for a fixed tax. For the first time, an attempt was made to determine who owned what, which allowed better social control and a more efficient taxation system, increasing the government's power.[22]

Article IV introduced a new system of taxation adopted from China based on three main types of taxes – agricultural produce paid in cereals, *corvée* labour, and service.[23] They were imposed on individuals in the households: a grain tax in kind (usually rice) – 3% of the crop produced, taxes on textiles and handicrafts, a tax in the form of compulsory labour covering 60 days of forced labour in the form of public works for the state (it was required by the provincial and central administration but could be converted into its equivalent value in cloth) and military service (soldiers were exempt from other taxes but went at their own expense). These additional state duties were the real hardship, especially the military service. One-third of the male inhabitants of each province, in the ages 20–59, had to spend in the active service one year at the capital and three years on the frontiers, providing their own equipment and provisions. This hard obligation encouraged people to desert their land to avoid conscription.[24] Labour for public works was required by the provincial and central administration, as it was already mentioned, it could be converted into its equivalent value in cloth.

The Taika Reform Edict (646) managed to create a centralized state. The old *uji* families had lost control over the *be* corporations and their private landholdings after their confiscation by the state in the period 645–646. The early Yamato system of administration was replaced by the *ritsuryō* model administered by officials.[25] It included a hierarchy of provinces (*kuni*) of four classes – great, superior, medium, and inferior; districts (*kori* or *gun*, originally called *agata* – arable land) of five classes – great, superior, medium, inferior, and small.[26] They were subdivided into *inaki* (granary) and *mura* or *sato* (village), each consisting of about 50 households (*ri* or *ko*). Mason and Caiger note that the basic administrative map of Japan (60 provinces and 600 districts, with their connecting system of land and water routes) of the Taika reformers remained until the institution of the current prefectures in the 1870s and 1880s.[27] Peasant communities were further blocked into groups of five families called an *association of five* (*goho* or *gonin-gumi*) with a recognized head (*hocho*). These groups were held mutually responsible for implementation of the official directives and their own control and protection.[28] The creation of districts and the structural reforms were of great institutional importance.

Provincial governors (*kokushi)* reappeared (go back to the 5th century) in the early 670s, becoming an integral part of the administrative system.[29] They were the highest-ranking officials in each province, connecting the Court and provinces. The emperor appointed them from men of high rank in the central bureaucracy, usually descendants of the old court nobility, at first for four-year and later for six-year terms. As income, they received two dozen acres of land for their rank and about five additional acres for their office. The governor's mission was to supervise the cult of deities, register the population, act as a father to the people, foster agriculture, rectify wrongs, supervise the police, and hear grievances, register households and rice fields, impose taxes, *corvée* labour, maintain irrigation systems, public buildings, and pastures, ensure that the province was able to defend itself by means of militias, arms, and signal fires. So, no aspect of the life of the population was expected to escape their control.[30]

Local lords and chiefs held lower-level positions serving under governors. Each district *(kori*), within the boundaries established in the period 680–685, was governed by a chief (*guncho* or *gunryo*). The district chiefs were imperial appointees, usually members of prominent local aristocracy, who collected taxes under the control of the imperial governor.[31] Thus, under governor were heads of districts, aldermen of townships (50 houses), elders of five households, and market commissioners. The latter supervised currency (in kind), trade, the originality of products, the validity of weights and measures, the prices of goods, and compliance with prohibitions.[32] The village had a village chief (*richo*) whose job was to record the number of people in each household, encourage agricultural and livestock productivity, resolve or report any offences, and initiate public services. The district chief's main obligation was to oversee *richo*.[33] Merchants, as leading townsmen, had the right to choose town elders (*otona*) who carried on local government through assemblies. All officials were salaried, paid in natural products, since no currency existed at that time.[34] In this way, traditional power holders, that is, clan leaders and local aristocrats, became the emperor's subordinates. The state created a well-functioning, hierarchical system of control and supervision over institutions and residents, which proves its good organization and strength.

The laws of the country emphasized social hierarchy, obedience, and responsibility. A complex system of codified rules and regulations underpinned a strongly hierarchical social order.[35] There were three types of social actors – the court nobles (descendants of the former powerful *uji* and now the highest-ranking officials in central government), the local lords (local powers with some military strength and position in provincial government), and the commoners who were at the bottom of the political and social structure.[36] The latter were free farmers (*ryomin*) who were the beneficiaries of the land redistribution policy during the Taika reform, often holding serfs and slaves (*semmin*) in bondage.[37] The Taika reforms liquidated the hereditary *be* and guilds and caused a reorganization of the *be* communities into households and townships. It was not possible to carry out this system in the case of the *kakibe* or labourers of the *uji*, and the domestic servants of a family, without preserving their former status.[38]

The Taika reform was a far-sighted policy forced from the top down by a small number of ruling elite under very dangerous conditions.[39] It was a political revolution and changed the social status of the masses from serfdom, as members of the *be* corporations, to free subjects and leaseholders (tenants) of the state.[40] It reinforced the government's power as the censuses attempted to determine who owned what, which allowed better social control and a more efficient taxation system, increasing the government's power.[41] It provided the state with regular income and enabled it to gain control over a large army.[42] Mason and Caiger argue that the *uji* was not destroyed by the reforms because the power and social status that *uji* leaders had lost with the abolition of corporations *be* and estates, were restored to them in the form of a monopoly on new bureaucratic positions. Because the income of an aristocrat depended mainly upon the grade of rank held, there was a great struggle among the courtiers for these grade-related degrees.[43]

The first Japanese *ritsuryō* code called Ōmi Code (668), based on rules and systems modelled on Chinese, contained 22 volumes which are said to establish the government system. Batten writes that, in 664, *uji* were classified according to status into three groups – great, small, and *be*-leader (*tomo-no-miyatsuko uji*). Heads of clans (*uji no kami*) were appointed as their leaders and provided with weapons representing their new status (long swords were given to the heads of large *uji*, short swords to the heads of small *uji* (*ko-uji* numbering between 50 and 90 relatives), and shields, bows, and arrows to the heads of *be*-leader uji). The emperor ordered a review and increase in the number of court ranks and appointments for heads of professional groups (*kakibe and yakabe).* Titles awarded in recognition of merit were to replace the former hereditary and office-related *kabane* (or *sei*).[44]

Emperor Tenmu (673–686), the first monarch of Japan who was called emperor (Tenno),[45] ruled state affairs by coercion, always with military assistance, but by appointing competent people to positions in the government. Until 684, *o-omi* and *o-muraji* stood between the throne and the two great uji classes, receiving instructions directly from the sovereign. The *uji* leaders recognized no control other than that of *o-omi* and *o-muraji*. During Tenmu's reign (673–686), a central administrative organ called the Office of Senior Controller (*daibenkan*) was established including a Chancellor (*daijō-daijin)*, a Minister of the Left, and a Minister of the Right. In the year 689, the name of this supervisory body was changed to Council of State (*daijokan*).[46] Emperor Tenmu raised the dignity and authority of the Court to an unprecedented degree. He expanded the obligation of decorum formulated in the Shōtoku Taishi code by publishing the Tenmu Law (685), containing guidelines for court ceremonies, behaviour, and forms of greeting of officials of all ranks.[47]

The Taika reform confirmed the recruitment of officials based on state examinations (based on China's bureaucratic system), which had already been promoted by Prince Shōtoku. According to the law, appointments to office and promotion should depend, not upon rank, but on the knowledge and skills of candidates. Prospective bureaucrats were required to study at university and to pass prescribed examinations. Brinkley and Kikuchi write that the university graduates were divided into three categories: those of eminent talent (*shusai*), those having extensive knowledge of the Chinese classics (*meikei*), and those advanced in knowledge (*shinshi*). Official vacancies were filled from these three classes in the presented order and promotion depended on proficiency. Candidates were first appointed chamberlains (*toneri*) and placed under observation. Their performance was evaluated once a year, and their rank and position were adjusted in accordance with the results.[48] However, in 682, emperor Tenmu issued the edict according to which the order of consideration in selecting men for office was to be birth, character, and ability.[49] Birth privileges were reinforced, allowing only nobility or the sons and grandsons of educated people to be admitted to university.[50] In this way, the *ritsuryō* system ensured that the bureaucracy was maintained by the hereditary aristocracy rather than by individuals vetted by the Chinese Confucian system of education, examinations, and meritocracy. The examinations were soon dropped as the aristocrats managed to abolish the system of public service and promotion, allowing offices to become hereditary and not open to competition on merit.[51]

To ensure that the highest ranks were monopolized by the great *uji*, the system of shadow ranks (*on'i*) was introduced, which offered concessions from the throne to nobles in the form of economic rewards, various stipends, and tax exemptions, preferential consideration in the granting of promotions, a special legal status guaranteeing nobles little or no penalty when they committed a minor crime.[52] The most politically strong *uji* leaders were appointed to high positions in the newly formed bureaucracy. The monopoly on new bureaucratic positions compensated them for the authority and social status they had lost with the abolition of *be* corporations and estates. They were awarded in the form of rice land and labour to cultivate them, which came from the emperor in the form of a benefice.[53] The new titles (*sei*) that replaced the *kabane* were obtained through a special grant from the emperor Tenmu, namely, *mahito, asomi, sukune, imiki, michi-no-shi*, *omi*, *muraji*, and *inagi*, and their nearest English equivalents are duke, marquis, count, lord, viscount, baron, and baronet. Later, they became hereditary but never indicated the holding of an office.[54]

The members of the imperial family and the leaders of the major *uji* were de facto nobles in the pre-Taika period, but they became de jure nobles whose economic rewards were sanctioned by the system which they helped to create and maintain. They suffered no economic losses from the adoption of the new order, so they accepted it.[55] In this way, the law became a compromise between the new principles of the *ritsuryō* system and the old respect for birth.[56] It was an excellent example of the use of hybridization, which had been quite often implemented in Japanese law and governance history. However, over time, these privileges proved to be the cause of the downfall of the *Ritsuryō* State.

The most important civilizing force introduced from China at that time were the formal institutions of education. The first schools in provinces as well as a state university (*daigaku*) in the capital and provincial ones (*kokugaku*) were established in the period 668–671.[57] The idea of the necessity of education has never left the Japanese.[58] The subjects taught in the universities were called the *shidō*, or *four paths of learning*, and were history, the Chinese classics, law, and mathematics.[59] The universities were placed under the jurisdiction of a special bureau (Taihō Code, 702). Their purpose was to educate the children of persons who held the fifth rank or higher, the children of lower-ranking officials were sometimes allowed to attend school with special permission, but the children of the common people were not admitted. The number of students was limited to 400, and the government *financed* their education and food.[60]

In the 8th century, rice-producing land took three forms: household or private fields (*kubunden*), public fields (*koden*), and reclaimed fields (*konden*). Household fields were allotted, or rearranged, every six years under the allotment system known as *handen*. They were allocated according to each household's size and composition, could not be sold, or exchanged, or used as security in making loans, but their crops could be mortgaged. Households kept them if they had the labour to cultivate them, as in early Japan private ownership of land was only recognized when it was actively used. This not only was inspired by the Chinese allotment system but also had traditional Japanese roots, which made the practice successful.[61]

Rice paddies that were not divided under the first national allocation system in the 690s were classified as public fields (*koden*) which covered about 5% of the total area under rice cultivation. They were to support rank holders, office holders, temples, shrines, and individual aristocrats. The best quality rice land was granted to the princes and the court nobles. The stipends of the imperial branch families, ranked from the first to the fourth class in order of succession to the throne, decreased as the rank fell. According to Yamamura, the 1st class, by virtue of their rank, received 80 *cho* of the best quality rice paddy, 800 households to cultivate the paddies, a total of 100 servants and guards, and annual stipends in cloth and iron plow while a fourth-ranked prince received 40 *cho* of rice paddy, 300 households, and 40 servants and guards. To compare, each free male received two *tan* of *Kubunden* was a rice field allocated to all citizens in the *Ritsuryō* system, the harvest of which was taxed by the government. The head and the leading members of *uji* received ranks ranging from those carrying stipends of 80 *cho* of rice paddy, 300 households (increased to 600 in 706), and 100 servants and guards, to the lower ranks coming with less of each type of stipend. The land granted was tax-exempt, and each of the household members given to the princes received his share of *kubunden* according to the established schedule.[62] Governors who managed land for the Court, as high-ranking officials, were granted *sustenance fiefs*, while other officials received gifts of hemp and silk. Murdoch writes that an official, in addition to rank land (*i-den*) and office land (*shoku-oun-den*), often received a four-class estate (*koden*) awarded for public service, free of all taxes. Land for the highest public merit was granted according to classes for various periods, that is, forever, or allowing it to be passed on to the third or second generation, or only to children, but always free of taxes. A courtier might be also gratified with a *shi-den*, or an estate created by a special decree of the sovereign. These tax-free estates contributed more than any other factor to the downfall of the imperial authority and the central government.[63] Thus, due to economic reasons, especially land tax exemptions, in the second half of the 8th century, the concept of a strong state based on extensive and well-organized economic, political, and administrative forms began to decline.[64] Later decrees such as the *Taihō* Code (702) and Yōrō Code (757) also introduced some significant status-related reforms.[65]

The reforms and new tax structure, culminated in 702 with the promulgation of the *Taihō* Code or Constitution, named after its enactment in the second year of the *Taihō* period. It unified the existing statutes and established the structure of the central government and its subordinate local governments.[66] The *Taihō* Code (Great Treasure) had two sections, the *ryō*, or administrative and civil codes, and the *ritsu*, or disciplinary and penal regulations, which concerned matters of arrest and imprisonment.[67] Up to 967, amendments to this code continued to be made to adapt it to changing circumstances.[68] It was modelled on the legislation (codes) of the Chinese Tang dynasty (618–907) and the doctrines of Confucius and Buddhism.

The *Taihō* Code provided Japan for the first time with a written code of law and a formal system of government administration. It contained no bill of rights, codified the fundamental laws, and took care of the smallest details. The framework of this code was oriented towards the creation of a strong central government and concentration of power, the prevention of large estates and the formation of a distinct warrior class, and ensuring that the government would be able to meet the needs of the people.[69] It imposed greater control over corruption among local officials and placed great emphasis on the promotion and regulation of court life, but little on the affairs of the common people.[70]

Carkeek writes that the Taihō Constitution established a complete framework of government. The head of government was the *mikado* (former title of the emperors of Japan), who exercised executive and legislative powers and was assisted by the legislative body, the Council of State. Laws were enacted or promulgated in his name by a ministry appointed by him, and the people had no say in the making of laws. Under the Council of State were eight departments – The Ministry of the Imperial Household, The Ministry of Court Ceremonies, A Department of Somewhat the Same Thing, The Home Department, The Ministry of War, The Ministry of Justice, The National Treasury, and The Treasury of the Imperial Household. The Taihō Code divided the country into 58 provinces, which were subdivided into more than 500 sub-divisions, each with a certain amount of self-government. Over each province, there was a governor appointed by the *mikado* and a governor was placed over each of the 500 districts.[71] These organizational changes, together with effective audit, were crucial for good corporate governance.[72] The Taihō Code stipulated that all lands were held by the *mikado* and were granted for a period of six years, at the end of which the land will be reallocated. Land was completely nationalized, and its private ownership was forbidden. It should be noted that the Taihō Code recognized the rights of the wife. It granted wives great freedom in managing property. The husband managed his wife's property, but in case of a divorce, he had to return it to her. The Taihō Code provided that the husband might obtain a divorce on seven grounds, but five of them were not available, when the husband was poor and humble when marrying, but subsequently accumulated wealth or was risen in office or distinction, as it was presumed in this case that the influence and help of the wife was a contributing cause.[73]

All real estate under the Taihō Code was held by the Mikado. The aristocracy was divided into five classes, whose members, according to their rank, received land (from 20 to 160 acres) as remuneration. The next class of land, the *office land*, was assigned for the support of the officials of the government. This was also exempt from taxation. The third class of land called *public merit land* was granted to distinguished persons. It was divided into three classes. The first class was given to a person and to his heirs forever; the second to a person and his heirs for three generations; the third only to a person and to his children.[74] In addition, various religious associations received certain tax-free lands in return for their support. Exempting such a large area of land from taxes did not matter much at first, but later, these large, tax-exempt estates began to cause serious fiscal problems, and with the increase in population, contributed to the impoverishment of the population and, consequently, to the fall of the *Ritsuryō* State. As far as tribute collection is concerned, before 680, it took the form of rice collected from a household according to the area of land that was cultivated, but after 680, tribute was collected from individuals. Therefore, the Taihō Code considered household registration as a very important and frequently revised matter.[75]

Three types of taxes were introduced by the Taihō Code – tax (*so*), forced service (*yo*), and tribute (*cho*).[76] Taxes were paid in produce from the soil, usually rice at about 3–5% of the value of the produce. The Code fixed the distribution of the proceeds due from the provincial rice tax. It was divided into three parts, the principal tax, the government tax, and the miscellaneous tax. The principal tax was further subdivided into three parts, one of which was sent to the capital, another was stored in the provincial or district granaries established by the government, and the third part was advanced to needy farmers as a loan by the government. The miscellaneous tax was used to repair government buildings, post stations, embankments, ponds and ditches, support of shrines and temples, provincial schools, and Ainu prisoners. A part of this tax was available for loans to needy farmers. There was no tax for war purposes. The soldier was lowest in the social scale, and the Ministry of War was the least prestigious and important of the eight ministries. Next to the nobility, the peasant occupied the highest position in the social hierarchy, and despite all the changes in Japanese law and jurisprudence, this principle has never changed. Farmers were supreme and protected in every code passed, and the taxes they paid were carefully adjusted so that they would not be crushed. This is true even at the present time.[77]

The Taihō Code divided crimes into those against the state, the Court, and those against family (private individuals). The order of their gravity was (1) high treason (against the State); (2) high treason (against the Crown); (3) treason; (4) parricide, fratricide, etc.; (5) offences against humanity; (6) use majesty; (7) unfilial conduct; and (8) crimes against society.[78] In the case of arrest for the first type of crime, the offender was placed in the care of a relative, while in the case of the second type, he was jailed. The Code defined 98 crimes and specified the penalties for committing them. The three greatest crimes were treason, unfilial conduct on the part of children towards their parents, adultery on the part of the wife. This gradation of crimes showed the influence of the doctrines of Confucius. It provided for six mitigations of punishment depending on the rank, official position, or public service of the perpetrator.[79] The main changes in judicial proceedings concerned the abolition of torture by boiling water, fire, and snakes.[80]

According to Carkeek, the Taihō Code provided for the following five forms of capital punishment – by strangulation, beheading, deportation, imprisonment with labour from one to three years, flogging with a stick (60–100 blows), and flogging with a whip (from 10 to 50 blows). It also regulated the law concerning insolvent debtors. Creditors had the right to make an insolvent debtor a slave. He became the property of the creditor, but only for a limited period of time, after which he regained freedom. If the creditor took the debtor into slavery, he could not charge any interest. Interest could be charged if the loan term was longer than 60 days. The legal reforms of the 8th century were deep and lasting, and the defects which arose were ingrained in human nature. The Taihō Code was the foundation of Japanese law until 1232, so approximately for 500 years, when a new code, known as the Shikomoku Code, was enacted.[81]

The basic principles of the Taihō Code stated that people, regardless of rank or lineage, had the same responsibilities to the state, that only those who had special rights to public benevolence were entitled to permanent exemptions, and that it was not noble birth that qualifies for office, but intellectual ability and achievement. Nevertheless, the Japanese legislators did not find it possible to fully apply these wise principles.[82]

The *Taihō* Code, implementing Confucianism into the Japanese code of ethics, differed from the Chinese Tang model only in two points – according to Japanese tradition government positions and class status were based on birth (merit in China) and the assertion that the emperor's power comes from his divine descent.[83] The imperial power was cemented, and the dogma of imperial succession (divinity of the emperor) from Amaterasu the Sun Goddess was codified in the *Kojiki* (An Account of Ancient Matters, 711–712) and *Nihonshoki* (The Chronicles of Japan, 720), the two oldest written documents of the history of the country.[84] Under the *ritsuryō* system, the Japanese emperor was not only an absolute monarch ruling the whole country as the head of the bureaucracy, active in political affairs, but also the traditional high priest who maintained peace for land and people by paying tribute to the deities and sounding out their will. Thus, those Chinese ideas that were similar or understandable to Japanese concepts, such as the notions of hierarchy titles, and court rituals, persisted in it while those less suitable or impractical were not adopted.[85] The enactment of the *Taihō* Code completed the transformation of ancient Japan into the *Ritsuryō* State, treating people and land as public property, and made Japan a highly centralized and unified state by the 9th century.[86] It was not only very important but also modern and established the principles of monarchy and the framework of government, the organization of which was brought to a perfect state. The lasting effect of the Taihō Code was administrative division; as in 1868, when Japan began its march towards modernity, it retained the division of the empire into prefectures and provinces, in accordance with this Code.[87]

In 710, the imperial capital was shifted from Asuka to Nara (according to the ancient custom of changing the seat after each new emperor ascended the throne) starting the Nara period (710–794) and the time of great influence of China. In Nara city (modelled after the Chinese capital), a permanent centralized government was established for the first time. The Nara era was a bridge between the establishment of the Japanese state, defining the basic characteristics of Japanese society, and the sophistication of the Heian period (784–1185) and the heyday of Japanese culture.[88] Its politics revolved around the sovereign and court life. The more refined the court became, the more it lost touch with reality. Aristocrats used to spend their time in the capital and delegated their administrative duties to subordinated officials. Service in any provincial post was regarded as an exile.

In 718, the Taihō Code was amended by the Yōrō Code to accommodate Japanese traditions and practical administrative needs, but it was not promulgated for four decades. The revision was carried out by a commission chaired by Prime Minister Fujiwara Fuhito, and the volumes they revised were known as *Code and Law* (ten volumes each) of the Yōrō period. It became fully operational from the Taihō era (701–704) and, with minor revisions, remained in force until the 15th century. The nature and scope of the Yōrō Code is characterized by the titles of its various sections, such as (1) Official Titles; (2) Duties of Officials; (3) Duties of Officials of the Empress' Household; (4) Duties of Officials in the Household of the Heir Apparent; (5) Duties of Officials in the Households of Officers of High Rank; (6) Services to the Gods; (7) Buddhist Priests; (8) the Family; (9) the Land; (10) Taxation; (11) Learning; (12) Official Ranks and Titles; (13) The Descent of the Crown and Dignities of Imperial Persons; (14) Meritorious Discharge of Official Duties; (15) Salaries; (16) Court Guards; (17) Army and Frontier Defences; (18) Ceremonies; (19) Official Costumes; (20) Public Works; (21) Mode of addressing Persons of Rank; (22) Stores of Rice and other Grain; (23) Stables and Fodder; (24) Duties of Medical Officers attached to the Court; (25) Official Vacations; (26) Funerals and Mourning; (27) Watch and Ward and Markets; (28) Arrest of Criminals; (29) Jails; and (30) Miscellaneous, including Bailment, Finding of Lost Goods, etc.[89] But it was much as the *Taihō* Code. Both of them placed no limits on imperial power, legalizing the emperor's despotic control.[90] They were supplemented by the rules (*kyaku*) and regulations (*shiki*), which were re-drafted, first, in the Konin era (810–824) by a commission under the direction of the grand councillor, Fujiwara Fuyutsugu; next, in the Jokwan era (859–877) by Fujiwara Ujimune and others, and finally, in the Engi era (901–923) by a committee chaired by Fujiwara Tadahira. These three sets of provisions were called in subsequent ages the *Rules and Regulations of the Three Generations* (*Sandai-kyaku-shiki*). These regulations owed their origin to Kamatari, the great founder of the Fujiwara family, and each successive revision was presided over by one of his descendants. Nara bureaucratic order lasted until about 850. It was headed by the emperor. By 750, about 10,000 people found employment in the Nara Government. According to the Yōrō Code (718), the central government consisted of the Council of Kami Affairs (Department of Worship – *Jingikan*) taking precedence over the Council of State (*Daijokan*). The first was of ceremonial importance as it concerned the great national religious ceremonies, the supervision of major temples and rites, and concerned Shinto only, despite the growing popularity of Buddhism. It was unique to Japan and helped to administer central political affairs.[91]

The Council of State was responsible for carrying out secular duties and dealing with all secular aspects of administration and the needs of the Court. It was the highest authority advising the emperor on all civil and military matters of the state. It was chaired by the chancellor (*dajō-daijin*), under whom was the Minister of the Left (*sadaijin*), the senior minister responsible for the entire administration. His deputy, and junior minister, was the Minister of the Right (*udaijin*).[92] It also comprised a Controller's Office, through which the Council supervised eight subordinate ministries: Central Affairs, Ceremonial, Civil Affairs, People's Affairs, War, Punishments, the Treasury, and the Imperial Household.[93] Six of them were based on Chinese prototypes and two – the Imperial Household and its Treasury – were added by the Japanese. They were headed by ministers and included from 2 to 18 specialized offices. The innovation was the appointment of a Buddhist priest and a literatus.[94] Appointments to central offices were made bureaucratically among qualified rank holders.[95] Thus, the administrative structure – from the heads of imperial offices to the heads of local offices in distant regions – ran a hierarchy of office titles and ranks.[96]

During the Nara period, Buddhism became the official national religion. Large Buddhist monasteries (seven-story pagodas) were built in the new capital and in each province, and free rest houses (ryokan) for poor travellers were built along the paths by Buddhist monks. They first appeared around Kyōto, as the centralized state system required people to travel there for business. The privileges granted the monasteries such strong political influence that Emperor Kanmu (reigned 781–806) decided to move the capital to Nagaoka in 784 in order to weaken the ties between the government and Buddhism, restore the supremacy of the government according to the *ritsuryō* system, protect the central government positions, and then to Heian (Peace and Tranquility) in 794, beginning the Heian period (794–1185). He managed to establish a powerful central government on the Chinese model, weaken the position of Buddhism, and show his strength and authority. Heian (later Kyōto) became the political centre of Japan for more than 1,000 years, until 1868. This era is regarded as Japan's classical age and is divided into two subperiods – the Early and the Late Heian.[97] The former was a continuation of the trends of the Nara period and the time of China's enormous influence on Japan, while the late Heian was a time of relative isolation and the fall of the *Ritsuryō* State. The erosion of the *ritsuryō* system accelerated during the reign of Emperor Kanmu (also called Kammu), when the Imperial Court was at the height of its political power and patronage of aristocratic culture.

The Court *paid* its members and officials holding hereditary court ranks with tracts of tax-exempt rice land, the size of which depended on their status within the aristocracy. They in turn passed it on to their heirs as rank land. Courtiers holding positions in the government were also allocated *office land* in accordance with the seniority of their appointments. It was not hereditary, but since the most significant court families monopolized the most important government positions, such land became a permanent family property. With the increase of the exemptions, the country's effective tax base was shrinking and the burden of raising revenues was falling on fewer peasants.[98] Life became hard for *kubunden* cultivators. Governors often assessed more *corvée* on *them* than legally prescribed (using them to open new fields), underreported the harvest, exaggerated natural disasters, and the consequent loss of population. Peasants strong attachment to their own plots of rice land caused their opposition to the bureaucratic system of periodic reallotment of it. All difficulties culminated in 776 in a revolt against the control of the central government. It took the government several years to end this conflict, which showed the weakness of the state. Therefore, in 792, emperor Kanmu reduced peasant burdens and reformed the land allocation system, halving the serfdom due to the government, and abolished peasant conscription. Compulsory service under the conscription system first appeared in 689, when the local governors were instructed that one-fourth of the able-bodied men in each province should be trained every year in warlike exercises.[99] Under the new system (*kondei*), military conscription was limited to national emergencies, and only the sons of district magistrates, local holders of tax-exempt land (by virtue of rank), and those who increased their landholdings were conscripted to the army. The military reform shifted the burden of military service from poor to rich farmers.[100] This can be considered the beginning of the formation of the later *samurai* class.

Another important step taken by Emperor Kanmu to solve the state's financial problems was to adapt the tax structure to changing economic conditions, as well as to improve control over those provincial governments that suffered the greatest loss of income.[101] He also introduced strict regulations regarding the office of the provincial governor. The inheritance of tenures for district chiefs and governors who held land grants exempt from taxes was abolished. Offices not listed in the administrative code were also abolished, causing the dismissal of numerous provincial and central government officials. All loans not authorized by provincial governors[102] were banned, in particular, those which benefited officials more than commoners. Stringent regulations were enacted for the control and guidance of the provincial governors. They were to consult with the people about the distribution of agricultural profits, not to act as judges in criminal cases or to accept bribes from suitors in civil ones; their staff, when visiting the capital, was strictly limited, and the use of public-service horses (bells) as well as the consumption of state provisions was vetoed unless they were travelling on public business. They had to carefully investigate all claims to titles and all alleged rights of land tenure. The district governors were obliged to act as tax collectors in their districts and to assess (unlike provincial governors) the legitimacy of appeals in legal terms, which enabled them to exert pressure on the underprivileged classes under their jurisdiction.[103]

Due to financial shortages in 805, emperor Kanmu demoted to the nobility over a hundred imperial princes and princesses eligible for statutory government assistance, who absorbed an increasing share of the country's revenue. This practice was followed by several succeeding emperors. Although the Imperial Court had been a political centre for four centuries, economic and political factors meant that, despite the emperors' best efforts, the power and effectiveness of its administration declined.[104]

Emperor Kammu installed in the capital three supervisory bodies to simplify and streamline the central government.[105] They were the Accounting Bureau (*Shukeiryō*), the Bureau of Tax Revenues (*Shuzeiryō*), and the Board of Discharge Examiners (*Kageyushi*). He also implemented land classification guidelines.

The Board of Discharge Examiners, also called the Audit Office (*Kageyushi*), was established between 795 and 797. It was a regular office with four levels of officials: one chief, two assistant chiefs, three senior clerks, and three junior clerks, which exercised unchallenged authority over provincial officers. The basic problem of those organizations was that officials in managerial positions tended to make uncontrolled decisions,[106] and they (firms) needed to find ways to control their managers or to reduce the level of private trade.[107] These problems can be seen as an implication of the conflict of interest arising from the relationship between the owner (the state) and its representatives (agents). The creation of a Board called Audit Office was part of a revision of the provincial administration, intended to limit the private control exercised by officials over the use of labour or the exchange of goods. It was dissolved in 806 but restored in 825, becoming a permanent office. District inspectors were reappointed to the Board to supervise provincial administration and its handling by the Controller's Office (*benkari*) of the Council of State. The Audit Office was obliged to audit a governor's accounts and the transfer of property to the incoming governor. This supervisory body had to check and approve dozens of documents. The governor and the vice-governor of a province were responsible for official property, and both needed a discharge certificate when they vacated their offices, as they were responsible for any discrepancies. In principle, no provincial administrator regardless of rank could receive his next appointment without leaving behind a completely clean slate.[108] Over time, this office expanded to regulate tax matters between the central government and the provinces.[109] Miller writes that the historical relationship between the state and corporate entities often involves the creation of *measurement institutions*, including accounting calculation practices, that facilitate the governance of the economy designed to protect and enhance the objectives of the state.[110]

In 810, emperor Saga (809–823) established the Repositors' Office or the Chamberlains' Office, also called the Household Treasury office (*Kurōdo-dokoro*) to regulate court procedures, issue imperial decrees, and arrange interviews with the emperor. Initially, the main duties of the office were to handle legal disputes, to ensure the confidentiality and integrity of imperial documents, and to secure the personal safety of the emperor.[111] During the Heian period, it became the government Council of State, assuming many of the executive and legislative functions of the administration.

A few trusted advisers worked with the emperor to control the government. It was used by the powerful Fujiwara family for issuing official ordinances on behalf of the emperor. Later, the Chamberlains Office passed on imperial edicts and oversaw the imperial archives, and then handled the emperor's domestic affairs.[112] Evolution of the Chamberlains Office in one of the main instruments through which the emperor exercised control over the court and government reflected the atrophy of government that was taking place in the 9th century and the shift in political power from public, bureaucratic statutory institutions towards governments that were based mainly on the emperor and a narrow circle of his relatives.[113] After the decline of Fujiwara power, the importance of this institution diminished, although it was not abolished till 1867.[114] Such great families as Soga and Fujiwara exerted indirect control over the monarchs for centuries causing the separation of ownership and control in the state. They also created a good corporate governance system.

During Saga's reign (809–823), a new imperial police force called the Offenses Investigation Agents (*kebiishi*) was established. Initially, it was restricted to police work and the maintenance of public order within Kyōto and its surroundings. About a decade later, to ensure law and order, Police Commissioners posts (*kebi ishicho*) were instituted (ca. 820) replacing the palace guards.[115] The new metropolitan police force spread to the provinces where all events and activities were closely scrutinized, especially land ownership and tax avoidance. The police had powers to deal with security matters, to apprehend criminals, investigate crimes, conduct trials, pass sentences, and imprison criminals. They issued laws from their base in the capital.[116]

As already mentioned, between 907 and 927, the legislation was improved by the *Regulations of the Engi Era* (*Engishiki*), which put administrative procedures into permanent statutory law, and by the *Regulations Relating to Official Replacements* (*Kōtaishiki*), the 50-volume work.[117] In the 30 sections of the Code, all 949 binding articles have been preserved, but only 322 articles of criminal provisions, placed in 12 sections.[118] The *Engishiki* chapters were arranged and distributed to be related to the structures of the *ritsuryō* bureaucracy (two councils and eight ministries). Chapters 1–10 dealt with the Jingikan (Department of Divinities); Chapters 11–40 concerned the *Dajōkan* (Council of State) and its eight ministries; Chapters 41–49 dealt with offices, such as the Bureau of Royal Police and the Bureau of Military Storehouses; and Chapter 50 with miscellaneous procedures. Rules concerning the Jingikan were voluminous and made nearly one-third of *Engishiki*. Other ministries referred to in many laws and regulations include the Ministry of Inner Palace Affairs (Nakatsukasashō), the Ministry of Popular Affairs (Mimbushō), and the Imperial Household Ministry (Kunaishō).[119] Several governmental offices were established in addition to the existing government system to make it more compatible with the Japanese needs.

According to Hérail, the Court was mainly concerned with the tax system, which supported the capital, its officials, and the judicial oversight of the local government. Provincial budgets, calculated in rice, were established for each province. Provincial tax revenues (*shōzei*), calculated in rice and collected as land tax (*sō*), were partly lent to peasants who were required to *borrow* a certain number of seeds and return it at harvest at very high interest (*suiko*-50% or more), which was allocated to the budgets of provincial governments or sent to the capital. Handicraft taxes (*chōyō*), an important part of the tax system, were fixed and calculated per individual taxpayer. Every able-bodied male (aged 26 to 60) had to pay tribute, a fixed quantity of silk fabric, pongee, raw silk, raw cotton, indigo (675 grains troy), rouge (the same quantity), copper (two and a quarter Ibs.), and a piece of 13-feet-long cotton cloth, in an Imperial domain.[120] The *Regulations Relating to Official Replacements* dealt with the preparation of annual population registers, the maintenance of public and religious buildings, irrigation systems, and the management of tax revenues, mainly the rice tax (*shōzeitō*), which was sent in full to the capital at the appointed time. In the late 10th and early 11th centuries, officials were appointed to one of the *kokushi* positions in order to obtain a salary or, in lower positions, tax exemptions. Such officials rarely visited their provinces and soon became absentee administrators (*yōnin*). The province had three to seven administrators, so individual accountability soon became an issue, as well as the distinction between responsibility and fault. The central administration established mutual supervision between officials. Only the *zuryo*, who took over the administration of the province from his predecessor, exercised power and was responsible for its people and public goods.[121] Zuryo could be called a governor (*kami*), a supernumerary governor (*gon no kami*), or a vice-governor (*suke*). The three to six other *kokushi* assigned to each province received an appointment – they were called *nin'yō kokushi* – but over the time these officials went increasingly rarely to their provinces and became absentee administrators (*yōnin*).[122] When tax arrears prevented expected revenue from flowing into the capital, the responsible officials made up the amount with deductions from their own salaries while the chief official was prosecuted.[123] Thus, a key feature of the control environment became the audit. Both the central audit and the manorial audit were, in essence, internal audits. They were institutional mechanisms set up by the state and landlord to ensure the accountability of the reporting officials. They were mainly concerned with stewardship and performance (management and efficiency).[124] It is worth noting that the concept of internal control relevant to accounting and finance may be traced back to the ancient times, some 3,000 years BC. It was a fundamental part of business management implemented by the generations of businessmen, government officials, accountants, and writers, thanks to whom this field of knowledge is so well developed and used today.[125]

A serious weakness of the Taika system was lack of good motivation to reclaim land. According to the law, new fields were the property of the emperor, not the persons that opened them. Due to the lack of rice fields to bestow on an ever-growing population, especially in more densely populated regions, the Land Law of 711 allowed aristocrats and local nobles to apply through the provincial governor for permission to cultivate a piece of virgin land reclaimed at their own expense (*shiko*).[126] These reclaimed paddy fields were owned by a developer, but after his death they were made available for distribution as household fields.[127] But in the year 723, a decree was issued stating that the newly opened rice fields at own expense would be the private property for three generations.[128] In turn, the decree of 743 not only allowed perpetual use of the newly opened land but also granted them with tax exemption, provided, however, that their owner incurred the costs of their recultivation.[129] The beneficiaries were mainly highly placed government officials and Buddhist temples and monasteries, because only they had sufficient resources to exploit the opportunities offered by the change in law.[130] Private initiative was also encouraged. An Imperial rescript promised that any farmer harvesting 3,000 koku (15,000 bushels) of cereals from land reclaimed by himself should receive the sixth class order of merit (kun roku-to), while a crop of over a 1,000 koku and less than 3,000 would carry lifelong exemption from forced labour.[131] State control was replaced by privatization, which was contrary to the original *ritsuryō* codes. After 743, there were three forms of private land acquisition, namely newly reclaimed rice land, virgin land for reclamation, and land received as a gift or purchased. Changes in land ownership and the use of new methods in agriculture management led to the creation of manors (*shōen*), which enabled their owners to become rich in the 11th and 12th centuries.[132]

During the Heian period, Chinese influence gradually decreased and in 894 Japanese rulers decided to stop sending official missions to China, which for hundreds of years had provided ideas influencing Japanese political and social development. The aristocratic culture developed being a style of social and artistic expression characteristic of the Japanese court at Heiankyō and limited primarily to its members. Preoccupation with beauty was the most visible feature new culture, influencing the perception of nature and standards judgments in art, assessments of human values, and norms of social behaviour.[133] However, the aristocratic Japan continued to borrow concepts from China shaping them to native needs.[134] Heian's court aristocrats adopted the Chinese code of decency, decorum, restraint, and self-control, but Japanese culture and thought flourished and developed. History started to play a major role in Japanese culture – Japan's emperors had found legitimacy in tradition, both mythic and historic, and scholars studied national morality and the value systems in their country's past.[135] Native Japanese culture was increasingly influencing art, poetry, literature, architecture, and religious learning. Heian was a time of courtly elegance in which the arts were blooming in a highly ceremonial atmosphere. The growing independence and uniqueness of Japanese culture was visible in every field. Nobles who had no governing duties spent their time playing games, writing poetry, practising calligraphy (a true mark of a person's level of refinement), painting, and distracting themselves with other pleasurable activities.[136] Gradually, there evolved a system of writing that used a purely phonetic, syllabic script formed by simplifying the Chinese characters. Another script was created by abbreviating Chinese characters. These two scripts, called *hiragana* and *katakana*, enabled writing in the national language with complete freedom. Their invention was an epochal event in the expression of ideas in Japanese.[137] The Heian period was a golden period and one of the most culturally rich eras in Japanese history, also called the period of development of national culture because cultural nationalism spread between the 8th and 12th centuries. Contacts with China also resulted in the development of new skills, such as the art of embroidery, playing the biwa (four-stringed lute), or playing go (Chinese chess). The latter was treated by Japanese warriors as training in military strategy.

During the Heian period, the institutions of *ritsuryō* evolved into a political and cultural system, but only nominal reforms were made to the operation of the central government. The rule of great families (Houses) through a divine emperor persisted, but the structure of government became more complex due to the custom of imperial abdications and the cloistering of former monarchs. According to Meyer, the Japanese evolved a system of government that met their requirements. After the first centuries of political centralization in the country, divisive factors became noticeable. Along with the weakening of the central authority, tendencies towards economic, military, and political decentralization grew, causing the importance of provincial areas to increase.[138] Chinese-style offices (established by Shōtoku Taishi) continued to function but lost their effective power. Appointment to official positions was not in line with the *ritsuryō* codes, and real power was transferred to newly created positions that were not provided for in these codes. The principle of direct rule by the emperor had not foreseen either the post of the regent (*sesshō*) who attended to state affairs during the minority of the emperor nor the *kampaku* (one who received reports prior to their transmission to the sovereign) post who dealt with the state affairs of the emperor even after his adolescence. In theory, *kampaku* was the adviser and spokesman of the Throne, but in practice a dictator.[139] Members of the powerful Fujiwara family were appointed chief ministers of state (*dajō-daijin*), the highest and most respected position reserved for an imperial prince of extraordinary virtue and ability.[140] The offices of the Ministers of the Right and of the Left, the Prime Minister, and the councillors continued into the 19th century, but they became hereditary and lost political significance.[141] The Heian period also set the foundations for a feudal system lasting in Japan for almost 700 years.[142]

The *ritsuryō* system increased the legitimacy and position of the emperor for centuries, but his economic and military power was systematically weakened by the continued growth of the power of the nobility. A serious drawback of the *ritsuryō* system was the reliance on family relationships. Brinkley and Kikuchi write that the sovereign reigned by virtue of his lineage, and that the hereditary nobility owed their high administrative positions to their ancestors. To discredit the titles of the nobles was to disturb the foundation of the Throne itself. Therefore, they were allowed to use the old, though now depreciated, *kabane* (titles), and the tradition of entrusting the management of *uji* affairs to their own *kami* was retained. The aristocratic families usurped the administrative power and encouraged some disastrous conflicts of interest.[143] The ambitions of the Soga, and later the Fujiwara clans, greatly weakened not only the *ritsuryō* system but also the power of the emperors, which had survived, thanks to legitimization of the throne, extensive bureaucracy, and cooperation with the nobility, as the cost of challenging it would be extremely high.[144] The gradual erosion of the *ritsuryō* system served best the economic and political interests of the nobles. They acquired larger rice fields, legally from the throne, illegally by opening new fields, by absorbing *kubunden*, or by purchase.

In Heian era, problems began to arise, due to the Court's inability to derive sufficient income from the provinces to maintain a luxurious standard of living. Although after 850 the established system still functioned well enough to preserve national peace and enable spectacular cultural achievements, the power of the emperor was weakening. Public ownership of land introduced by the *ritsuryō* system began to crumble, causing increasing instability of government and of the system of governance.[145] The central government's control of the provinces steadily declined, and so did the revenues. The reasons for this were excessive spending on the construction of a new capital, wars with the Ainu, an increase in the number of *shōen* enjoying tax immunity, but above all, the emergence of a powerful and wealthy class in provinces that the central authorities were unable to control and exploit.[146]

In the early 10th century, the court abandoned a centralized, bureaucratic pattern of governance in favour of a more flexible approach to local governments. The central government limited its powers to the provincial governors, who gained the right to independently govern their provinces in exchange for the secure transfer of taxes due to the state. The province became the governor's *household* under his personal authority.[147] However, the lack of fiscal responsibility left the *kokushi* with no incentive to leave the capital and take over positions that were mainly used to receive wages and privileges.

Provincial governments were organized like the central administration and had offices. Usually, four of them were common in every province: the Bureau of Land (*Tadokoro*), which kept the registers of rice fields and their owners' names, plans, and the results of on-scene inspections; the Bureau of Tax Revenues (*Saisho*), whose name expresses its function; the Bureau of Official Documents (or Archives, *Kumonjo*), and the Bureau of General Affairs (*Mandokoro*). If necessary, a governor used both his own men (the *rōdō*) and local men.[148] The local officials were able to enrich themselves through harsh taxation and by imposing other additional duties on farmers.[149] By the mid-9th century, provincial governors became important in Heian society and played an essential role, both in national administration and in court life.[150] Many of them stayed in the capital to enjoy the cultural life and luxuries, exercising virtual control over their provinces and treating their governorship only as a source of income. Those holding other high positions in the central bureaucracy and court aristocrats could not leave the capital, but using their court connections, they could obtain fiscal immunities and independence from the civil officials administration system. But they understood well that the quality of their court life depended on the skill with which their local officials administered the provinces and collected taxes.[151] Increasingly, the governors living in Kyōto delegated their duties to local administrators and entrusted the generation of their revenues to their subordinates – the district magistrates and the *dogo* (*do*-soil and *go*-powerful), a new and growing group of provincial landowners who in remote regions were the only source of law and order. Some of the *dogo* became district magistrates and cooperated with the provincial governors, often in exchange for tacit consent to their illegal land reclamation. The class of local (district) administrators underwent organizational changes but did not lose any of its power and privileges. Absentee governors were well connected to the powerful nobility at Court and supported by the central government. For this reason, challenging them was too dangerous for the local officials and *dogo*, who sought the protection of other powerful nobles in the capital to neutralize the power of the absent governors.[152] Powerful landowners (aristocrats and monastic orders) who accumulated large landholdings in the provinces were often given imperial appointments as vice-governors.[153] The main attraction of the provincial post was the possibility of obtaining large profits by people with sufficient support or skills. Private landowners made their land more secure and profitable by aligning their interests with those of the ruling upper nobility and transforming public land into *shōen*.[154]

The system of periodic reallocation of rice land (*handen*) ended in the 9th century due to abuses by provincial and local officials, manipulation of population records, monopolization of a vast area of public land by aristocratic families and religious institutions, large migration, and the search for a more secure form of tenure.[155] Governors who went to the provinces of their appointment were eager to enrich themselves by maximizing the difference between the tax collected and forwarded to the central government. They expanded their landholdings and increased their political and financial power. It became important for them to appoint reliable district magistrates, usually relatives or leaders of minor local *uji*, ready to increase revenues for them. During the second half of the 9th century, the political power started to shift from the provincial governors to the district officials and the *dogo*. During this time, the estates of the nobility expanded rapidly due to land reclamation, field purchases, illegal use of rice fields abandoned by *kubunden* farmers, and land allotted to them by district magistrates, *dogo*, and other cultivators. In consequence, the tax revenues sent to the capital were steadily declining. The number of *kubunden* cultivators working for the nobles, temples, magistrates, and *dogo* also began to surrender their land to the highest ranked nobles in return for protection from the local officials or governors oriented towards increasing their own economic base. Since the weak central authority was still able to quell local unrest, the nobility occupying the highest positions in the central bureaucracy saw no need to change the status quo that was so favourable to them.[156]

As already noted, in the late 9th century, allotment of rice land was not required any longer by the government. All rice land, except that given to appointed *shōen* owners, was leased from provincial governments. Rent was paid in the form of a provincial land tax, on which the *shōen* tenancy system was modelled. The unit for taxation of public lands and manorial lands was the *myo* (nominal), on which taxes were calculated and collected. Therefore, the provincial authorities only recorded the area of taxable land within each *myo*, and not the number of people cultivating that land or the division of cultivation rights among them.[157] Each *myo* unit had a *myoshu* who acted as the tax collector and leader of the cultivators of the rice paddies within each *myo*. Many of the *myoshu* (so called in the 10th century) were cultivators (*tato)* who contracted to work and to oversee others working on small strips of public, or already privatized land. Some of them were descendants of lesser nobles; others managed to reclaim a small piece of land but failed to establish themselves among the local powers.[158]

The destruction of the *Ritsuryō* State proceeded slowly but steadily, causing that around 950, the Court no longer was able to maintain peace in Kyōto, and the aristocratic absentee landlords were unable to protect their property without the help of military forces supported by local magnates.[159] In Japan, there was a distinction between nominal power (authority) and real power.[160] An important noble family residing in the capital might have had enough wealth and power to mobilize resources to obtain land, but not enough to maintain real control over it. The destruction of the central government was blamed on the powerful Fujiwara clan, the largest holder of extensive manorial rights.[161] The failure of the central government, unable to keep order, brought the warriors into prominence.[162] In the second half of the 9th century, armed men specializing in defending the interests of the *dogo* and nobility appeared, but it took several decades before they became *samurai*, who in 1185 established their own government.[163]

Emperor Go-Sanjo, the first emperor in 170 years whose mother was not a Fujiwara, was enthroned in 1068. He wanted to rule without clans interference and restore administrative power to the Crown, which had been either usurped or depreciated by the Fujiwara clan (until the 19th century, regents were traditionally chosen from the Fujiwara five main branches).[164] He abdicated in 1073, after six years of reign, in favour of his son, starting the practice of royal abdications and the *cloistered emperors* (19 from 33 emperors of the Heian period withdrew to monasteries). Retired emperors left the throne at a relatively young age to become Buddhist monks, but they usually did not limit themselves to religious rituals. They tried to rule the country from the Buddhist temples, retaining varying degrees of political power.[165] The advantages of being a cloistered emperor were greater personal freedom, less obligation of ceremony, retention of mystical authority, independent advisers, and spokesmen chosen by him outside the official hierarchy.[166] A child being emperor gave no trouble, allowed decisions to be made by a small group of high-ranking nobles, the majority of whom supported the retired emperor. In this way, although the reigning emperor was a figurehead, control over this position returned to the imperial family, enabling it to compete more effectively for the power and wealth. Sansom writes that *the emperors at that time reigned but did not rule*.[167] The Throne was divided by the struggle for power and threatened by political instability, weakening further the *ritsuryō* system. The practice of Cloister Government (*insei*) lasted at the turn of the 11th and 12th centuries.[168] The idea of a transcendent state, to which all elite groups were subordinated, embodied in the person and authority of the emperor, lost its importance.[169] During the Nara (710–784), and especially the Heian (794–1185) periods, the emperor was *supreme over all the Empire* only in name as power was held by some court families, monastic institutions, or retired emperors.[170] A system was created, in which weak emperors without political power were subject to manipulation at Court by powerful families exerting indirect control over them. The monarchs seldom exercised authority directly, relying on the court officials to oversee the administrative affairs, or on regents. They became the symbol of the state and performed Shinto (a religion originating from Japan) rituals. The Court was so self-absorbed with power struggles and elaborate rituals and ceremonies (social behaviour and costumes were regulated to the minutest point. Solemn edicts fixed the colour of official robes, the length of swords, and the nature of salutations. Women could wear no more than six skirts) that it neglected the government administration outside the capital.[171]

The Heian period was very civilized and peacefully inclined. The law of feudal Japan was a blend of the codified law of China and the customary laws of the Japanese clans.[172] Sansom argues that it was administered in a lenient manner and there was great reluctance to inflict the death penalty or any drastic punishment, and that amnesties were common (Buddhist sentiment). For these reasons, crime flourished.[173] Theft became a major problem in both the capital and the provinces, and law and order began to break down. The decline of central authority in the provinces caused a rise in lawlessness. Some local chieftains began to cause unrest and some soldiers (*bushi*) roamed the countryside hunting travellers and farmers. Pirates operated on the sea and in coastal areas. Clergy wars added to the military turmoil, as wealthy and strong militant Buddhist temples, maintaining their own guards of armed monks (*akuso*) for self-defense, fought each other, the nobility, and the court. The monks, who should show compassion and respect for life, carried weapons openly and often took part in slaughters. By the end of the Heian period, Buddhism became not only a religious force but also a political and military power. The highest positions in the religious world were occupied by members of the imperial family and former aristocrats excluding the lower-ranking monks from promotion. In cases of disagreement, they went to the capital and forced the Court to accept their demands.[174] The central government, in order to minimize the danger of unrest, ordered the confiscation of war weapons from private individuals, locking them in purpose-built arsenals on wasteland. The landowners had to take measures to protect their property, and therefore, they started to engage armed guards.

Around the mid-12th century, conflicts between the aristocracy were resolved by force, which contributed to the increase in the status of warriors recruited for the sole purpose of fighting. The warriors (*bushi*) guaranteed military protection in exchange for a portion of the proceeds from the cultivation of the land.[175] *Samurai* took primary responsibility for maintaining public order and collecting rent on local estates. Their actions were authorized by the highest manors owners, who were the nobility, the imperial family, or temples. For their services, *samurai* required rents.[176]

From the end of the 9th century until the end of the 12th century, the regency was occupied by the Fujiwara family members. They established a system of governance that lasted until the Meiji Restoration in 1868, but even then the power of the emperor was limited because he had to rely on trusted and able advisers. However, by depriving the emperor of effective power, the imperial institution was protected. The divine emperor was not involved in politics, which meant that he did not create enemies. Japanese aristocracy did not adopt the Chinese idea of *mandate of heaven*, where an emperor could be removed through revolution, if he or she failed to provide good government. This allowed the imperial family to survive for many centuries and supported a system of separating the head of state from the government for much of Japan's history.[177]

The process leading to the rise of the *bushi* class on the Japanese political scene was enhanced by the Genpei War (1180–1185), the culmination of a decades-long struggle for power and dominance of the Imperial court and control of Japan, between the Taira and Minamoto clans. It resulted in the fall of the Taira clan after the legendary sea battle of Dannoura (1185) on the Inland Sea in Western Japan. The Taira were finally defeated, and the emperor Antoku was drowned in it, losing a famous sword being one of the three Imperial Treasures of Japan supposedly brought from heaven by the first Japanese emperor. In consequence, the Kamakura *Shōgunate* under Minamoto no Yoritomo was established in 1192.[178] In this way, the first *bakufu*, the military government (dictatorship) in Kamakura, was created. The warriors were placed under *shōgun*, a unique military authority, and officially became the rulers of the country.[179]

Notes

1 J. Murdoch, History of Japan. From the Origins to the Arrival of the Portuguese in 1542 A.D., Vol. I. *The Asiatic Society of Japan*, London 1910, p. 148.
2 B. L. Batten, Foreign Threat and Domestic Reform: The Emergence of the *Ritsuryō* State. *Monumenta Nipponica* 1986, Vol. 41, No. 2, pp. 199–219.
3 C. J. Kiley, State and Dynasty in Archaic Yamato. *Journal of Asian Studies* November 1973, Vol. XXXIII, No. 1, pp. 25–49.
4 B. L. Batten, Foreign Threat, and Domestic Reform . . . op. cit.
5 C. Andressen, A Short History of Japan. From Samurai to Sony. *Allen & Unwin,* Canberra 2002, p. 35.
6 M. W. Meyer, Japan A Concise History. *Rowman & Littlefield Publishers Inc*, Plymouth 2009, p. 41.
7 F. Brinkley, D. Kikuchi, A History of the Japanese People from the Earliest Times to the End of the Meiji Era. *The Encyclopaedia Britannica Co*, New York, London 1912, p. 160.
8 M. W. Meyer, Japan. A Concise History . . . op. cit., p. 49.
9 R. H. P. Mason, J.G Caiger, A History of Japan. *TUTTLE Publishing*, Tokyo; Rutland, VT; Singapore 1997, pp. 42, 43.
10 J. Murdoch, History of Japan, From . . . op. cit., p. 181.
11 Ch. Holcombe, Ritsuryō Confucianism. *Harvard Journal of Asiatic Studies* 1997, Vol. 57, No. 2, pp. 543–573. *JSTOR*, https://doi.org/10.2307/2719487.
12 K. Yamamura, Y. Murakami, Ie Society as a Pattern of Civilization . . . op. cit.
13 H. G. Wren, The Legal System of Pre-Western Japan. *Hastings Law Journal* 1968, Vol. 20, No. 1, pp. 217–244.
14 C. D. Totman, A History of Japan. *Blackwell Publishing*, Malden; Oxford; Carlton 2005, p. 76.
15 R. H. P. Mason, J.G Caiger, A History of Japan . . . op. cit., pp. 43, 44.
16 K. Yamamura, The Decline of the *Ritsuryō* System: Hypotheses on Economic and Institutional Change. *Journal of Japanese Studies* 1974, Vol. 1, No. 1, The Society for Japanese Studies, pp. 3–37. J. Murdoch, History of Japan. From . . . op. cit., p. 172.
17 B. L. Batten, Foreign Threat, and Domestic Reform . . . op. cit.
18 W. S. Morton, J. K. Olenik, Japan. Its History and Culture . . . op. cit., p. 24.
19 C. Andressen, A Short History of Japan . . . op. cit., p. 36.
20 www.britannica.com/event/Taika-era-reforms.
21 J. Murdoch, History of Japan. From . . . op. cit., pp. 149–155.
22 C. Andressen, A Short History of Japan . . . op. cit., p. 36.
23 W. S. Morton, J. K. Olenik, Japan. Its History and Culture. *McGraw-Hill Companies Inc,* New York 2005, p. 24; J. Tubilewicz, Historia Japonii. *Zakład Narodowy Imienia Ossolińskich*, Wrocław 1984, p. 63.
24 B. L. Batten, Foreign Threat, and Domestic Reform . . . op. cit.
25 M. W. Meyer, Japan. A Concise History . . . op. cit., pp. 41, 42; R. H. P. Mason, J. G. Caiger. A History of Japan . . . op. cit., p. 80.

26 F. Brinkley, D. Kikuchi, A History of the Japanese People . . . op. cit., pp. 180, 181.
27 R. H. P. Mason, J. G. Caiger, A History of Japan . . . op. cit., p. 75.
28 J. Murdoch, History of Japan. From . . . , op. cit., pp. 149, 154, 155.
29 Ibidem, p. 161.
30 F. Hérail, The Position and Role of Provincial Governors at the Height of the Heian Period. *French Journal of Japanese Studies* 2014, No. 3.
31 R. H. P. Mason, J. G. Caiger. A History of Japan . . . op. cit., p. 45.
32 F. Brinkley, D. Kikuchi, A History of the Japanese People . . . op. cit., p. 164.
33 Ibidem, pp. 180, 181.
34 K. Hara, An Introduction to the History of Japan. *Yamato Society Publication, G. P. Putnam's & Sons. The Knickerbocker Press*, New York, London 1920, p. 116.
35 C. Andressen, A Short History of Japan . . . op. cit., p. 34.
36 K. Yamamura, Y. Murakami, *Ie* Society as a Pattern of Civilization: Introduction. *Journal of Japanese Studies* 1984, Vol. 10, No. 2, The Society for Japanese Studies, pp. 279–363.
37 M. W. Meyer, Japan. A Concise History . . . op. cit., p. 49.
38 F. Brinkley, D. Kikuchi, A History of the Japanese People . . . op. cit., p. 172.
39 R. H. P. Mason, J. G. Caiger, A History of Japan . . . op. cit., p. 44.
40 B. L. Batten, Foreign Threat, and Domestic Reform . . . op. cit.
41 C. Andressen, A Short History of Japan . . . op. cit., p. 36.
42 M. L. Nagata, Brotherhoods and Stock Societies: Guilds in Pre-Modern Japan. *International Review of Social History* 2008, Vol. 53, pp. 121–142.
43 J. Murdoch, History of Japan, From . . . , op. cit., p. 168.
44 B. L. Batten, Foreign Threat, and Domestic Reform . . . op. cit.
45 C. J. Kiley, State and Dynasty in Archaic Yamato . . . op. cit.
46 J. Murdoch, History of Japan, From the Origins . . . op. cit., p. 149.
47 F. Brinkley, D. Kikuchi, A History of the Japanese People . . . op. cit., pp. 170, 171.
48 Ibidem, p. 181.
49 W. S. Morton, J. K. Olenik, Japan. Its History and Culture . . . , op. cit., p. 26.
50 F. Brinkley, D. Kikuchi, A History of the Japanese People . . . op. cit., p. 181.
51 W. S. Morton, J. K. Olenik, Japan. Its History and Culture . . . op. cit. p. 48.
52 K. Yamamura, The Decline of the Ritsuryō System . . . op. cit.
53 B. L. Batten, Foreign Threat, and Domestic Reform . . . op. cit.
54 F. Brinkley, D. Kikuchi, A History of the Japanese People . . . op. cit., pp. 170, 171.
55 K. Yamamura, The Decline of the Ritsuryō System . . . op. cit.
56 J. Murdoch, History of Japan. From . . . , op. cit., p. 171.
57 M. W. Meyer, Japan. A Concise History . . . op. cit., p. 42.
58 V. M. Carkeek, The Taiho Code, the First Code of Japan. *Washington Law Review* 1926, Vol. 1, No. 3, pp. 181–194.
59 K. Asakawa, Japan. From the Japanese Government History. Vol. 7. In: H. C. Lodge (ed.), The History of Nations. *The Collier Press*, New York 1906, p. 35.
60 V. M. Carkeek, The Taihō Code . . . op. cit.
61 D. Morris, Land and Society. In: J. W. Hall, M. B. Jansen, M. Kanai, D. Twitchett (eds.), The Cambridge History of Japan. Vol. 2. Heian Japan. D. H. Shively, W. H. McCollough (eds.). *Cambridge University Press,* Cambridge 2008, p. 215.
62 K. Yamamura, The Decline of the Ritsuryō System . . . op. cit.
63 J. Murdoch, History of Japan. From . . . op. cit., pp. 169, 170.
64 W. S. Morton, J. K. Olenik, Japan. Its history and Culture . . . op. cit., p. 37.
65 B. L. Batten, Foreign Threat, and Domestic Reform . . . op. cit. K. Hara, An Introduction to the History of Japan . . . op. cit., p. 116.
66 K. Hara, An Introduction to the History of Japan . . . op. cit., p. 117.

67 www.britannica.com/topic/Taiho-code
68 W. S. Morton, J. K. Olenik, Japan. Its History and Culture . . . op. cit., p. 47.
69 V. M. Carkeek, The Taiho Code . . . op. cit.
70 K. Yamamura, The Decline of the Ritsuryō System . . . op. cit.
71 V. M. Carkeek, The Taihō Code . . . op. cit.
72 M. J. Jones, Internal Control, Accountability and Corporate Governance: Medieval and Modern Britain Compared. *Accounting, Auditing & Accountability Journal* 2008, Vol. 21, No. 7, pp. 1052–1075.
73 V. M. Carkeek, The Taihō Code . . . op. cit.
74 Ibidem.
75 N. Kojiro, The Nara State. In: D. M. Brown (ed.), The Cambridge History of Japan. Vol. 1. Ancient Japan. *Cambridge University Press*, Cambridge 2008, p. 232.
76 F. Brinkley, D. Kikuchi, A History of the Japanese People . . . op. cit., p. 183.
77 V. M. Carkeek, The Taihō Code . . . op. cit.
78 F. Brinkley, D. Kikuchi, A History of the Japanese People . . . op. cit., p. 178.
79 Ibidem.
80 V. M. Carkeek, The Taihō Code . . . op. cit.
81 H. G. Wren, The Legal System of Pre-Western Japan . . . op. cit.
82 F. Brinkley, D. Kikuchi, A History of the Japanese People . . . op. cit., p. 178.
83 M. W. Meyer, Japan. A Concise History . . . op. cit., p. 48.
84 The Kojiki and Nihon Shoki of Japan, www.kcpinternational.com/2015/12/the-kojiki-and-nihon-shoki-of-japan/. K. Hara, An Introduction.to the History of Japan . . . op. cit., p. 54; M. W. Meyer, Japan. A Concise History . . . op. cit., pp. 55, 56.
85 K. Hara, An Introduction.to the History of Japan . . . op. cit., pp. 117, 124.
86 C. Andressen, A Short History of Japan . . . op. cit., p. 40.
87 V. M. Carkeek, The Taihō Code . . . op. cit.
88 C. Andressen, A Short History of Japan . . . op. cit., p. 38.
89 Brinkley, D. Kikuchi, A History of the Japanese People . . . op. cit., p. 177.
90 N. Kojiro, The Nara State. In: The Cambridge History of Japan. Vol. 1. Ancient Japan . . . op. cit., pp. 231–233.
91 Ibidem, p. 233.
92 F. Brinkley, D. Kikuchi, A History of the Japanese People . . . op. cit., p. 163.
93 W. S. Morton, J. K. Olenik, Japan. Its History and Culture . . . op. cit., p. 25; C. D. Totman, A History of Japan . . . op. cit., p. 76.
94 D. M. Brown, The Yamato Kingdom. In: The Cambridge History of Japan. Vol. 1. Ancient Japan . . . op. cit., p. 149.
95 B. L. Batten, Foreign Threat, and Domestic Reform . . . op. cit.
96 N. Kojiro, The Nara State. In: The Cambridge History of Japan. Vol. 1. Ancient Japan . . . op. cit., p. 236.
97 C. Andressen, A Short History of Japan . . . op. cit., pp. 39, 40.
98 W. S. Morton, J. K. Olenik, Japan. Its History and Culture . . . op. cit., p. 26.
99 F. Brinkley, D. Kikuchi, A History of the Japanese People . . . op. cit., p. 95.
100 K. Yamamura, The Decline of the Ritsuryō System . . . op. cit.
101 W. H. McCullough, The Heian Court, 794–1070. In: The Cambridge History of Japan. Vol. 2. Heian Japan . . . op. cit., pp. 37, 38.
102 F. Brinkley, D. Kikuchi, A History of the Japanese People . . . op. cit., p. 165.
103 K. Yamamura, The Decline of the Ritsuryō System . . . op. cit.
104 D. H. Shively, W. H. McCullough, Introduction. In: J. W. Hall, M. B. Jansen, M. Kanai, D. Twitchett (eds.), The Cambridge History of Japan. Vol. 2, Heian Japan. (eds) D. H. Shively, W. H. McCullough, *Cambridge University Press* 2008, pp. 1 and 7.

105 C. Andressen, A Short History of Japan . . . op. cit., p. 40.
106 K. Rost, E. Inauen, M. Osterloh, The Corporate Governance of Benedictine Abbeys. What Can Stock Corporations Learn from Monasteries? *Journal of Management History* 2010, Vol. 16, No. 1, pp. 90–115.
107 A. M., Carlos, S., Nicholas, Agency Problems in Early Chartered Companies: The Case of the Hudson's Bay Company. *The Journal of Economic History* 1990, Vol. 50, No. 4, pp. 853–875.
108 F. Hérail, The Position and Role of Provincial Governors . . . op. cit.
109 C. J. Kiley, Provincial Administration, and Land Tenure in Early Heian. In: The Cambridge History of Japan. Vol. 2, Heian Japan, op. cit., pp. 269–272.
110 P. Miller, On the Interrelations between Accounting and the State. *Accounting. Organizations and Society* 1990, Vol. 15, No. 4, pp. 315–338.
111 C. Andressen, A Short History of Japan . . . op. cit., p. 41.
112 D. H. Shively, W. H. McCullough, Introduction. In: The Cambridge History of Japan. Vol. 2. Heian Japan . . . op. cit., p. 7.
113 W. H. McCullough, The Heian Court, 794–1070. In: The Cambridge History of Japan. Vol. 2, Heian Japan, op. cit., p. 41.
114 www.britannica.com/topic/Kurodo-dokoro.
115 M. W. Meyer, Japan. A Concise History . . . op. cit., p. 69.
116 W. H. McCullough, The Heian Court, 794–1070. In: The Cambridge History of Japan. Vol. 2. Heian Japan . . . op. cit., p. 43.
117 G. B. Sansom, A History of Japan to 1334. Vol. 1. *Stanford University Press*, Stanford 1963, p. 112.
118 A. Kojiro, The Nara State. In: The Cambridge History of Japan. Vol. 1. Ancient Japan . . . . op. cit., p. 233.
119 T. Hiroshi, Encyclopedia of Shinto. Chronological Supplement. *Institute for Japanese Culture and Classics Kokugakuin University*, Tokyo 2016.
120 F. Brinkley, D. Kikuchi, A History of the Japanese People . . . op. cit., p. 183.
121 F. Hérail, The Position and Rol of Provincial Governors . . . op. cit.
122 F. Brinkley, D. Kikuchi, A History of the Japanese People . . . op. cit., p. 165.
123 F. Hérail, The Position and Rol of Provincial Governors . . . op. cit.
124 M. J. Jones, Internal Control, Accountability and Corporate Governance . . . op. cit.
125 T. A. Lee, The Historical Development of Internal Control from the Earliest Times to the End of the Seventeenth Century. *Journal of Accounting Research* 1971, Vol. 9, No. 1, pp. 150–157.
126 K. Yamamura, The Decline of the Ritsuryō System . . . op. cit.
127 D. Morris, Land and Society. In: The Cambridge History of Japan. Vol. 2. Heian Japan . . . op. cit., p. 216.
128 T. Toshiya, Nara Economic and Social Institutions. In: The Cambridge History of Japan. Vol. 1, Ancient Japan . . . op. cit., pp. 438, 439.
129 K. Yamamura, The Decline of the Ritsuryō System . . . op. cit.
130 www.britannica.com/place/Japan/The-Taika-reforms#ref168017 21.04.2020.
131 F. Brinkley, D. Kikuchi, A History of the Japanese People . . . op. cit., p. 49.
132 T. Toshiya, Nara Economic and Social Institutions. In: The Cambridge History of Japan. Vol. 1. Ancient Japan . . . op. cit., pp. 448, 449.
133 H. Craig McCullough, Aristocratic Culture. In: The Cambridge History of Japan. Vol. 2. Heian Japan . . . op. cit., p. 390.
134 M. W. Meyer, Japan. A Concise History . . . op. cit., p. 69.
135 General Editors' Preface. In: The Cambridge History of Japan. Vol. 2. Heian Japan . . . op. cit., p. V.
136 C. Andressen, A Short History of Japan . . . op. cit., p. 43.

137 K. Asakawa, Japan. From the Japanese Government History . . . op. cit., p. 42.
138 M. W. Meyer, Japan. A Concise History . . . op. cit., p. 69.
139 R. H. P. Mason, J. G. Caiger. A History of Japan . . . , op. cit., p. 70; K. Asakawa, Japan. From the Japanese Government History . . . op. cit., p. 113.
140 W. H. McCullough, The Heian Court. 794–1070. In: The Cambridge History of Japan. Vol. 2. Heian Japan . . . op. cit., pp. 59–61.
141 M. W. Meyer, Japan. A Concise History . . . op. cit., p. 55.
142 C. Andressen, A Short History of Japan . . . op. cit., p. 40.
143 F. Brinkley, D. Kikuchi, A History of the Japanese People . . . op. cit., pp. 164, 171, 172.
144 K. Yamamura, The Decline of the Ritsuryō System . . . op. cit.
145 www.britannica.com/place/Japan/The-Taika-reforms#ref168017 21.04.2020.
146 R. H. P. Mason, J. G. Caiger. A History of Japan . . . op. cit., p. 70.
147 B. L. Batten, Foreign Threat, and Domestic Reform . . . op. cit.
148 F. Hérail, The Position and Role of Provincial Governors . . . op. cit.
149 J. P. Mass, The Kamakura *bakufu*. In: K. Yamamura (ed.), The Cambridge History of Japan. Vol. 3. Medieval Japan. *Cambridge University Press*, Cambridge 2008, p. 49.
150 F. Hérail, The Position and Role of Provincial Governors . . . op. cit.
151 M. L. Nagata, Brotherhoods and Stock Societies: Guilds in Pre-Modern Japan. *International Review of Social History* 2008, Vol. 53, pp. 121–142.
152 K. Yamamura, The Decline of the Ritsuryō System . . . op. cit.
153 W. S. Morton, J. K. Olenik, Japan. Its History and Culture . . . op. cit., p. 50; R. H. P. Mason, J. G. Caiger. A History of Japan . . . op. cit., p. 122.
154 K. Nagahara, Landownership under the Shōen-Kokugaryō System. *Journal of Japanese Studies*, 1975, Vol. 1, No. 2, pp. 269–296.
155 D. Morris, Land and Society. In: The Cambridge History of Japan. Vol. 2, Heian Japan . . . op. cit., pp. 218–221.
156 K. Yamamura, The Decline of the Ritsuryō System . . . op. cit.
157 D. Morris, Land and Society. In: The Cambridge History of Japan. Vol. 2, Heian Japan . . . op. cit., pp. 223, 224.
158 K. Yamamura, Tara in Transition: A Study of a Kamakura Shoen. *Journal of Japanese Studies*, 1981, Vol. 7, No. 2, The Society for Japanese Studies, pp. 349–391.
159 G. B. Sansom, A History of Japan to 1334. Vol. 1. *Stanford University Press*, Stanford 1958, p. 237.
160 M. W. Meyer, Japan. A Concise History . . . op. cit., p. 62.
161 K. G. Henshall, A History of Japan: From Stone Age to Superpower, *Palgrave Macmillan*, London 2012, p. 31.
162 G. B. Sansom, A History of Japan to 1334 . . . op. cit., p. 236.
163 K. Yamamura, The Decline of the Ritsuryō System . . . op. cit.
164 G. B. Sansom, A History of Japan to 1334 . . . op. cit., p. 199.
165 M. W. Meyer, Japan. A Concise History . . . op. cit., p. 48.
166 W. S. Morton, J. K. Olenik, Japan. Its History and Culture . . . op. cit., p. 49.
167 G. B. Sansom, A History of Japan to 1334 . . . op. cit., p. 201.
168 K. Yamamura, The Decline of the Ritsuryō System . . . op. cit.
169 G. B. Sansom, A History of Japan to 1334 . . . op. cit., p. 8.
170 M. P. Caleddu, The Evolution of the Ancient Way of the Warrior: From the Ancient Chronicles to the Tokugawa Period. *Asian Studies* 2018, Vol. 6 No. 2, pp. 87–109.
171 www.britannica.com/place/Japan/The-Heian-period-794-1185.
172 H. G. Wren, The Legal System of Pre-Western Japan . . . op. cit.
173 G. B. Sansom, A History of Japan to 1334 . . . op. cit., p. 239.
174 C. Andressen, A Short History of Japan . . . op. cit., p. 45.

175 H. G. Wren, The Legal System of Pre-Western Japan . . . op. cit.
176 M. Nakabayashi, Institutions, and Economic Development of Early Modern Japan. *ISS Discussion Paper Series F-146* August 2009, Institute of Social Science, The University of Tokyof-146.pdf.
177 C. Andressen, A Short History of Japan . . . op. cit., pp. 38–41.
178 www.britannica.com/event/Gempei-War.
179 M. P. Caleddu, The Evolution of the Ancient Way . . . op. cit.

Bibliography

Andressen, C., A Short History of Japan. From Samurai to Sony. *Allen & Unwin*, Canberra 2002.

Asakawa, K., Japan. From the Japanese Government History. Vol. 7. In: H. C. Lodge (ed.), The History of Nations. *John D. Morris and Company*, *The Collier Press*, New York 1906. www.gutenberg.org/ebooks/45645.

Batten, B. L., Foreign Threat and Domestic Reform: The Emergence of the *Ritsuryō* State. *Monumenta Nipponica* 1986, Vol. 41, No. 2, pp. 199–219. www.jstor.org/stable/2384665.

Batten, B. L., Provincial Administration in Early Japan: From Ritsuryō Kokka to Ōchō Kokka. *Harvard Journal of Asiatic Studies* 1993, Vol. 53, No. 1, pp. 103–134. Harvard-Yenching Institute. https://doi.org/10.2307/2719469.

Brinkley, F., Kikuchi, D., A History of the Japanese People from the Earliest Times to the End of the Meiji Era. *The Encyclopaedia Britannica Co, New York*, London 1912. https://archive.org/details/historyofjapanes00briniala/page/n5/mode/2up.

Carkeek, V. M., The Taiho Code, the First Code of Japan. *Washington Law Review* 1926, Vol. 1, No. 3, pp. 181–194.

Carlos, A. M., Nicholas, S., Agency Problems in Early Chartered Companies: The Case of the Hudson's Bay Company. *The Journal of Economic History* 1990, Vol. 50, No. 4, pp. 853–875. *JSTOR*. www.jstor.org/stable/2122458.

Culeddu, M. P., The Evolution of the Ancient Way of the Warrior: From the Ancient Chronicles to the Tokugawa Period. *Asian Studies* 2018, Vol. 6, No. 2, pp. 87–109. https://doi.org/10.4312/as.2018.6.2.87-109.

Hara, K., An Introduction to the History of Japan. *Yamato Society Publication, G. P. Putnam's & Sons. The Knickerbocker Press*, New York, London 1920.

Henshall, K. G., A History of Japan: From Stone Age to Superpower. *Palgrave Macmillan*, London 2012. www.gutenberg.org/files/37186/37186-h/37186-h.htm.

Hérail, F., The Position and Role of Provincial Governors at the Height of the Heian Period. *French Journal of Japanese Studies* 2014, No. 3. https://journals.openedition.org/cjs/658.

Hiroshi, T., Encyclopedia of Shinto. Chronological Supplement. *Institute for Japanese Culture and Classics*, *Kokugakuin University*, Tokyo 2016. https://d-museum.kokugakuin.ac.jp/eos/detail/?id=8612.

Holcombe, Ch., *Ritsuryō* Confucianism. *Harvard Journal of Asiatic Studies* 1997, Vol. 57, No. 2, pp. 543–573. *JSTOR*. https://doi.org/10.2307/2719487.

Kiley, C. J., State and Dynasty in Archaic Yamato. *The Journal of Asian Studies* 1973, Vol. 33, No. 1, [Cambridge University Press, Association for Asian Studies], pp. 25–49. Published by: Association for Asian Studies www.jstor.org/stable/2052884.

Lee, T. A., The Historical Development of Internal Control from the Earliest Times to the End of the Seventeenth Century. *Journal of Accounting Research* 1971, Vol. 9, No. 1, pp. 150–157. https://doi.org/10.2307/2490208

Mason, R. H. P., Caiger, J. G., A History of Japan. *TUTTLE Publishing*, Tokyo; Rutland, VT; Singapore 1997. file:///D:/Users/wzr/Downloads/A_History_of_Japan_Mason_Caiger%20(5).pdf

Meyer, M. W., Japan A Concise History. *Rowman & Littlefield Publishers Inc*, Plymouth 2009. file:///D:/Users/wzr/Downloads/epdf.pub_japan-a-concise-history-4th-edition.pdf.
Miller, P., On the Interrelations between Accounting and the State. *Accounting, Organizations and Society* 1990, Vol. 15, No. 4, pp. 315–338.
Morton, W. S., Olenik, J. K., Japan. Its History and Culture. *McGraw-Hill Companies Inc*, New York 2005. https://vdocuments.mx/japan-its-history-and-culture-56811b380a71d.html.
Murdoch, J., History of Japan, From the Origins to the Arrival of the Portuguese in 1542 A.D. Vol. I. *The Asiatic Society of Japan*, London 1910. file:///D:/Users/wzr/Documents/Japonia%20Ks1/Ksi%C4%85%C5%BCki%20Hist/A%20history%20of%20Japan%20Volume%201%20(1903).pdf.
Nagahara, K., Landownership under the Shōen-Kokugaryō System. *Journal of Japanese Studies* 1975, Vol. 1, No. 2, pp. 269–296. *JSTOR*, www.jstor.org/stable/132127.
Nagata, M. L., Brotherhoods and Stock Societies: Guilds in Pre-Modern Japan. *International Review of Social History* 2008, Vol. 53, pp. 121–142. *JSTOR*. www.jstor.org/stable/26405470.
Nakabayashi, M., Institutions and Economic Development of Early Modern Japan. *ISS Discussion Paper Series F-146* August 2009, pp. 1–26. Institute of Social Science, The University of Tokyof-146.pdf.
Rost, K., Inauen, E., Osterloh, M., Frey, B. S., The Corporate Governance of Benedictine Abbeys. What Can Stock Corporations Learn from Monasteries? *Journal of Management History* 2010, Vol. 16, No. 1, pp. 90–115. https://doi.org/10.1108/17511341011008331.
Sansom, G. B., A History of Japan to 1334. Vol. 1. *Stanford University Press*, Stanford 1958.
The Cambridge History of Japan. Vol. 1. Ancient Japan. D. M. Brown (ed.). *Cambridge University Press*, Cambridge 2008.
The Cambridge History of Japan. J. W. Hall, M. B. Jansen, M. Kanai, D. Twitchett (eds.). Vol. 2. Heian Japan. D. H. Shively, W. H. McCollough (eds.). *Cambridge University Press*, Cambridge 2008.
The Cambridge History of Japan. Vol. 3. Medieval Japan. K. Yamamura (ed.). *Cambridge University Press*, Cambridge 2008.
Totman, C. D., A History of Japan. *Wiley* 2014. www.perlego.com/book/1006239/a-history-of-japan-pdf.
Tubilewicz, J., Historia Japonii. *Zakład Narodowy Imienia Ossolińskich,* Wrocław 1984.
Wren, H. G., The Legal System of Pre-Western Japan. *Hastings Law Journal* 1968, Vol. 20, No. 1, pp. 217–244. https://repository.uchastings.edu/hastings_law_journal/vol20/iss1/5.
www.britannica.com/event/Gempei-War
www.britannica.com/event/Taika-era-reforms
www.britannica.com/place/Japan/The-Heian-period-794-1185.
www.britannica.com/place/Japan/The-Taika-reforms#ref168017 21.04.2020.
www.britannica.com/topic/Kurodo-dokoro.
www.britannica.com/topic/Taiho-code
Yamamura, K., The Decline of the *Ritsuryō* System: Hypotheses on Economic and Institutional Change. *Journal of Japanese Studies* 1974, Vol. 1, No. 1, The Society for Japanese Studies, pp. 3–37. https://doi.org/10.2307/133435.
Yamamura, K., Tara in Transition: A Study of a Kamakura Shoen. *Journal of Japanese Studies* 1981, Vol. 7, No. 2, The Society for Japanese Studies, pp. 349–391. https://doi.org/10.2307/132206.
Yamamura, K., Murakami, Y., *Ie* Society as a Pattern of Civilization: Introduction. *Journal of Japanese Studies* 1984, Vol. 10, No. 2, The Society for Japanese Studies, pp. 279–363. www.jstor.org/stable/132142.

5 The corporate governance system in the *Ritsuryō* State

During the period described earlier, the *Ritsuryō* State emerged, developed, and collapsed. It was an organized structure linking the emperor with the ordinary people through a hierarchy of central, provincial, district, and local governmental units staffed by aristocrats. Japan established for the first time a rational and centralized bureaucratic government, based on the principle of universal rule, land allocation, and taxation. Good governance was based on a balance of imperial virtue, bureaucratic industry, and divine protection.[1] In around 500 years, this system (governance) went full circle on the macro level. The centralized, law-based state that the enlightened elites had built in the 7th century gradually weakened due to its political weaknesses, until it was finally destroyed by the families seeking material and political dominance.

The weakness of central control and the inadequacy of Chinese practices in Japanese reality caused that from the 10th-century governors were able to govern their provinces without the interference of the central government.[2] Thus, two stages of state management can be distinguished in the period under consideration – a stage of fully centralized management and a two-level management system. The first existed from the 7th to 9th centuries, when Japan was centrally managed and provinces were under strict central control. The second stage began in the 9th century and lasted until the fall of the *Ritsuryō* State, during which time the state functioned as a two-tier supervisory structure, consisting of the central government and local governments. The central government appointed governors, giving them great freedom in managing their provinces, but only if they carried out the tasks imposed on them (financial plans) by the authorities. The length of this period and the many significant, revolutionary changes that took place during it mean that the analysis of the then-existing corporate governance will only be outlined later.

The first centralized state established by Emperor Tenji (668–672) from clan-based agricultural communities (*uji*) gave him direct control over the people and the rice fields they cultivated. The Taika reform introduced a system of equal fields in which land was distributed to peasants in the form of a lease that expired after six years. It was paid for from rice production, according to a scale adapted

DOI: 10.4324/9781003497936-7

to the gender, age, and status of each member of the household.[3] The entire nation became the public people of the empire, and the whole of the land became the property of the Crown, while the hereditary nobles became state pensioners. The changes required an accurate census of the population, a survey of the land, fixing the boundaries of provinces, districts, and villages, appointing officials to administer the affairs of these local divisions, and organizing the central and local government councils and offices, as well as creating a strong system of governance and control. Japan managed to accomplish all these extremely difficult tasks, adopted and implemented codified law (*ritsuryō*), nationalization and equal distribution of land, a uniform tax system, and institutionalization of government bodies.[4] A complex system of codified rules and regulations formed the basis of a strongly hierarchical society that promoted obedience and responsibility. The legal reforms (646, 702, 757, and 927) greatly developed the Japanese political system, increasing the power of the emperor and the central government through an efficient system of land ownership, levying and collecting taxes, and a well-organized administration.[5] The developed institutions had distinct Japanese characteristics.[6]

The *Ritsuryō* State may be viewed as a hybrid of the two organizational principles, as it adapted the Chinese legal codes (historic civilization), modified to allow for Japanese conditions, and the heritage of Japanese *uji* (clan) society.[7] The Chinese concept of the scholar-bureaucracy was adopted. However, the Japanese system of government at that time was very conservative, because it allowed the elite to oppose unsuitable changes and maintain beneficial traditions, which slowed down social and economic changes throughout the country's history. In the *Ritsuryō* State, as in the Yamato, religion was an important factor in gaining hegemony and political consolidation. The new imperial order was supported by the religious obligations of monarchs, based on the emperor's divine legitimacy, and reinforced by secular rituals of respect and reward. Opposition to imperial authority was to be punished by law and deities. The monarch and the elite groups used their divine roots to justify their superiority and right to benefits and power. The emperor also maintained his hegemony by gaining the support of potential competitors in exchange for economic and political benefits. The important instrument of governance became the *uji–kabane* system. The nobility accepted the change of the system because it was compatible with their interests. What changed was the source of high benefits for the hereditary nobility, who lost the land they controlled and the income generated from it, but were granted state benefits (pensions) in return. Conflicts of interest were avoided so long as the revenues of aristocrats were sufficient (steadily increasing) to satisfy their needs. In this system, all farms, the *ko*, or families functioned as economic units. Also, shrines and temples could be regarded as families who lived a self-sufficient economic life and were engaged in land economy. But despite all the fundamental changes, the new system was economically unsound, socially limited, and therefore started slowly to decay by the end of the 8th century.

In the macroeconomic aspect, the vertical relations between the emperor, government, ministers, provinces, and districts officials may be considered, as in the preceding eras, in the light of the Resource Dependency Theory, the Social Networks Theory, and the Managerial and Class Hegemony Theory. The Agency Theory may also be used to explain the governance relations between them.

The Resource Dependency Theory (RDT) emphasizing the strength and tactics available to organizations regards an organization as a stable alliance, *pursuing joint objectives, coordinating activities, sharing knowledge and resources*.[8] The state built internal and external social, institutional, and industrial networks to obtain synergy benefits. They influenced its solidarity, relationships, and integrity.[9] The aristocratic class, headed by the emperor, was interested in obtaining synergies that would maximize its income. A strong and well-organized government was necessary for this. Obtaining the synergy effect was conditional on the cooperation (or domination) of the nobility with the emperor, who was the source of titles, positions, and related income. A conflict with the monarch could result in the loss of all these privileges and degradation. Another condition for maximizing revenues was to build strong local structures throughout the country, responsible for accurate calculation and collection of all taxes levied and for their safe transfer to the government. The knowledge absorbed from China made it possible to create a rational tax system, expand, and increase the efficiency of agriculture, which in turn enabled the emergence of craftsmen. All these goals required good cooperation, especially from the ruling class, and were achieved by the central government and the nobility.

The Managerial and Class Hegemony Theory (MCHT) which sees corporate governance as an interpersonal, political process,[10] may be looked at in the *ritsuryō* period. The key was the aristocrats' (directors') view of themselves and their influence on the court, organization, and management of the country. They perceived themselves as an elite group with divine roots to whom all privileges, the highest positions, and honours were due. Their dominance in the state was legally confirmed, which translated into the high income based on birth privileges. Their main goal was to maximize benefits in the form of top positions and fortunes, which in turn were conditioned by their position in the aristocratic class.

Therefore, the most powerful members of the aristocracy were determined to gain hegemony in their class and at court. Some clans (Soga, Taira, Minamoto, Fujiwara) succeeded and gain hegemony, influence over the emperors, and politics of the country. At the highest level, the struggle for hegemony took place between emperors and great aristocratic families, as well as between these families and within them. The hegemon (monarch) could strengthen his position (hegemony) by implementing the proper organization of the state and its institutions as well as effective systems of motivation and supervision. Such efforts were made by successive emperors, undertaking intense, though usually unsuccessful, struggles for power and private benefits within the highest court elite.

The history of the *Ritsuryō* State has proven that the personality of the monarch and his determination to wield power have a great influence on the behaviour and operation of the government (board). In Japan, powerful families were able to dominate not only the government (board) decisions but also weak emperors (ruling and cloistered) and were able to achieve their purposes, if not by requests, then by force and wars. Their ambitions (or greediness) were the main reasons for the collapse of the centralized state. At a lower level (second), the struggle for hegemony was fought at the provincial, district, and *shōen* levels between aristocrats, local nobility, and high and low officials. The aims of this fight were to maximize the landed property (interests), secure it, obtain tax privileges, and dominate local structures. The third level of the struggle for hegemony was the family, whose leader had a hegemonic position, which he often had to fight hard to gain or maintain.

As earlier noted, according to the Theory of Social Networks (TSN), those involved in corporate governance processes are linked through networks. In the *Ritsuryō* State, social groups united, building their own networks to protect and enhance their interests. Members of each network belonged to a particular social class, had similar income sources, education level, family, institutional or corporate affiliations, backgrounds, lifestyles, and shared the same values. Social networks and their subnetworks had varying degrees of influence over their goals, governance, and development. They had their own self-government, forms of organization, duties, and responsibilities, usually defined in internal codes. Leaders played a key role in the networks, because they had to connect them with the strategic environment – the state and local authorities. They formed alliances, eliminated enemies, sought to gain, maintain, and strengthen their position and sphere of influence, improve organization, increase income, and acquire strong patrons. In the period under consideration, the network created by the village strengthened and networks organized by craftsmen and merchants began to gain more and more importance. However, they were independent in creating internal relations but not in shaping external ones. They had to fully adapt to the requirements from above.

At the macro and micro levels, the Agency Theory may be used to define the relations between the nobles, their leaders, and agents. The law of the *Ritsuryō* State distinguished the ruler, the government, and the people that made up the state, and defined the duties and rights of each as well as of each branch of government. The rulers of the *Ritsuryō* State built its vertical and horizontal structures and defined their goals, powers, and responsibilities, making the state function as a corporation. A formal, well-constructed, and effective system of governance was established in the form of a nationwide, multi-level system of state control headed by an emperor, his government, ministers, governors, and their subordinates. The hierarchical dependences were strictly defined and obeyed. The administrative structure outlined in the previous chapter, from the imperial offices to the local offices in remote regions, was based on a hierarchy of titles and office ranks.

There was a separation of ownership and control in the vertical governance system. The emperor (principal) may be compared to the CEO and his government (court) to the board of directors – his agents. During the considered half of the millennium, the emperors' position, as CEOs in contemporary companies, varied in time, being either strong or weak, able or unable to gain support of the governments, but finally limited to ceremonial and religious duties; however, their social primacy was never denied. The emperor who formally exercised supreme power was not accountable because of his divine empowerment and the weaknesses of his governance position (reign but not rule).

The Council (board) was the ultimate authority to advise the emperor on all civil and military affairs of state. The strongest fraction was always the leader. The most influential families (Soga and Fujiwara) shaped the history of the *Ritsuryō* State. Weak, quarrelsome, selfish boards lead to the bankruptcy of enterprises, just like the leading aristocratic families that fiercely competed for power, plunged the country into turmoil, wars, and ruin. Each of them tried to display power, rights to benefits, and skills in achieving them. Conflicts of interest were mitigated during periods of cooperation, for example, at the beginning of the *Ritsuryō* State, but exacerbated during its decline. The main aim of the nobility (agents) was to maximize their status and interests of their families. The intensity of agency conflicts and their resolution depended on the strength of the principal and agents and their ability to compromise interests. The conflicts were resolved through diplomacy, the ability to conclude and implement contracts (peacefully or through wars), maintaining good relations with superiors, and with competitors. When the hegemon (central authority) was weak, conflicts of interest exacerbated and resulted in wars (e.g. the Genpei War) fought for power and wealth.

The family treated as a corporation was ruled by a head (principal or CEO) focused on increasing its wealth, position, and power. The head coordinated politics, managed the clan's (corporate) assets, fully controlled its members, and distributed the income among them. He was responsible for the effective management of the family and its affairs (corporation), its solvency, maintaining its perpetual succession (business continuity), and separateness (position). The family acted as a single individual, thus, had corporate characteristics. Religious, financial, and traditional bonds united these families. Nothing was allowed that could undermine the family's collective strength.[11] However, conflicts of interests, or rather the battles for power, sometimes divided the family and families, leading to open conflicts and to extinction of the losers.

The local administrative structure was divided into three levels of administrative units (*kuni, kori*, and *sato*), governed by *kokushi, gunji*, and *richo*, respectively. The governance of the provinces was entrusted to governors (*kokushi) who* became an integral part of the administration, responsible for governance and justice in their *kuni*. They were the highest-ranking officials in the province, and their subordinates were the heads of the districts called district governors, whose subordinates were heads of the village (*richo*), heads of the homesteads (50 houses), and the elders of five households. The *richo* had to keep records of the number of people in each household; encourage diligence in farming the land and rearing animals; reprimand and, if necessary, report any abuse, and encourage public service. In districts, special officials (*choshu-shi*) were nominated and obliged to observe and report on the conduct of the new officials with respect to their diligence, honesty, and to ensure that the operation and integrity of the new system were maintained. They were also responsible for maintaining order and peace, checking that producers were paying the government a fixed tribute, overseeing efficiency, competitiveness, and development by recording and controlling business transactions, and administering penalties. Peasant and townsmen communities, blocked into groups of five families, were held mutually responsible for the implementation of the official directives and paying taxes. Thus, the leased land was administered and controlled by the appointed officials accountable to their superiors. The vertical governance relations were clear, and the chain of responsibility was well defined. Initially, this system was supported by law and harsh punishments for breaking it, but the ability of the government to provide law and order declined in time.

In early Heian era, three new supervisory bodies were established to strengthen control by the central government – the Accounting Bureau (*Shukeiryō*), the Bureau of Tax Revenues (*Shuzeiryō*), and the Board of Discharge Examiners (*Kageyushi*). The latter audited a governor's accounts and the transfer of property to the incoming governor (discharge certificates). Both the governor and the vice-governor of a province were accountable for any discrepancies found. In time, the audit office began to regulate tax matters, between the central administration and the provinces. District inspectors supervised provincial administrators and their handling by the Controller's Office (*benkari*) of the Council of State. In the central administration, at the provincial level and lower levels, up to five household units, persons (bodies) were designated responsible for control, division, and efficiency of work as well as compliance with laws and rules. Officials at the provincial and district levels, as agents of the central government, were obliged to control the population of the country through a regular censuses and paddy surveys. New systems of internal controls were created to monitor managers at all levels and books of accounts had to be kept and verified. Since the land was governed by officials appointed by the emperor (principal) and the estates (*shōen*) by the proprietor's appointees, there was a separation of ownership and control. Initially, this system did not cause serious agency conflicts. Absentee aristocrats realized that they had to rely on their agents, high-level managers responsible for the production process and revenue generation, as well as local officials. They therefore had to meet the expectations of their agents in terms of obtaining benefits and guaranteeing security.

This required the *shōen* owner to have a powerful position at court and a strong state capable of enforcing the established rights and privileges. Therefore, a new metropolitan police force spread to the provinces to watch any events and activities concerning land ownership and tax avoidance. The principle of internalizing problems in all units (corporations) was still in force, but the whistle-blowing was accepted. The country was reasonably well governed by using strict governance mechanisms. The administration and inhabitants were under a sophisticated, well-organized system of vertical governance and control. The economic consequences resulting from changes in land ownership rights not yet had a significant direct impact on the financial situation of the Kyoto elite and the maintenance of its old privileges. The following changes continued to transfer most of the surplus production to the ruling class and elite (i.e. the court nobility and higher clergy), who continued to benefit most from the Taika reforms. The aristocracy was able to create policy, and especially the tax policy of the country, oriented towards optimization of their revenues. They retained their dominant position for the next few centuries.

As far as the micro level of governance is concerned, the *shōen*, characterized in the next subchapter, became most important. They were production units very well organized, managed, and oriented towards efficiency, increased productivity, and tax optimization. They were mostly tax-free estates, economically independent units, having some features of companies, created to protect ownership and organize highly specialized efficient and profitable production. The *shōen* were managed by professional managers, and all its stakeholders shared the same aims. Therefore, the risk of internal conflicts was not high in them. *Shōen* were under strict control, audited and assessed internally and externally by special officials. Tax optimization was used as a low-risk method to increase income from these manors. *Shōen* gradually resulted in the development of new centres of power, brought financial benefits, and implied significant social and political consequences for many decades to come. The lower-ranking nobility saw an opportunity to increase their position and wealth by entrusting themselves to the care of a chosen high-ranking aristocrat or by allying themselves with a local authority that controlled the tax-producing lands. *Shōen* may prove the existence of corporate governance in Nara and Heian Japan.

However, there were conflicts of interest between *shōen* owners, managers, and outsiders. The emergence of *shōen* and the *shōen-koguaro* system was the result of a conflict of interest between leading ambitious aristocrats and monks who competed not only for the most lucrative positions but also to expand their estates by opening new rice fields, obtaining tax exemptions, and strengthening their position at court. In order to achieve their goals, the owners of *shōen* had to hire loyal agents able to protect their interests in the provinces and maximize their wealth (income). Tradition and the law safeguarded this system. However, the agents gained more and more power, using their knowledge of agriculture, planning, management, law, and accounting, and using more or less nepotism and local contacts. Aligning one's own interests with those of one's superiors became a way to eliminate agency conflicts. This policy brought benefits to both sides of the conflict.

By the end of the 9th century, the power of *shōen* had grown so strong that they began to promote local separatism, which was also helped by the weakening of the central government's power in most provinces. With this trend, serious agency problems emerged. The power and wealth of landowners in the provinces increased, thanks to which they were able to assert and defend their interests by force. Imperial power weakened, and the strong, centralized state system began to disintegrate. The main reason for this was the conflicts of interest between the emperor, secular and religious aristocracy, and their agents, resulting from the deteriorating economic situation of the ruling class and a strong determination to remedy this situation. Changes in land ownership and the struggle of powerful clans for the dominance of family interests led to a significant weakening of the centralized monarchy and the development of Japanese feudalism in the Kamakura *Bakufu*.

The analysis of the literature on the *Ritsuryō* State allows us to realize that already during the Yamato period certain features specific to the modern Japanese model of corporate governance, such as strong group identity – with family, group, and community, the ability to cooperate, organize teamwork, commitment (self-sacrifice) – were formed or strengthened. Respect for superiors, knowledge, education, and tradition are other features of Japanese corporate governance dating back to ancient times. Emphasizing the importance of loyalty has been a hallmark of Japanese culture for centuries. It focuses on the duty of care, diligence (lack of it was severely punished), submission, responsibility, obedience, and respect in the relationship between superiors and subordinates, and this mutual duty has become an established pattern supporting the values of morality and discipline. Other characteristics are internalization of problems, unity against outsiders, respect for law, and recognition of social differences.[12] It can be argued that these values are still among the most important features of Japanese corporate governance.

Although during the Heian period the Japanese showed exceptional respect for their own tradition and culture, the *Ritsuryō* State proved their great ability to use hybridization. Ideas that could be absorbed into Japanese society and culture at the time were modified or directly implemented, while those that were inappropriate or impractical were rejected or lost importance over time. Hybridization played a key role in the formation of Japanese civilization. This was a very important determinant of shaping corporate governance in the *Ritsuryō* State. The centuries-old ability to adopt diverse innovations and apply them in unique[13] ways continues to play a very important role in shaping corporate governance and the development of Japan, and has not lost its importance so far.

Notes

1 Ch. Holcombe, *Ritsuryō* Confucianism. *Harvard Journal of Asiatic Studies* 1997, Vol. 57, No. 2, pp. 543–573.
2 G. B. Sansom, A History of Japan to 1334. Vol. 1. *Stanford University Press*, Stanford 1958, p. 234.
3 M. W. Meyer, Japan A Concise History. *Rowman & Littlefield Publishers Inc*, Plymouth 2009, p. 45.
4 K. Yamamura, Y. Murakami, *Ie* Society as a Pattern of Civilization: Introduction. *Journal of Japanese Studies* 1984, Vol. 10, No. 2, The Society for Japanese Studies, pp. 279–363.
5 W. S. Morton, J. K. Olenik, Japan. Its history and Culture. *McGraw-Hill Companies Inc,* New York 2005, p. 27.
6 C. Andressen, A Short History of Japan . . . op. cit., p. 38.
7 K. Yamamura, Y. Murakami, Ie Society as a Pattern of Civilization . . . op. cit.
8 W. R. Scott, G. F. Davis, Organizations and Organizing: Rational, Natural, and Open System Perspectives. *Pearson Prentice Hall,* Upper Saddle River, NJ 2007.
9 G. F. Davis, J. A. Cobb, Resource Dependence Theory: Past and future. *Research in the Sociology of Organizations* 2010, No. 28, pp. 21–42.
10 B. Tricker, Corporate Governance. Principles, Policies, and Practices. *Oxford University Press*, Oxford 2015, pp. 68, 69.
11 R. H. P. Mason, J. G. Caiger. A History of Japan. *TUTTLE Publishing,* Tokyo; Rutland, VT; Singapore 1997, p. 71.
12 K. Paramore, Confucianism as Cultural Capital (Mid-first Millennium CE – Late Sixteenth Century CE). In: Japanese Confucianism: A Cultural History (New Approaches to Asian History). *Cambridge University Press*, *Cambridge* 2016, pp. 16–40.
13 J. McEldowney, Hybridization: A Study in Comparative Constitutional Law . . . op. cit.

Bibliography

Andressen, C., A Short History of Japan. From Samurai to Sony. *Allen & Unwin*, Canberra 2002.

Davis, G. F., Cobb, J. A., Resource Dependence Theory: Past and Future. *Research in the Sociology of Organizations* 2010, No. 28, pp. 21–42. http://dx.doi.org/10.1108/S0733-558X(2010)0000028006G.

Holcombe, Ch., *Ritsuryō* Confucianism. *Harvard Journal of Asiatic Studies* 1997, Vol. 57, No. 2, pp. 543–573. *JSTOR*. https://doi.org/10.2307/2719487.

Mason, R. H. P., Caiger, J. G., A History of Japan. *TUTTLE Publishing*, Tokyo; Rutland, VT; Singapore 1997. file:///D:/Users/wzr/Downloads/A_History_of_Japan_Mason_Caiger%20(5).pdf.

McEldowney, J., Hybridization: A Study in Comparative Constitutional Law. *Penn State International Law Review* 2010, Vol. 28, No. 3, Article 5, pp. 355–376. http://elibrary.law.psu.edu/psilr/vol28/iss3/5.

Meyer, M. W., Japan A Concise History. *Rowman & Littlefield Publishers Inc*, Plymouth 2009. file:///D:/Users/wzr/Downloads/epdf.pub_japan-a-concise-history-4th-edition.pdf.

Morton, W. S., Olenik, J. K., Japan. Its History and Culture. *McGraw-Hill Companies Inc*, New York 2005. https://vdocuments.mx/japan-its-history-and-culture-56811b380a71d.html.

Paramore, K., Japanese Confucianism: A Cultural History. New Approaches to Asian History. *Cambridge University Press*, Cambridge: 2016, pp. 16–40. https://doi.org/10.1017/CBO9781107415935.004.

Sansom, G. B., A History of Japan to 1334. Vol. 1. *Stanford University Press*, Stanford 1958.

Scott, W. R., Davis, G. F., Organizations and Organizing: Rational, Natural, and Open System Perspectives. *Pearson Prentice Hall*, Upper Saddle River, NJ 2007.

Tricker, B., Corporate Governance. Principles, Policies, and Practices. *Oxford University Press*, Oxford 2015.

Yamamura, K., Murakami, Y., *Ie* Society as a Pattern of Civilization: Introduction. *Journal of Japanese Studies* 1984, Vol. 10, No. 2, The Society for Japanese Studies, pp. 279–363. www.jstor.org/stable/132142.

6 *Shōen* and their importance for the economy and corporate governance

In the 8th century, the imperial government did move towards centralized governance. According to the Imperial Legal Codes, any piece of land in Japan belonged to the emperor, any kind of private property right over land was excluded, and any tax revenue belonged to the central government. However, technological constraints on transportation and development did not allow the imperial government to directly govern the reclamation and management of rice fields and farms. Local leaders, some of whom worked for local governments as minor officials, had no claim to agricultural income either as private owners or as officials. Therefore, they had no incentive to develop wastelands and effectively manage rice fields and farms, and as a result, the neglected fields were getting devastated. In response to this failure and the need to acquire new rice fields, institutional change was necessary to adapt imperial law to Japanese reality. The newly formed institution was the Japanese manorial system (*shōen*), where the supreme ownership and the sovereignty still belonged to the emperor, but considerable portion of tax and rent were received by intermediary agents.[1] *Shōen* were established and developed through the joint endeavours of court aristocrats, religious institutions, and members of the local gentry who combined their interests to make these estates more secure and profitable.[2] Their inner structure was complex as they were made up of a number of smaller holdings, known as *myo*.[3] The expansion of the *shōen* from the 8th century was built on mutual benefits, respect for power, ability of ranks, and the importance of relational capital. Public ownership of land began to transform into private ownership, causing the origins of *shōen* to be associated with the beginning of the disintegration of the *Ritsuryō* state. The increase of private ownership of land undermined the political and economic power of the emperor, contributed to the growth of powerful local clans, and led to the emergence of new regional centres of wealth and power.[4] It created a system based on the family as an economic unit.[5] Thus, the two great institutional developments of the period, familism and *shōen*, grew up within the Taika system.[6]

In the 11th century, more land in Japan was controlled by *shōen* owners than by the central government (around 70%). Power was thus decentralized, restoring

DOI: 10.4324/9781003497936-8

the ancient Japanese structure of powerful provincial leaders. According to Sato, after the establishment of tax immunities, *shōen* became a complex and hierarchical system of ownership, aimed at managing property as an economic unit, adequately distributing its income, and maintaining social control.[7] In this way, *shōen* became important economic institutions, corporations, or states within a state. The *shōen* system was stopped around the mid-15th century, when villages became self-governing units, owing loyalty to a feudal lord – *daimyō*.[8] These private, tax-free, autonomous estates may serve as an example of the development of corporate governance, but establishing their strong position was a long process.[9]

Origins and development of *shōen*

The privately owned and managed large rural estates (manors) excluded from public governance were called *shō*, or *shōen*, where *shō* meant a *country house*, and *en* – *well-kept grounds*.[10] *Shōen* became hereditary private property, enjoying financial and administrative privileges.[11] They were estates outside the direct state control, with immunity excluding them from state taxation and direct supervision by state officials. They were a tool for direct transferring tax revenues to designated aristocratic households (absentee landlords), religious institutions, and local managers, as form of private income. *Shōen* originates from the land officially assigned to approve Shintō shrines or Buddhist temples. In the second half of the 8th century, to ensure that they get the support from the government, some provincial public land (*koden*) was designated to provide these dues directly (on a permanent or a floating basis) to the religious institutions. In this way, approved Shintō shrines or Buddhist temples exchanged their state grants for officially acquired rights to taxes from this land, in whole or in part. These fields were called exempt fields (*menden*) or *floating exempt fields (ukimeri)* because they were designated for this purpose each year.[12]

Shōen were created from public *privatized* land (*kokugaryō*), which resulted from the opening of new fields, obtaining rights to various taxes and *corvée*, and through commendation.[13] S*hōen* created by the first method consisted of new paddy fields opened by court nobles, temples, and shrines, or created by the central government and then given by the emperor to his own family, friends, nobles, state officials, or religious institutions. The 743 central government decree stated that reclaimed rice fields (*konderi*) were to be held in perpetuity by those who opened them at their own expense. The main political families of the capital, wanting to increase their income, developed ties with provincial governors to establish *shōen* on their own behalf or through the temples and shrines with which they were associated. The maximum size of reclaimed fields that aristocrats of various ranks, commoners, and temples could own was set in 749, but in the late 8th century, the government limited reclamation of fields to all except the imperial family. In the period 828–886, it was granted nearly

7,000 hectares of the developed (20%) as well as not developed farmland. From 795 to 878, over 3,700 hectares were granted to 33 imperial princes and princesses, to be developed into farmland. By 770, the great Todaiji temple held 92 *shoen* in 23 provinces and half of them had their origin in commendation by the central government.[14] By the 10th century, central government withdrew support for the *shōen*. Cooperation between owners and managers of landed estates began to deteriorate. Proprietors depended on the loyalty of their estate managers for whom developing reclaimed fields for themselves became more profitable. Estates managed by the owners often went bankrupt, but estates managed by local notables survived, because agricultural workers could only be obtained with the cooperation of the local nobility. Therefore, the early *shōen*, like the *ritsuryō* order within which they had developed, were declining during the 9th century.

From the late Heian period, the *shōen* system started to develop at an increasing rate (new *shōen*), but it took another 200 years before they dominated Japan.[15] Most of the new *shōen* were formed according to the *Kinai shō* pattern, because especially in this region, most *shōen* were organized into units called *myo*. Each such unit was assigned to a single *mioshu* who was responsible for collecting and paying taxes and other fees from this *myo*. *Myo* were administered by local officials and *myoshu*, with little or no involvement of the proprietor in managing local agricultural affairs.[16] Around the second half of the Kamakura period, these units began to divide into smaller ones and this disintegration process lasted until the end of the 14th century.[17]

The second method of creating *shōen*, especially popular in the 11th–12th centuries, involved nobles and temples obtaining the right to use serfdom imposed on farmers who cultivated public lands and paid the government a rice tax. The next step of these prominent people was to claim the rights to take over public lands cultivated by peasants providing them with serfdom, which usually ended with the seizure of these lands. Commendations, the third, most important method of *shōen* creation, were closely related to the development of those estates. The commander converted a piece of *public* land into a *shōen* to improve his political and economic position. It did not mean that he handed over his exclusive proprietary rights to that land to the court noble. Thanks to the commendation agreements, the imperial family, the aristocracy, and temples were owners in name, while the families in the provinces retained rights as actual administrators of the property. The possibility of concluding commendation contracts (agreements) resulted in a significant increase in the wealth and income of the aristocracy. Local tax managers reported directly to the owners of these estates and did not forward the revenues to the provincial government office.[18] By the late Heian period, some proprietors were able to obtain complete tax and juridical immunity for their holdings, *becoming states in state*. Each case of commendation was used to obtain greater concessions from provincial officials. Local tax managers did not have the power to keep tax revenues for themselves – any attempt to do so put them in rebellion against the imperial government. But through the power of commendation they could determine that the taxes they collected went to the political master of their choice (ruling class) and thus choose the best possible financial and patronage protection. This resulted in significant growth in the power and influence of local magnates and the local tax managers' group.[19]

Development and running a *shōen* did not rely on slaves but on employed labour.[20] Reischauer writes that each employee of a *shōen* possessed documents (contracts) guaranteeing them rights of office and rights in the land. The hierarchy of the estate structure began with cultivators (*shomin*) at the very bottom. Above them, acting as managers and overseers were the *shoke* or *shokan*, either residents appointed by the proprietor or agents sent out from the capital. These administrative officials, classified into *upper* (*joshi*), *middle* (*chushi*), and lower *family officials* (*geshi*), governed the *shōen*. The main landowner (*ryoke*) was the central figure in the *shōen* and had rights of disposal, administration, and taxation.[21] He usually was a member of the court aristocracy or a large prestigious religious institution located in the capital. To prevent interference and possible problems from the provincial governor, the *ryoke* usually commended again the land to the more politically influential *honke* (legal guardian of the manor) at the top of the power hierarchy.[22] A great *honke*, well and highly connected at court, was the ultimate protector (defender) of *shōen* and its immunities.[23] The result was the multi-layered proprietorship over *shōen*. *Honke* families (aristocrats and senior clergy) or institutions (great temples) received by contract an agreed share of the production of the lands under their protection.[24]

Thus, the basic tax was paid to the *shōen*-holder (*ryoke*) not to the government. During this period, the relationship between the landlord and its managers was strong. The principal landowner (*ryoke*) was dependent on managers (stewards) who focused on managing the estate and protecting its people, and on local nobility for land reclamation and management. Local nobility, in turn, needed support from the court aristocracy or great temples to obtain permission to take over a piece of wasteland or newly opened, usually high-yielding rice fields, for their own use. Developing rice fields without formal permission risked their confiscation, so the local nobility obtained the support of court aristocrats to allocate and secure the recultivated land and prevent its confiscation. In return for paying their obligations, peasants received a place in local manorial society that entitled them to such rights as security of tenure, access to village resources (i.e. land), and a system for the redress of grievances. According to Goldsmith, the estate system was a highly effective method for extracting revenues from the countryside. The aim of it was to confine and control subjects, but it also gave cultivators access to power. This cycle of obligations defined the status of both, the patron and the client, and that status in turn accorded privileges.[25]

However, the growth of the non-taxable estates (a departure from the *ritsuryō* system) worsened the conditions of peasants cultivating fields and craftsmen who had to bear an increasing burden of ad hoc payments in the form of taxes.[26] They were subject to authority, and strictly controlled with respect to efficiency, diligence, and all the other aspects of their life. Farmers were oppressed by the tax system and legal and illegal requirements. The central government set tax quotas for each province, leaving the governor free to judge what the farmers could pay. The increasing number of complaints against governors since then indicated that they often tried to extort taxes from the peasants. Manipulations were made mainly at lower management levels, using legal loopholes and accounts. Such actions aroused the hostility of the peasants who showed dissatisfaction by abandoning their land, escaping to frontier areas becoming socially displaced people (*ronin*), or putting themselves under the protection of powerful persons by commending own land to them. These were the only methods of seeking security, less demands, and tax optimization available to peasants. Through the process of commendation, peasants started to work land on the private tax-free estates of the temples and nobles, in return for fiscal immunity and protection for them and their descendants.[27] By concluding such agreements, farmers agreed to pay rent in the form of part of the harvest, but this agreement did not involve a change in land ownership.[28] Thus, they shared the financial benefits and greater security of the *shōen*. Under these conditions, the owner of a provincial *shōen* could take over estates from many local peasants.

Kiley writes that landowners could extend their influence over *shōen* land and farmers in three ways intended to increase rental income equivalent to the land tax that would otherwise go to the provincial government.[29] By imposing additional rent (*kajishi*) on all exempt fields, in parallel with additional burdens imposed by provincial governments, by obtaining a limited exemption from the second component of provincial taxes, *miscellaneous exactions*, which they could collect themselves because they were not covered by *shōen* certificates, were negotiated directly with the provincial government. Granting exemptions depended on the provincial governor but could be revoked by his successor. A third way to extend the owner's influence over *shōen* was to gain control over granting rights to the *shōen* fields.[30]

The formal procedure for creating a *shōen* required either a certification record (*dajo-kanfu*) from the central government or a validating certificate issued by a provincial governor. The *shōen* were thus divided into *provincially exempted manors* (*kokumenshō)* when the rights were recognized by the *kokushi*, and *imperially exempted manors (chakumenshō)* when the rights were recognized by the Great Council of State (*dajōkon*). The latter estate was a completely independent political and economic unit.[31] The lack of a certificate of transfer of state land to the *shōen* resulted in the confiscation of the estate by the government.

In the 8th and 9th centuries, the central government expected the expansion of *shōen* through the development of new lands, but around 900 it decided that further expansion of areas exempt from provincial taxes was not desirable. The rise of *shōen* as a tax instrument (distinct from its earlier role as a land-development estate) stemmed from the evolution of a tax structure adjusted to the shrinking provincial quotas.[32] Due to the rapidly diminishing amount of taxable land, government revenues steadily declined.[33] These decreasing provincial revenues still had to cover the stipends and emoluments of aristocrats, the costs of running the government, maintaining the imperial household and the capital of Heian.[34] Therefore, high officials began to halt *shōen* development and revoke improper exemption certificates. The central government edicts restricting property gave the governor an excuse to scrutinize an estate's immunities and declare them invalid, often on very poor grounds.[35] Morris writes that, in 902 and 915, *shōen* registration and tax exemptions were ordered to be controlled through annual review and assessment by provincial and local officials. Accreditation of exempt fields was always done by the central government not by provincial officials. But under the new system of registration, provincial governments gained the power to recognize or reject new land-development applications submitted by *shōen* owners or local officials. This system addressed three key aspects of *shōen* that significantly influenced their fate – the recognition of the certification of exempt fields and of new reclaimed fields, and the exemption of *shōen* people or, later, *shōen* land, from provincial miscellaneous exactions. The owners could appeal against the provincial decision to the central authorities only in the first case, the other two were entirely under the jurisdiction of the province but the decision could be changed by the next governor.[36] Asakawa writes that from the 10th century, *shō* holders initiated the legal custom of referring to the statutes of the central and provincial governments, which clearly recognized *shōen* ownership, defined its boundaries, scope, and exemptions from various taxes. Statutes usually specified what taxes (all or part) the property was exempt from and prohibited provincial officials from invading the estate.[37] Most *shōen* originally had only partial tax immunity, being excused the labour and *other produce* taxes, but not the rice tax.[38] In the 10th century, the most important thing for *shōen* was tax exemption, not land development.[39]

According to Yamamura, the early (old) *shōen* from the Nara period differed from the Heian *shōen* (new) in three ways. The owners and managers of the Heian *shōen* were entitled to tax exemptions (*fuyu-keri*) and were not controlled by the state. In this way, not just the land of the *shōen* but also their workers were removed from that control. Such rights had not existed in the Nara period. This caused conflicts with the state, which tried to maintain and strengthen control over the assessment and collection of taxes to cover government and law enforcement costs. The increase in the number and size of Heian *shōen*, especially those belonging to powerful institutions, caused social, economic, and political instability at the end of this period. The second characteristic of Heian *shōen* was that their spread was linked to the deterioration of the *ritsuryō* order, unlike the early *shōen* which were established by the officials of the well-organized *Ritsuryō* State. A third feature of Heian *shōen* was a tendency to expand and become increasingly independent of outside control.[40] Financial gain was a motivating factor in transferring provincial public lands to the *shōen* owner, but even more important was gaining patronage, a powerful source of political support.

Around 1000, the political power started to shift gradually from the central government to the large independent provincial landowners who exercised rights of private ownership over land and jurisdiction over people, all of which were legally the sole prerogative of the Crown.[41] However, emperor Go-Sanjo (1034–1073) wanted to re-establish a strong position of emperor and renew the *Ritsuryō* State and principles. He decided to repair the economy and the crumbling structure of the imperial state. With fiscal and judicial immunity, *shōen* destroyed the centralized administrative system and created quasi-autonomous domains beyond the jurisdiction of provincial governors. As already noted, provincial budgets, calculated in rice, were established for each province. Provincial tax revenues (*shōzei*), calculated in rice and collected as a land tax (*so*), were partially loaned out at interest (*suiko*). The interest was allocated to various budget items intended either for provincial government use or to be sent to the capital. Handicraft taxes (*chōyō*), an important part of the tax system, were also meticulously fixed and in principle calculated per individual taxpayer. Emperor Go-Sanjo was determined to hamper the development of local autonomy by introducing restrictions on the establishment of landed estates and the power to decide on the validity of claims for immunities, since they belonged to the prerogatives of the central government, not the provincial governors.[42]

The relationship between *shōen* proprietors and provincial governments deteriorated in the 1040s. The central government established a standard rate for the provincial land tax (6 *soku* per *tan*). *Shōen* proprietors were permitted to collect as rent all or part of this rate for the certified exempt fields, but in either case, the amount allowed was a standard rate. Any provincial land-tax exactions above 6 *soku* per tan (there were many) were to go to the provincial government, favouring provincial governments over *shōen* holders. In the same period, the levy of miscellaneous exactions shifted from persons to land units. The exactions were called *provincial levies* (*kuniyak*u), or miscellaneous levies (*zoyaku*). This change simplified the assessment and collection of taxes. But this modification resulted in competition among highest officials in the capital for limited sources of taxation, in which the organized temple bureaucracy had an advantage over the aristocratic bureaucrats of the civil government.[43]

In 1069, Emperor Go-Sanjō (he broke the strong grip on power by the Fujiwara) established a new office, the *Shōen* Records Office (*Kirokuyo*), specifically to review the validity of estate documentation for their privileged status as lands immune from taxation and supervision by government officials.[44] He issued two separate ordinances for the regulation of *shōen*. They stated that all *shōen* established after 1045 were illegal and would be confiscated and returned to the public domain while those created prior to that date would be subject to confiscation, if their documents were not in order or if they were an obstacle in running provincial affairs. The guarantee of continued ownership of lands, called chartered estates (*kanshobu shien*), was to obtain confirmation from the central government. This required two charters, one from the Grand Council of State and the other from the Ministry of Popular Affairs. Estates known as *provincially exempt estates* (*kokumen shien*), which only had documents containing guarantees from the provincial authorities, were not safe.[45] Although all *shōen* with state-uncertified fiscal privileges (immunities) were abolished, these decrees had little effect in practice, because the main culprits were high-ranking court officials. It is worth noting that the imperial family retained a strong economic base because a large area of land was still registered as taxable public domain, and because it created its own *shōen*.

Shōen was a complex ownership and economic structure.[46] It not only was the mechanism for land management and ownership but included the social order of the *shiki* hierarchy, possession of which gave the right to income and a place in this hierarchy. However, it ceased to keep pace with economic changes because the estate proprietors were not able to exploit new sources of income using traditional methods. The confusion in the social arrangement of *shiki* was one of the most important problems in the late 13th and 14th centuries.

The *shōen–kokugaryō* system – characteristics and influence on corporate governance

As already mentioned, the manors (*shōen*) gained such a strong position that they began to encourage local separatism (political power depended on the wealth of the country), causing the collapse of the authority of the central government in most provinces. The power and prestige of the provincial and local landowners increased because growing wealthier they were becoming more capable of defending their property and privileges by force.

During the 9th and 10th centuries, the people management system (including the ancient family registration system, the creation of the yearly tax registers, and the periodic reallocations of rice fields), which supported the *ritsuryō* system, began to collapse, and the governance on a single-person basis became difficult to maintain. The government therefore introduced a local governance system in which the basic unit of tax collection from the *koden* (a field administered directly by the ruler) was the *myoden* or *myo*, meaning rice fields assigned (named) to a nominal holder. It was a basic unit of the governance and tax collection in the *shōen–koryo* system established in the 11th century.[47]

The governance of land and people after the 11th century took place through *shōen* and *koryo*. This governing form was called *shōen–koryo sei* (The System of Public Lands and Private Estates) or the *shōen–kokugaryō* system.[48] In addition to governance, this system also included a *myoden*-based tax collection system called *myo-taisei* (the local tax management system based on rice fields). Under it, the tax base was changed from people to land units, and the basic tax unit became *myo*.[49] The evolution of cultivation and land use rights into a *myo* (right attached to a name) was first accepted by provincial governors as the basic taxable unit of their domains, and later by the *ryoshu* as the basic rent-paying *shōen* unit.[50] The departure from a system of land ownership based on the number of consumers in each household initiated governance problems for the metropolitan aristocracy.[51]

The *myo*, also called *myoden*, spread widely in the 11th and 12th centuries at the height of the estate system as the basic unit of the *shōen* structure and taxation.[52] There were two main types of the *myo* – held by the agents and officials of the central proprietor (*shōen-myo*) and *myo* held by ordinary peasants having permanent tenure (*hyakusho-myo*). It was already said that this system greatly simplified the imposition and collection of taxes. Provincial governments and landlords were concerned only with the assessment of taxable land divided into *myo*, not the distribution of rights to cultivate the land or the identity of the farmers. It was common to assign to *myo* uniform *shōen* dues. For many *shōen* owners, generating a steady income from central government-certified fields required a constant fighting with provincial governments. Powerful lords of the manor usually divided their *myoden* equally and allotted each farmer a portion of the *myo* to manage it efficiently for them. Each *myo* had a named holder usually a wealthy peasant who was low-level *shōen* official (tax manager), a landholder (not landowner) and cultivator called *myoshu* (appeared in 1047). *Shōen* owners entrusted them with the responsibility of collecting taxes assessed by the provincial government and delivering them in the required form. This included an annual tax on rice (*nengu*), and other dues in kind, corvée, or services (*kuji*) collected from each *myo*[53] in the *shōen* and from each of the cultivators working under his supervision (usually several *myo*). Tax-exempt land and other privileges gave *myoshu* additional resources that they could use to improve rice fields, help farmers in need, or provide some assistance to cultivators who needed seeds, tools, or food. *Myoshu*'s land rights included keeping *myo* in *shōen*, working on it, and reporting on his land. They managed several industries such as agriculture, fishery, handicraft manufacturing, and employment of subordinate labourers. It did not matter whether the *myoshu* farmed his own land or not, as long as his *myoden* remained a taxable unit. Yamamura writes that *myoshu* was a leader in undertaking small but necessary tasks to maintain the quality of the land, ensured that each rice field was cultivated and met the highest labour requirements. He decreased the costs and risks of tax collection and *shōen* management, and motivated cultivators to make the most productive use of their land and labour, exploiting the threat of diversion of cultivated rice fields.

The *myoshu* were dependent on *shōen* managers and local rulers. As those responsible for collecting assessed taxes, they faced the risk of poor harvests. In the event of severe crop failures, dues could be reduced, but *myoshu* were obliged to remit agreed tributes to nobility, temples, local officials, and others with rights to *shōen* revenues. Some of the *myoshu* who completed the required military service later became local *samurai*. Taxes from farmers on *myo* land were also collected and remitted to the *shōen* owner by the local tax manager (*fumyo*). Part of these taxes was allocated to the purchase of certain necessary products, which were then transferred, along with the rest of the taxes, to the provincial government. *Myo* and *myoshu* continued to exist because they embodied an efficient system of tax collection, land management, and because of their administrative and economic efficiency.[54]

At the end of the Heian period, the central government increased support for *shōen* development, but only local officials could guarantee that taxes would be properly assessed and collected. As a consequence of this, the entire ruling hierarchy became reliant on *shōen* support. Public land that did not yet belong to the *shōen* (40–60% of the country's tax base) still supported government offices, aristocratic and imperial householdings, in the same way as the *shōen*.[55] By the end of the Kamakura period, *myoshu* enjoyed secure tenure in land and had improved their land using more of their own capital. As long as the expected dues were paid, neither the *shōen* managers nor the *ryoke* were able to challenge his right to pass the land to his heirs. *Myoshu* rights were restricted in various ways, but in the second half of the 13th century, their rights to land were equalized with those of private owners. The *myoshu* could require farmers working in the *myoden*, which he maintained and improved with his own resources, to pay him a certain rent in addition to the contributions paid to the *ryoke* and *jitō*.[56] The appearance of *kajishi* (rice delivered as a tax to owner of rice fields like *myoshu*) began an important change for the medieval peasants, which affected the intertwined political, economic, and institutional history in the following centuries.

Since the 10th century, provincial governors or *shōen* owners granted the right (revocable at any time) to control the cultivation of a specific parcel of land to managers called *tato* (managers of farms leasing public fields from provincial lords and producing agricultural products), who could also act as tax managers (*fumyo*) for the same land. If he had the right to collect taxes, his position was higher and more profitable compared to other farmers. Wealthy farmland peasants (*handen*), families of old district officers (*gunji*), and local (district or provincial) governors (*kokushi*) formed the wealthy *tato* class.

Tato, if he had enough land under his control, could assign the rights to cultivate it to other peasants (*sakushu* or *sakujin*) for whom he would be the landlord, or include adjacent *myoden* fields managed by other *tato*. They did not *own* the *myoden* fields but had only cultivation rights to it.[57] The provincial government decided that it was more effective to collect taxes by a small number of *tato* who owned significant wealth, had many subordinates and managed large farms, and also because they managed people very effectively.[58] However, the *tato's* right to control the cultivation of the land could be revoked at any time by the provincial government or *shōen* owner.

Morris writes that the *tato* played an important role in *myoden* farming. They paid a rice field tax to the provincial government office (*kokuga)* on behalf of other peasants in *myoden*. This tax payment style was called *fumyo* and created debtor–creditor relations between *tato* farmers and other peasants. They became wealthy, which allowed them to strengthen their position enough to unofficially rule over other peasants and improve their professional *myoden* management skills.[59] The sources of the wealth of *tato* were farming activities and *suiko*. From the 7th to the 12th centuries, *suiko* was a system, according to which seed-rice (*ine*), officially (*ku-suiko*) or privately (*shi-suiko*), was lent to farmers in spring, obliging them to pay it back with interest after the harvest.[60] The *ritsuryō* codes stated that *suiko* should not be administered by the government but should be a private and free contractual relationship. But transformation of the tax structure at the end of the 9th century made *suiko* a land tax applied to reclaimed and household fields. It became a land tax on reclaimed land and households, with very high interest rates (up to 100%). Local authorities imposed it to acquire financial resources for provincial governors' salaries. *Suiko* became an important reason for the fall of the *shōen*.

Cultivators who were appointed *tato* could not treat their household fields as divisible and tradable. After 900, provincial authorities stopped issuing ownership (title) certificates that had previously guaranteed these rights to developers of new agricultural land. This central government policy started a period of a century and a half, during which land *ownership* was not recorded in the provincial land surveys (*kokuzu*). In consequence of this, holders of reclaimed fields, who paid taxes on the *myo* containing them, were often expropriated from the land they cultivated. But in the 11th century, permanent farmers (*eisakushu*) could obtain recognition of rights to the land they farmed from provincial governments or *shōen* owners. They were able to sell, exchange, or bequeath their land in perpetuity, but full *permanent cultivator* rights were rarely granted.[61] In the 12th and 13th centuries, lords of manors, local government officials (*kokugi*), and *samurai* appointed as local overseers, appreciated the role of the *tato*, and granted them the ownership of *myoden* in exchange for constant payment of land tax and undertaking public duties. Thus, the *tato* farmers developed into *myoshu* who owned the permanent tenure of the *myoden*.[62] The *tato* farmers and the *myoden* fields were administered within the manor grounds and supervised by a *shokan* (a manor officer) appointed by the lord of the manor. Imperial estates were administered within a district (*gun*), village (*go*), or settlement (*ho*) and overseen by a *gunji* (district official), *goji* (village official), and *hoji* (land official), respectively. More and more *samurai* were assigned to these positions as military tensions increased in local societies.[63]

Land conditioned the existence of various social groups and was a source of material wealth and political influence for the ruling class, consisting of courtiers, clergy, and warriors. In the 12th century, changes occurred among the lower ranks of society and local land officials and peasants became involved in land administration, supervising the cultivation of the land and ensuring income from it. Farmers ceased to be only tax subjects but began to form associations in village communities and articulate their demands to the rulers.[64] Officials who acted on behalf of their superiors – members of the imperial court, religious institutions, or provincial governors – evolved into influential local land proprietors and warriors. The erosion of the financial and administrative power of the central government challenged the principles of Taika Reform and monarchy, which promoted full, direct state control over all subjects throughout the empire, a state governed by a central bureaucracy, and paid for by public taxes.[65] Asakawa writes that within Kyōto reigned luxury and pomp, but outside it, unrest, and discontentment. The main reason of this sharp contrast between the capital and country was the failure of the system of equal land allotment upon which the great Taika reform had been constructed.[66] The government relied on this system because it provided the Crown with revenue, military service, and calmed competing clans. The Imperial Court delegated all regional affairs to provincial governors, intervening only to ensure that tax revenues continued to be collected from imperial lands. The local government, except the governor, consisted of subordinate officials, such as district administrators (*gunji*) and junior employees (comprising from two to six men), and his clerks (*shishō*), all of whom came from the capital and a large staff of locally recruited personnel.[67] The *shōen* were not controlled politically and economically; they were closed and independent entities that existed within the framework of the national political authority which empowered the *shiki* structure.[68] They were organized into a single self-sufficient system. However, the items and quantities of goods that each *shōen* was expected to provide for court ceremonies held throughout the year were precisely defined.

In the 12th century, the *ritsuryō* system was replaced by a new land tenure system called *shōen–kokugaryō* (provincial government territory or non-*shōen* holding). Another name for it was the *shōen–koryo* system.[69] It was a multi-layered land governance structure, based on *shōen* (manors) and lands under *koryo* (feudal government) control. By the 12th century, most provinces in Japan had complex pattern of landholding in which public and private holdings were intermingled. The reason for its development was the emergence of local powers as private landowners in many regions of Japan. They were unable to claim exclusive ownership of land, but they could improve their position by developing the *shōen–kokugaryō* system. *Kokugaryō* was not a private estate but land on which provincial governors imposed due taxes and corvée and had the right to levy additional tax. Provincial governors also received land from the *shōen* in the form of a stipend due to the *geshi* (local official managing the *shōen* estate), so they had no incentive to commend land and create *shōen*.

Both, *shōen* and *kokugaryō*, were based on tiered land ownership, with multi-layered *shiki* underpinning the positions and rights of higher- and lower-level proprietary lords. Court nobility and temples formed the upper level of property lords in the *kokugaryō*. This multi-layered system of proprietorships was one of the hallmarks of the medieval Japanese *shōen* system.[70] The underdeveloped legal status of land ownership by local authorities and *myoshu*, and the dominance of the ruling class in asserting property rights, characterized the *shōen-kokugaryō* system. The court aristocracy was also the basis for the formation and maintenance of the *shiki* structure and their support by the power of the central government.[71] The process of undermining the *ritsuryō* principles that accelerated after 850 had a significant impact on the development of a flexible *shōen–shiki* system.

In the manorial system, the privilege to acquire rent accompanied by a specific delegated duty was called *shiki* (title).[72] Thus, shiki was a right to a fixed amount of income resulting from the performance of administrative and public functions, formalized by means of *appointment*, recognized and sanctioned by the central government. After the establishment of the Kamakura *Bakufu*, Minamoto no Yoritomo asked the emperor to appoint him as the chief national *jitō* for all 66 provinces of the country, so that he could 'divide' his *shiki* among his vassals without violating the established formal procedure, at least in form.[73] They were divisible, freely bought and sold, and could be inherited by women and men. *Shiki* was a private property right and an officially recognized position and an institution maintained, thanks to the competences granted by the central authority.[74] By means of *shiki*, local powers transformed a bureaucratic position into private property rights.[75] Sato writes that with the development of commendation-type *shōen* and the spread of *shiki*, allocation of the *shōen* income became very complex. Originally, it was associated with a specific office or position on the estate and a specified income due according to the level of the *shōen* hierarchy. For example, there were *shomin shiki* that went to cultivators, *shoke shiki* for managers, and so on. Since *shiki* were alienable and divisible, it was possible for *shōen* income to be widely distributed through sale, inheritance, or donation. Because they became detached from their nominal office or function, a single individual could hold several levels of *shiki* in the same *shōen* or in several different *shōen*. The use of *shiki* as a means of the estate income allocation gave the *shōen* system flexibility, and this was one of the reasons for its longevity. There may have been changes regarding *shiki* holders at *ryoke* or *honke* level, but they had little effect on the day-to-day running of the estates. Changes in the tenure of farmers and the methods of *shōen* governance did not affect the high amount of income due to the central owner. *Shōen* owners had no incentive to take an interest in managing their estates as long as they received the *shiki* assigned to them. They only became interested in *shōen* when their managers reported a threat to their tax exemptions, which could always be questioned by the provincial governor or his agents.[76] The land ownership model under the *shōen–kokugaryō* system focused on the control of rice fields (*kokugaryō* land occupied at least 25–29% of all land). Public paddy fields established by the surveys (each new governor was obliged to verify and register them) were taxed by the provincial government or by the *shōen*. A *shōen* owed its rice tax and the major part of its serfdom to the *honjo*, while the *kokugaryō* owed these obligations to the provincial governor.[77] Provincial governors rarely possessed political power equal to that of the *honjo, of shōen (the lords exercising effective authority over the shōen)*, and governors tended to give a free hand in administering the *kokugaryō*. This meant that their course of action was more beneficial to these local powers than it would have been for them to turn the land into *shōen*. In *shōen*, influential families had the exclusive right to levy taxes, while in *kokugaryō* the *zuryō* were responsible for determining and collecting them. Under this system, the higher-level proprietary lords holding the rights of administration took most of the total revenue from the *public paddy fields*. They exercised administrative powers and had the most important rights of property control. *Zaicho kanjin*, provincial administrative officials, exercised effective power in the administration. The units under their administrative control were called *kokugaryō*.

The *shiki* holdings were often scattered geographically, and the power to give or to withhold s*hiki* was not the same as the power to have command over persons. During the 13th century, it became increasingly difficult to conduct surveys, and therefore, the proportion of *public* paddies declined relative to other paddies.[78] Although the rice lands became the principal economic base for the rise of local powers and leaders among the peasants, they caused instability in political conditions and weakened the power of managers and *ryoke*. Their income began to decline, and they were unable to increase the revenue.

At the end of the 13th century, the members of the *buke* class were less able to commit their time and resources for active governance of their *shōen* as they became preoccupied with political, economic, and the military problems, such as the weakened authority of the *shōgunate*, conflicts among the retainers of the *shōgun* (*gokenin*), an increased reliance on the market economy (an increasing consumption of commercial products and services, debts, and loss of land used as collateral), and especially, the high cost of defending Japan against the Mongols (both actual and anticipated invasions). These problems resulted in the growing power of the *myoshu* over the rice fields they cultivated and managed. As long as compulsory contributions were made to the manager and *jitō* (lord of the estate), the *myoshu* was free to manage the rice fields as he saw fit. But to ensure that agreed dues were transferred, the landlords competed in offering *myoshu* incentives in form of the tax-exempt rice fields and other privileges. This further strengthened the *myoshu's* rights over the *myoden* (named rice fields). *Myoden* consisted of several smaller farms which were not legally subject to sale but could be fragmented, which allowed ownership rights to be dispersed among a larger group of people.[79] The size of a *myoden* within a manor depended on the region and consisted of equal-sized *myoden* fields (ranging from one to two *cho*

(2,45 acres) – 9,917 to 19,834 square meters). Manors in the distant provinces consisted of unequal-sized *myoden, often* larger than several *cho* because their proprietors (*honjo*) had less involvement in the management of their manors due to the great distances from their permanent place of residence.[80] Between 1254 and 1256, under the *shōen–koryo* system, *myo* were equalized in size to facilitate tax collection and estate management. Such manors called *kinto-myo-shōen* (a manor consisting of equal-sized *myo*), existed till the 14th century, and were based on the *shiki*. They were still a mixture of different types of fields, with tax and labour responsibilities evenly divided. In *shōen* in which a *myo* structure did not exist, the tax burden was borne by local farming households (*zaike*).[81] In the process of *myo* development, the concept of freely disposed property was created, which became an important link in Kamakura feudalism.[82] *Myo* began to lose its importance with the rise of the *samurai*.[83]

To counteract the semi-autonomous farming activities of the *myoshu* and *tato*, the *ryoshu* (descended from the nobles of the *ritsuryō* period) maintained parts of their *shōen* as directly managed fields (*tsukuda*). For their maintenance, all the people within his domain, including the *myoshu* and *tato*, had to contribute various labour services and taxes.[84] In the 13th century, both *shōen* and *kokugaryō* used the *hanyu* system, under which the rice tax was paid to the provincial government and *corvée* to the proprietary lord.[85] It is worth noting that the internal structure of the *shōen and kokugaryō* was significantly different.

The *shōen* underwent significant changes during the second half of the 13th century and the first decades of the 14th century. The size of the *myo* unit decreased as the population grew faster than the number of available rice fields, making agriculture more labour intensive and causing the productivity (value) of the land to increase. Small *myo* could be managed and supervised closely by someone with a strong incentive and sufficient resources to maintain and improve the quality of the paddies. Managers and *jitō*, focused on increasing own income, noticed that *myoshu*, by managing smaller units of land, could better coordinate the use of farmers' labour, increase land productivity, and the effective tax base. Therefore, to obtain maximum efficiency per unit of land, they encouraged a reduction in the size of the *myo* unit.[86] Although the division of *myo* did not cause the decline of *shōen*, it did imply changes in society that began to undermine the old order based on *shōen*.[87] The *shōen–kokugaryō* system gradually disappeared because, with the development of peasant property rights, the differences between *myoden* (fields in which more than one tax was paid) and *isshikiden* (fields in which only the rice tax was paid) leased to cultivators on annual basis disappeared.[88] Its dues were collected directly by the estate manager. *Myo* field holders enjoyed permanent tenure, and the *myoshu* charged them fees at a lower rate because they also paid various other contributions (*kuji*). Cultivators of *isshikiden* relied on *myoshu* or local *shōen* officials for tools and seeds. Before the growth of the village community in the late medieval period, these cultivators were not full members of the village community but rather had access to communal property through their ties to *myoshu*. The uniquely Japanese *shōen–kokugaryō* system that grew out of the *ritsuryō* system began to gradually disappear.

The local lord-owners grew in strength and gradually succeeded in exerting increased control over the peasants and in undermining the authority of the higher level of property lords. The *shiki* structure, the basis of the *shōen–kokugaryō* system, disintegrated and it became very difficult to maintain scattered *shiki* holdings. Following its disintegration, the *kokujin ryoshu* (local *samurai* lords who directly ruled the farmers) system emerged and *shugo* grew into *daimyō* controlling larger units of territory. In the second half of the 14th century, a new system of *daimyō* domains was created, in which many remnants of the *shōen–kokugaryō* system survived.[89] In the Muromachi period, the *myoden* fields were gradually integrated into the government of *shugo* (a military provincial governor). During the Sengoku (warring states) period, the *myoden* system declined as the central government strengthened and ceased to exist after a cadastral census commissioned by Hideyoshi Toyotomi during the Azuchi–Momoyama period.[90]

Shōen, regardless of whether it was privately owned or a component of private and state property, can be treated as a corporation with a diversified internal structure. They can be called corporations because they have met (in a manner adequate to the civilizational development of the analysed historical period) most of the features that, according to Hein (1963),[91] constitute the essence of corporation. *Shōen* were artificial beings – invisible and existing in law, they had the right of perpetual succession, they could sue and be sued, purchase and hold real property, and they had a common seal and were govern by making by-laws and private statutes. The separation of ownership and control usually took place and they were managed by professional managers. These attributes and features must be considered in historical terms, taking into account the level of institutional and economic development at that time. However, based on their occurrence in *shōen*, the concept of treating *shōen*, as corporations competing on the market for resources, privileges, and markets can be put forward.

The nature of *shōen* as a corporation is best described by the definition stating that a corporation is a *nexus of contracts* or a *compromise of interests* formulated by Jensen and Meckling (1976).[92] Shoen was a real bundle of contracts that were concluded at all levels of ownership and management, by representatives of all social classes (stakeholders) of it. These contracts were also governed and monitored internally and externally what may evidence the use of accounting and external and internal audits. They were written down and then monitored and enforced, and the results of the audits influenced the position, income, or punishment of the stakeholders. It can therefore be concluded that the agency costs were borne by *shōen*, and that corporate governance mechanisms were used by them, as well as accounting methods that helped in the flow of business information.

Literature analysis allows to conclude that *shōen* developed sophisticated corporate governance, both external and internal. Strict vertical supervision over *shōen* exercised by the central government and its supervisory institutions, the court and military aristocracy, local officials, managers at various levels, and the peasants themselves. The framework of governance was determined by legal regulations, as well as tradition, absorption of innovations, and the power of individual stakeholders of the *shōen*-corporation. Their supervision involved strict control and enforcement of responsibility for income and was aimed at maximizing results for stakeholders, but above all, their owners. The *shōen* administrators resided in the *main place*. Those persons who provided the *shōen*, often on a part-time basis, with various non-agricultural products and specialized services lived in the *sanjo*. Due to the tasks these people performed in *sanjo* they were usually located at local transport hubs. They grew in number, first in and around the capital (Kyōto). Those in the *sanjo*, like those in the *miyaza*, provided their services to the *shōen* either instead or in addition, to the usual *shōen* fees. Membership in groups working in *sanjo* was usually established at the time of birth.[93]

The second level of governance and supervision concerned internal management and control in *shōen*. It was exercised by the managers of the *shōen* and their subordinates responsible for the effectiveness and tax efficiency of the manors. They were oriented towards budgeting as they were obliged to achieve the planned (centrally or locally) drawn budgets. The scope of duties and responsibilities of *shōen* managers, and especially the opportunities facing them, varied in particular periods of *shōen* activity in almost 800 years of their existence.

Overall, there was a separation of ownership and control in *shōen*, which led to agency conflicts, that ultimately resulted in the collapse of the system. The agents were qualified local managers, oriented strongly towards tax optimization as the most important method of satisfying their principals (state-level – *honke, ryoshu*, local-level governors and managers) expectations, increasing their own returns, and offering as small as possible return to cultivators. They used planning, accounting methods to tighten control and stimulate production to increase efficiency and profitability of the entities they managed. Innovative methods of management, supervision, and exploiting peasants were being worked out. They promoted the use of innovative methods in agriculture that brought benefits to innovative farmers. The *shōen* system also included motivation mechanisms at all levels of organization. Over time, many local agents became owners of the land they farmed, managed, or supervised.

The household economy of *shōen* was a complex, self-sufficient structure.[94] Sato writes that for much of the *shōen* long history (from 8th to 15th centuries), it was a microcosm of medieval Japanese society. According to Sato, *shōen* played a key role in achieving the political and financial goals of the ruling class. Not only were they the main source of income for the aristocracy in Kyōto, but they also provided housing, jobs, and income for the peasants who farmed them, and to the administrators and managers of these manors. Workshops and craftsmen in *shōen* produced tools needed by farmers, as well as weapons for the warrior class who had its roots in the estate system. However, as markets developed, the self-sufficiency of *shōen* was undermined by their owners, who increasingly purchased necessary products from Kyōto and other markets rather than using those produced on the estates. The maintenance of each class and subclass of the *shōen* stakeholders depend on the *shōen*. They tried to pursue their own goals, which over time led to conflicts of interest. In periods of prosperity, the symmetry of interests of particular social classes and groups, as well as the use of strict systems of supervision and motivation, limited conflicts. However, the situation changed with the development of political conditions, productive forces, markets, and the increase in the potential and economic awareness of *shōen* stakeholders, which led not only to a conflict of interests but also to the liquidation of *shōen*. Their owners fought to acquire and protect their privileges, that is, to preserve them as independent and tax-free entities. Property privileges were fragile because they were threatened by actions taken by local officials competing for positions and benefits. During the Heian period, most disputes (claims) between proprietors and provincial governors were settled in the court, thus within the legal system, not by armed force. This indicates the strength of the state and governance system, which were able to legally resolve and enforce property (land) and tax disputes through the *Shōen* Records Office or *Dajokan*. The flexibility and the endurance of the landed manors as an institution stemmed from the ability to adapt and survive in the changing economic environment.[95]

Notes

1 M. Nakabayashi, Institutions and Economic Development of Early Modern Japan. *ISS Discussion Paper Series F-146* August 2009, pp. 1–26, Institute of Social Science, The University of Tokyof-146.pdf.
2 T. Toshiya, Nara Economic and Social Institutions. In: D. M. Brown (ed.), The Cambridge History of Japan. Vol. 1. Ancient Japan. *Cambridge University Press*, Cambridge 2008, p. 444.
3 O. Kyohei, Medieval *shoen*. In: K. Yamamura (ed.), The Cambridge History of Japan. Vol. 3, Medieval Japan. *Cambridge University Press*, Cambridge, p. 101.
4 C. Andressen, A Short History of Japan. From Samurai to Sony. *Allen & Unwin,* Canberra 2002, p. 44.
5 E. Honjo, The Economic Development of Japan. *Kyoto University Economic Review* 1931, Vol. 6, No. 1, pp. 14–28.
6 K. Nagahara, Landownership under the Shōen-Kokugaryō System. *Journal of Japanese Studies* 1975, Vol. 1, No. 2, pp. 269–296.
7 E. Sato, Ōyama Estate and Insei Land Policies. *Monumenta Nipponica* 1979, Vol. 34, No. 1, pp. 73–99.
8 www.britannica.com/topic/shoen.
9 Y. Takekoshi, The Economic Aspects of the History of the Civilization of Japan. *Routledge*, London 2004, p. 132.
10 R. K. Reischauer, The Japanese *Shōen,* or Manor: Some Useful Terminology. *Journal of the American Oriental Society* 1937, Vol. 57, No. 1, pp. 78–83.

11 Y. Takekoshi, The Economic Aspects of the History . . . op. cit., p. 113.
12 O. Kyohei, Medieval shōen. In: The Cambridge History of Japan. Vol. 3. Medieval Japan . . . op. cit., p. 101.
13 N. Keiji, Landownership under the *Shōen-Kokugaryō* System. *Journal of Japanese Studies*, 1975, Vol. 1, No. 2, pp. 269–296.
14 D. Morris, Land and Society. In: J. W. Hall, M. B. Jansen, M. Kanai, D. Twitchett (eds.), The Cambridge History of Japan. Vol. 2. Heian Japan. D. H. Shively, W. H. McCollough (eds.). *Cambridge University Press,* Cambridge 2008, pp. 224–225.
15 T. Toshiya, Nara Economic and Social Institutions. In: The Cambridge History of Japan. Vol. 1. Ancient Japan . . . . op. cit., p. 452.
16 D. Morris, Land and Society. In: The Cambridge History of Japan. Vol. 2. Heian Japan . . . op. cit., p. 229.
17 T. E. Keirstead, Fragmented Estates: The Breakup of the Myō and the Decline of the Shōen System. *Monumenta Nipponica* 1985, Vol. 40, No. 3, pp. 311–330.
18 O. Kyohei, *Medieval shoen*. In: The Cambridge History of Japan. Vol. 3. Medieval Japan . . . op. cit., p. 101.
19 D. Morris, Land and Society. In: The Cambridge History of Japan. Vol. 2. Heian Japan . . . op. cit., pp. 234, 235.
20 M. W. Meyer, Japan: A Concise History. *Rowman & Littlefield Publishers Inc*, Plymouth 2009, p. 61.
21 R. K. Reischauer, The Japanese *Shōen* (莊 園), or Manor: Some Useful Terminology. *Journal of the American Oriental Society* 1937, Vol. 57, No. 1, pp. 78–83.
22 N. Keiji, Landownership under the *Shōen-Kokugaryō* . . . op. cit.
23 E. Sato, Ōyama Estate and Insei Land Policies. *Monumenta Nipponica* 1979, Vol. 34, No. 1, pp. 73–99.
24 K. Nagahara, Landownership under the *Shōen- Kokugaryō* System . . . op. cit.
25 B. Goldsmith, Amassing Economies: The Medieval Origins of Early Modern Japan, 1450–1700. *Stanford University*, Stanford 2008, p. 96.
26 M. W. Meyer, Japan. A Concise History . . . op. cit., p. 45.
27 K. G. Henshall, A History of Japan: From Stone Age to Superpower, *Palgrave Macmillan*, London 2012, p. 17–25.
28 G. B. Sansom, A History of Japan to 1334 . . . op. cit., p. 235.
29 C. J. Kiley, Provincial Administration, and Land Tenure in Early Heian. In: The Cambridge History of Japan. Vol. 2. Heian Japan . . . op. cit., pp. 236–340.
30 Ibidem, pp. 227, 228.
31 R. K. Reischauer, The Japanese Shōen . . . op. cit.
32 Y. Takekoshi, The Economic Aspects of the History of the Civilization of Japan. Vol. 2, *Routledge*, London 2004, p. 132.
33 J. Murdoch, History of Japan, From the Origins to the Arrival of the Portuguese in 1542 A.D., Vol. I. *The Asiatic Society of Japan*, London 1910, p. 210.
34 D. Morris, Land and Society. In: Cambridge History of Japan. Vol. 2. Heian Japan . . . op. cit. p. 232.
35 E. Sato, Ōyama Estate and Insei Land Policies . . . op. cit.
36 D. Morris, Land and Society. In: The Cambridge History of Japan. Vol. 2. Heian Japan . . . op. cit., pp. 230, 231.
37 K. Asakawa, The Origin of the Feudal Land Tenure in Japan. *The American Historical Review* October 1914, Vol. 20, No. 1, pp. 1–23.
38 R. H. P. Mason, J. G. Caiger. A History of Japan . . . op. cit., p. 76.
39 D. Morris, Land and Society. In: The Cambridge History of Japan. Vol. 2. Heian Japan . . . op. cit., pp. 225–228.

40 K. Yamamura, The Decline of the *Ritsuryō* System: Hypotheses on Economic and Institutional Change. *Journal of Japanese Studies* 1974, Vol. 1, No. 1, The Society for Japanese Studies, pp. 3–37.
41 G. B. Sansom, A History of Japan to 1334 . . . op. cit., p. 234.
42 E. Sato, Ōyama Estate and Insei Land Policies . . . op. cit.
43 D. Morris, Land, and society. In: The Cambridge History of Japan. Vol. 2. Heian Japan . . . op. cit., p. 230.
44 E. Sato, Ōyama Estate and Insei Land Policies . . . op. cit.
45 C. G. Hurst, The Reign of Go-Sanjō and the Revival of Imperial Power. *Monumenta Nipponica* 1972, Vol. 27, No. 1, Sophia University, pp. 65–83.
46 O. Kyohei, Medieval shoen. In: The Cambridge History of Japan. Vol. 3. Medieval Japan. . . . op. cit., p. 102.
47 B. L. Batten, Provincial Administration in Early Japan: From Ritsuryō Kokka to Ōchō Kokka. *Harvard Journal of Asiatic Studies* 1993, Vol. 53, No. 1, pp. 103–134.
48 K. Nagahara, Landownership under the *Shōen- Kokugaryō* System, op. cit.
49 K. Kito, Brief History of Development of Ancient and Medieval Land Systems in Japan. *Dialogues d'histoire ancienne Année* 1986, No. 12, pp. 457–469.
50 T. E. Keirstead, Fragmented Estates: The Breakup of the *Myō* . . . op. cit.
51 M. W. Meyer, Japan: A Concise History . . . op. cit., p. 61.
52 T. E. Keirstead, Fragmented Estates: The Breakup of the Myō . . . op. cit.
53 D. Morris, Land and Society. In: The Cambridge History of Japan. Vol. 2. Heian Japan . . . op. cit., pp. 222, 223.
54 K. Yamamura, Tara in Transition: A Study of a Kamakura Shoen. *Journal of Japanese Studies* 1981, Vol. 7, No. 2, The Society for Japanese Studies, pp. 349–391.
55 K. Nagahara, Landownership under the Shōen- Kokugaryō System . . . op. cit.
56 K. Yamamura, Tara in Transition: A Study of a Kamakura *Shoen* . . . op. cit.
57 D. Morris, Land and society, in: The Cambridge History of Japan. Vol. 2. Heian Japan . . . op. cit., p. 223.
58 www.japanese-wiki-corpus.org/history/Myoden.html.
59 D. Morris, Land and Society. In: The Cambridge History of Japan. Vol. 2. Heian Japan . . . op. cit., p. 223.
60 E. Hondo, On the Financial Development of Japan. *Kyoto University Economic Review* 1930, Vol. 5, No. 2 (10), Kyoto University, pp. 66–79.
61 D. Morris, Land and Society. In: The Cambridge History of Japan. Vol. 2. Heian Japan . . . op. cit., pp. 223, 224.
62 O. Kyohei, Medieval shoen. In: The Cambridge History of Japan. Vol. 3. Medieval Japan . . . op. cit., p. 102.
63 www.japanese-wiki-corpus.org/history/Myoden.html.
64 J. Frohlich, Land Administration in Medieval Japan: Ito no shô in Chikuzen Province, 1131–1336. *University of Zurich, The Historical Association and Blackwell Publishing Ltd.,* Oxford 2003.
65 R. H. P. Mason, J.G Caiger. A History of Japan . . . op. cit., p. 76.
66 K. Asakawa, Japan. From the Japanese Government History . . . op. cit.
67 F. Hérail, The Position and Role of Provincial Governors at the Height of the Heian Period. *French Journal of Japanese Studies* 2014, No. 3.
68 K. Nagahara, Landownership under the *Shōen- Kokugaryō System,* op. cit.
69 O. Kyohei, Medieval shoen. In: The Cambridge History of Japan. Vol. 3. Medieval Japan . . . op. cit., p. 89.
70 Ibidem, p. 100.
71 K. Nagahara, Landownership under the *Shōen- Kokugaryō* System . . . op. cit.

72 M. Nakabayashi, Institutions and Economic Development of Early Modern Japan . . . . . . op. cit.
73 N. Keiji, Landownership under the *Shōen-Kokugaryō* . . . op. cit.
74 K. Nagahara, Landownership under the *Shōen- Kokugaryō* System . . . op. cit.
75 R. H. P. Mason, J. G. Caiger. A History of Japan . . . op. cit., pp. 75, 76.
76 E. Sato, *Ōyama Estate and Insei Land Policies* . . . op. cit.
77 K. Nagahara, Landownership under the Shōen-Kokugaryō System . . . op. cit.
78 Ibidem.
79 T. E. Keirstead, Fragmented Estates: The Breakup of the *Myō* and the Decline of the *Shōen* . . . op. cit.
80 www.japanese-wiki-corpus.org/history/Myoden.html.
81 O. Kyohei, Medieval shoen. In: The Cambridge History of Japan. Vol. 3. Medieval Japan . . . op. cit., p. 101.
82 T. E. Keirstead, Fragmented Estates: The Breakup of the Myō . . . op. cit.
83 M. Nakabayashi, Institutions, and Economic Development of Early Modern Japan . . . op. cit.
84 D. J. Lu, Japan: A Documentary History. Vol. 1. The Down of History to the Late Tokugawa Period. *An East Gate Book, M.E. Sharpe, Inc*, London 2005, pp. 98, 99.
85 K. Nagahara, Landownership under the *Shōen- Kokugaryō* System . . . op. cit.
86 K. Yamamura, Tara in Transition: A Study of a Kamakura *Shoen* . . . op. cit.
87 T. E. Keirstead, Fragmented Estates: The Breakup of the *Myō* . . . op. cit.
88 The Origins of Japan's Medieval World: Courtiers, Clerics, Warriors, and Peasants in the Fourteenth Century. J. P. Mass (ed.). *Stanford University Press*, Stanford 1997 p. 396.
89 K. Nagahara, Landownership under the *Shōen- Kokugaryō* System . . . op. cit.
90 www.japanese-wiki-corpus.org/history/Myoden.html.
91 L. W. Hein, The British Business Company: Its Origins and Its Control. *The University of Toronto Law Journal* 1963, Vol. 15, No. 1, pp. 134–154.
92 M. C. Jensen, W. H. Meckling, Theory of the Firm: Managerial Behavior, Agency Costs and Ownership Structure. *Journal of Financial Economics* (JFE) 1976, Vol. 3, No. 4, pp. 305–360.
93 K. Yamamura, The Development of za in Medieval Japan . . . op. cit.
94 O. Kyohei, Medieval shōen. In: The Cambridge History of Japan. Vol. 3. Medieval Japan . . . op. cit., p. 102.
95 E. Sato, *Ōyama* Estate and *Insei* Land Policies . . . op. cit.

Bibliography

Andressen, C., A Short History of Japan. From Samurai to Sony. *Allen & Unwin*, Canberra 2002.

Asakawa, K., Japan. From the Japanese Government History. Vol. 7. In: H. C. Lodge (ed.), The History of Nations. *John D. Morris and Company*, *The Collier Press*, New York 1906. www.gutenberg.org/ebooks/45645.

Asakawa, K., The Origin of the Feudal Land Tenure in Japan. *The American Historical Review* October 1914, Vol. 20, No. 1, pp. 1–23. https://doi.org/10.1086/ahr/20.1.1.

Batten, B. L., Provincial Administration in Early Japan: From Ritsuryō Kokka to Ōchō Kokka. *Harvard Journal of Asiatic Studies* 1993, Vol. 53, No. 1, pp. 103–34. Harvard-Yenching Institute. https://doi.org/10.2307/2719469.

Frohlich, J., Land Administration in Medieval Japan: Ito no shô in Chikuzen Province, 1131–1336. *University of Zurich, The Historical Association and Blackwell Publishing*

Ltd., Oxford 2003. file:///D:/Users/wzr/Downloads/Land_Administration_in_Medieval_Japan_It%20(1).pdf.

Goldsmith, B., Amassing Economies: The Medieval Origins of Early Modern Japan, 1450–1700. *Stanford University*, Stanford 2008.

Hein, L. W., The British Business Company: Its Origins and Its Control. *The University of Toronto Law Journal* 1963, Vol. 15, No. 1, pp. 134–154. *JSTOR*. https://doi.org/10.2307/824910.

Henshall, K. G., A History of Japan: From Stone Age to Superpower. *Palgrave Macmillan*, London 2012. www.gutenberg.org/files/37186/37186-h/37186-h.htm.

Hérail, F., The Position and Role of Provincial Governors at the Height of the Heian Period. *French Journal of Japanese Studies* 2014, No. 3. https://journals.openedition.org/cjs/658.

Honjo, E., On the Financial Development of Japan. *Kyoto University Economic Review* 1930, Vol. 5, No. 2 (10), pp. 66–79. www.jstor.org/stable/43216724.

Hurst, G. C., The Reign of Go-Sanjō and the Revival of Imperial Power. *Monumenta Nipponica* 1972, Vol. 27, No. 1, pp. 65–83. https://doi.org/10.2307/2383478.

Jansen, M. B., The Making of Modern Japan. *The Belknap Press of Harvard University Press*, Cambridge, MA, London, England 2000. *JSTOR*. https://doi.org/10.2307/j.ctvjf9vr7.

Keiji, N., Landownership under the Shōen-Kokugaryō System. *Journal of Japanese Studies* 1975, Vol. 1, No. 2, pp. 269–296. https://doi.org/10.2307/132127.

Keirstead, T. E., Fragmented Estates: The Breakup of the Myō and the Decline of the Shōen System. *Monumenta Nipponica* 1985, Vol. 40, No. 3, pp. 311–330. https://doi.org/10.2307/2384763.

Kito, K., Brief History of Development of Ancient and Medieval Land Systems in Japan. *Dialogues d'histoire ancienne Année*, 1986, No. 12, pp. 457–469. www.persee.fr/doc/dha_0755-7256_1986_num_12_1_1735.

Lu, D. J., Japan: A Documentary History, Vol. 1. The Down of History to the Late Tokugawa Period. *An East Gate Book, M.E. Sharpe, Inc*, London 2005, pp. 98–99. https://books.google.pl/books?id=maXRLaADxLsC&printsec=frontcover&source=gbs_ge_summary_r&cad=0#v=onepage&q&f=false.

Mason, R. H. P., Caiger, J. G., A History of Japan. *TUTTLE Publishing*, Tokyo; Rutland, VT; Singapore 1997. file:///D:/Users/wzr/Downloads/A_History_of_Japan_Mason_Caiger%20(5).pdf

Meyer, M. W., Japan A Concise History. *Rowman & Littlefield Publishers Inc*, Plymouth 2009. file:///D:/Users/wzr/Downloads/epdf.pub_japan-a-concise-history-4th-edition.pdf.

Murdoch, J., History of Japan, From the Origins to the Arrival of the Portuguese in 1542 A.D. Vol. I. *The Asiatic Society of Japan*, London 1910. file:///D:/Users/wzr/Documents/Japonia%20Ks1/Ksi%C4%85%C5%BCki%20Hist/A%20history%20of%20Japan%20Volume%201%20(1903).pdf.

Nagahara, K., Landownership under the Shōen-Kokugaryō System. *Journal of Japanese Studies* 1975, Vol. 1, No. 2, pp. 269–296. *JSTOR*, www.jstor.org/stable/132127.

Nakabayashi, M., Institutions and Economic Development of Early Modern Japan. *ISS Discussion Paper Series F-146* August 2009, pp. 1–26. Institute of Social Science, The University of Tokyof-146.pdf.

Reischauer, R. K., The Japanese Shōen (莊 園), or Manor: Some Useful Terminology. *Journal of the American Oriental Society* 1937, Vol. 57, No. 1, pp. 78–83. *JSTOR*. https://doi.org/10.2307/594783.

Sansom, G. B., A History of Japan to 1334. Vol. 1. *Stanford University Press*, Stanford 1958.

Sato, E., Ōyama Estate and Insei Land Policies. *Monumenta Nipponica* 1979, Vol. 34, No. 1, pp. 73–99. *JSTOR*. https://doi.org/10.2307/2384282.

Takekoshi, Y., The Economic Aspects of the History of the Civilization of Japan. Vol. 2. *Routledge*, London 2004.

The Cambridge History of Japan. Vol. 1. Ancient Japan. D. M. Brown (ed.). *Cambridge University Press,* Cambridge 2008.

The Cambridge History of Japan. J. W. Hall, M. B. Jansen, M. Kanai, D. Twitchett (eds.). Vol. 2. Heian Japan. D. H. Shively, W. H. McCollough (eds.). *Cambridge University Press*, Cambridge 2008.

The Cambridge History of Japan. Vol. 3. Medieval Japan. K. Yamamura (ed.). *Cambridge University Press*, Cambridge 2008.

The Origins of Japan's Medieval World: Courtiers, Clerics, Warriors, and Peasants in the Fourteenth Century. J. P. Mass (ed.). *Stanford University Press*, Stanford 1997. www.sup.org/books/title/?id=1015

www.britannica.com/topic/shoen

www.japanese-wiki-corpus.org/history/Myoden.html

Yamamura, K., The Development of Za in Medieval Japan. *Business History Review* December 1973, Vol. 47, No. 4, pp. 438–465. www.jstor.org/stable/3113366?seq=1&cid=pdf-reference#references_tab_contents.

Yamamura, K., The Decline of the *Ritsuryō* System: Hypotheses on Economic and Institutional Change. *Journal of Japanese Studies* 1974, Vol. 1, No. 1, The Society for Japanese Studies, pp. 3–37. https://doi.org/10.2307/133435.

Yamamura, K., Tara in Transition: A Study of a Kamakura Shoen. *Journal of Japanese Studies* 1981, Vol. 7, No. 2, The Society for Japanese Studies, pp. 349–391. https://doi.org/10.2307/132206.

Part 3

The rise, development, and destruction of the Kamakura *Shōgunate* (1185–1333) and its corporate governance system

7 The rise and fall of the Kamakura *Shōgunate*

From the end of the 12th century on, Japan was ruled through a dual government structure – the emperor who retained cultural and religious sovereignty over the nation, and the military elite who assumed political and economic leadership. This system of governance remained in place until the late 1800s. In the early years of the Kamakura era (1180s), feudalism started to develop. It was distinguished by fiefdoms, vassalage, and military ethos in culture and politics, but was still a mixture of a complicated administrative system borrowed from China and an indigenous Japanese clan society.[1]

The Kamakura era (1185–1333) can be considered as the grand modification of the Heian political order.[2] Despite some conflicts between the imperial court and the new warrior government, such as the *Jôkyû* war (1221), the Kamakura Era was a relatively peaceful time, characterized by economic growth and flourishing cultural activities. At that time, Japan had to face great external threats, namely two Mongol invasions in 1274 and 1281. The large and long-term military investments necessary to repel these incursions and protect against possible further attacks led to the collapse of the Kamakura *Bakufu* in 1333. Andressen argues that the range of social practices identified with modern Japan have their origins in this period.[3]

During the Heian period (794–1185), tendencies towards political, economic, and military decentralization intensified, increasing the independence of the provinces and weakening the power of the emperor. The process of military decentralization began with the rise of the *shōen* power (from the 10th century). The imperial court, suffering from declining tax revenues, was unable to finance the national army and maintain public order, so the owners of the *shōen* had to set up their own armies of *samurai* warriors (*bushi*), to protect their interests and safety.[4] Due to disruptions and unrest, the provincial governors (civilian officials) and rich residents had to acquire military skills and defend their lands.[5] Minor local nobles (provincial warriors) appointed as estate managers were growing more powerful in relation to the loss of power by the central government.[6] As a result, the weakening central government became increasingly dependent on the

DOI: 10.4324/9781003497936-10

military power of these families. Over time, their descendants became powerful regional forces, forming the basis of Japan's warrior class – the *samurai*.[7] They were the main component of a feudal society and the feudal age which lasted in Japan at least until the mid-19th century.

The term *samurai* evolved from the word *saburahi* (to serve) meaning *the mounted warriors who serve*.[8] The warriors came mainly from the guards of aristocratic families, police in the urban areas, especially Kyōto, men authorized by the central government to protect their landholdings in outlying areas and the borders from *barbarians*, and local administrators and managers of the *shōen*.[9] *Samurai* did not have their settled territories where they could rule as feudal lords before the *shōen–koryo* system was established in the 11th century. Thus, the system in which *shōen* and *kokugaryō* (*koryo)* evolved into *gun* (local district), *go* (sub-local district), *ho* (imperial estate) as tax units, was called *shōen koryo sei* (system of public lands and private estates). This system allowed *samurai* to own manors or estates in the aforementioned areas, which became their settled territories and the basis for the origin of the *samurai* surname (called *honganchi*). The pattern of surname formation was taken over by high-ranking *samurai* of the *gokenin* class (direct vassals of the *shōgun*) in the Kamakura period, who were joined by a class of local samurai (*kokujin*) in the Muromachi period. The status of the *samurai* as a fighting man was defined and regulated, and none could claim this status without permission of Yoritomo. The *samurai* was generally a mounted warrior, with full armour and a flag bearing his insignia.[10] *Samurai* performed military service on battlefields, and in peacetime, apart from running farms, they were engaged in hunting and constantly developing a durable and practical character, which was their duty. Training in the martial arts was central to their lives (refinement of Japanese swordsmanship, archery, and horseback riding).[11]

Samurai valued the pride of family name, cherished ideals of courage and of loyalty above their lives. The motivation for their incredible bravery and endurance came from personal pride and honour, and from loyalty to one's lord, which took precedence over loyalty to the emperor, religion, and family. Loyal service to one's overlord became the fundamental ethic and tie that existed between *samurai* and their lords. The code of behaviour of the *samurai*, known as *bushido* (*the way of the warrior)* containing elements of Confucianism, Shinto, and Zen Buddhism, established the basis for the *samurai* culture.[12] *Bushido* means that in a man's sword resided his honour, and he would sooner die than part with it.[13] This virtue is held in very special esteem by the Japanese, whose society exhibits to this day a network of obligations and loyalties that serve as an intangible but strong binding force. Its practitioners were offered a direct road to enlightenment and release through discipline, austerity, and inner control, which closely fitted the warrior code.[14] The only respected alternative to dishonour or defeat, enabling the *samurai* to demonstrate courage, self-control, strong determination, and honesty, was suicide through the process of disembowelment (*seppuku*) or abdominal incision (*harakiri*).[15] Zen came to Japan in 1191 and declared that enlightenment came through sudden inner experience. Its anti-scholasticism, simplicity, austerity, discipline, and close relationship between master and disciple appealed particularly to the military. It was most suitable for a feudal system, in which land was held in return for military service to an overlord granting protection to all in his domain.[16] Thus, bushido was the representation of a lifestyle, mindset, and conduct code of the warrior class.[17]

The samurai became Japan's economic basis, because they were closely connected with the ownership of land and the production of rice. Many of them were appointed managers (*shoji* or *shokan*), *gunji, goji*, or *hoji*, and had *tato* and *fumyo* under their control.[18] They were given an economic base which allowed them to keep their military power strong enough to maintain public order. S*amurai* started to be increasingly influential from the second half of the Heian period. The local landowners assumed military functions and organized a military police force in each province, commanded by a capable man. They focused on developing their military prowess and became an effective military force. As a result, the preservation of order shifted from the central government to powerful local landowners.[19] The ability of the local nobility to use military skills and their connections with the court aristocracy led to the formation of military alliances by warrior chiefs.[20] After consolidating their power in the provinces, the *samurai* gradually moved to the capital, where they served the military needs of the state, protecting it against potential rebellions, as well as acting as bodyguards of great noble families and as guards of the emperor's residence (Taira clan).[21] The Chief Commissioner had to recruit armed men from among the provincial leaders of private warriors for the police service in Kyōto. Soon, members of the emerging military class began to enter civilian power, becoming the central government's effective military force to establish order and security.[22]

The economic basis of feudalism was the development of tax-free estates as economically independent units, provincial landowners focused on their own interests and expanding their land holdings, and estate managers representing absentee court or monastic landowners, who managed estates and provided income to their proprietors. Members of the court wanting to strengthen their position began to build fortunes in the provinces. Hereditary power and imperial origins gave them prestige and loyalty, enabling them to initiate new economic ventures in the country's peripheral rural areas.

Vassalage evolved slowly in court-dominated government structures. The strong bond between military commanders and subordinates, created by the loyal service of warriors and the rewards bestowed upon them by their leaders, turned warriors into vassals. This institution and the conduct and loyalty of individual vassals enabled the heads of the military Houses to displace the civilian aristocracy and rule Japan.[23] Confucianism strongly supported the development of a hierarchical order of higher and lower persons and the maintenance of relationships that ensured social harmony. The social imperative reinforced the emergence of *samurai* as the dominant social group in the late 12th century.

According to Hara, the end of the Heian period was an important turning point in the history of Japanese civilization, due to the revival of the conservative spirit that had always existed in the lower strata of the nation, expressing itself in strength and energy. Members of the lower social class sympathized much more with the military men than with the courtiers.[24] They were innovators because, not being bound by the ages-old formalities of the Japanese court, they developed their own practical culture and restructured Japanese society. This made their attitude towards ordinary people more flexible and enabled the spread of elite culture to Japanese society. During the Kamakura period, the *samurai* class replaced the ancient civilian aristocracy but retained the classical culture. The highly centralized government, established on the Chinese model by the Taika reform, collapsed at the end of the Heian period and a new system emerged, in which a new military class played a key role.

In 1156 during the Hogen Rebellion, followed by the Heiji Rebellion (1159–1160) and the Gempei War (1180–1185), regional clans intervened military in a political dispute for the first time (called to support rivals for the throne). The name of this war between the chief clans is compounded from the Chinese form of their names, *Gen*, in native Japanese form 'Minamoto', and *Hei*, pronounced as *-pei* stands for *Taira*. The compound for phonetic reasons emerges as *Gempei*. From then on, warrior families (military leaders) played a key role in ruling Japan and exercising effective control, except in ceremonial matters. During the Kamakura period, there was a gradual transfer of power from the nobility to military landowners in the provinces. As the new regime took shape, it fought hard to build unity and control over the entire country.[25]

The Taihō Code ordered that the sixth-generation descendants of emperors be deprived of the rank of prince, and they were to take the family name and start an independent life.[26] From 1156, for several dozen years, the two largest and most powerful military clans, Taira and Minamoto (both served the Fujiwara clan), descended from the emperors, fought each other for power.[27] Their struggle for power was decided in the Gempei War (1180–1185), which ended with the great naval battle of Dan-no-ura and the defeat and extermination of the Taira clan in 1185, after which the Minamoto family took control over Japan.[28] In 1192, the cloistered emperor Go-Toba awarded Minamoto no Yoritomo, the title of *shōgun* (abbreviated form of *seii tai-shōgun* – barbarian-suppressing supreme general), first awarded to Sakanoue no Tamuramaro in 797 for achievements in the conquest of the Ainu.[29] The emperor had then conferred the office on a particular general for a limited period. Later, the position of *shōgun* was usually held by a prince of imperial blood. It was the highest honour a warrior could obtain, and the most desired among the military for the next millennium. Yoritomo, however, considered the title permanent and giving him and his descendants the right to rule Japan in the name of the emperor and thus *shōgun* eventually became the title of the head of the *bakufu*.

The ancient monarchical court and aristocratic system ended when Yoritomo established a military government, called the *bakufu* (tent government, the field headquarters of a campaigning warrior) or *shōgunate*, in his hometown of Kamakura in 1192, leaving the monarchy and weak government in Heian.[30] He chose his support base as his *bakufu* headquarters because he wanted to stay away from the sybaritic Kyōto court and its intrigues and undesirable influences.[31] Yoritomo became master of Japan,[32] starting a period (1185–1333) of the *samurai* rule, during which an independent warrior government successfully opposed the political power of the civilian aristocracy, which had previously exercised power indirectly through the imperial line.[33]

The civil power in Heian (the official capital) and the military power in Kamakura shared authority for governing the nation, but the emperor had lost effective power, playing mainly a ceremonial and legitimizing role.[34] The real power passed to the military class, and the *shōguns* held effective political control until the Meiji Restoration of 1868. The primary tasks of the *bakufu* were to restore order and to create a new balance between central and local authority. Soon *bakufu* became the greatest real power as Yoritomo managed to transform the *shōgunate* from a simple military organ into an effective military body of indirect rule.[35] The new government used the practice of leaving the imperial family as a symbol of supreme power in the country, while real power was exercised behind the scenes. Minamoto no Yoritomo, the most powerful person in the country, held the imperial court in high regard, because of the prestige of the imperial House.[36] The inviolable and sacred emperor legitimized the *shōgun* by entrusting him with power, and the *bakufu* was to constitute the military force of the imperial government. The divine character of the ruler was the moral basis for the *shōgun*, the highest political authority and the emperor's deputy. Yoritomo continued to issue decrees in the name of the reigning monarch, from whom he and his successors derived authority. The court retained authority in bureaucratic matters, religious institutions continued to play a significant role in the political world, and the old central institutions remained largely intact, although weakened. Old titles were retained but often given new meanings.[37] He did not eliminate the powerful Fujiwara family, still supplying regents in Kyōto, nor did he restrict the possessions or ritual duties of the court families over which he kept tight political control. Yoritomo formulated a government based on the old *ritsu* system, retaining many of the traditional political and administrative structures of the inherited central government. He maintained the posts of provincial and local administrators from the Nara era and the *shōen* system. The Heian pattern of government lasted into the 14th century and was destroyed along with the Kamakura *bakufu* rather than by it.[38] However, this form of government survived until the 19th century with only minor modifications.[39] Thus, during the Kamakura period, Japan was a diarchy with two capitals and two interconnected centres of power. This was the specificity of the relationship between the developing feudal system and the ancient monarchy based on written legal codes.[40] As a result, the principle of cooperation prevailed during the Kamakura period. If a higher authority is the guarantor of the legitimacy of those in power, it gives that higher authority a guarantee of protection. Recipients of legitimization may in turn legitimize those below them, and so on. On the one hand, it disperses responsibility, but on the other hand, it organizes power hierarchically. In this way, the government became a mixture of old and new due to the need for legitimacy and the Japanese practice of maintaining some degree of continuity with the past during change.[41]

Yoritomo used the administrative structure, as well as his (often personal) connections with his vassals to preserve his authority and peace in the country. This created a well-established system of loyalty to a leader just as it had been in the days of the family clans. Their unions were based on formal contracts financially rewarding the vassal for his services. The loyalty imposed by the court, the Taika reform, and feudal laws were not easily accepted, but feudal duties in the early Kamakura period were paramount.

Initially, the main financial base of Kamakura *Bakufu* was *shōen* taken from the defeated Taira family plus limited administrative income derived from public estates in the provinces granted to Yoritomo by the imperial court. Then, the *bakufu* expanded its influence over lands controlled by the civil provincial governors and the private estates of the civil aristocracy, temples, and shrines. Other sources of revenue used by the *bakufu* included taxes on merchants, patronage of *za* (guilds), road and border tolls, and tribute trade with Ming China. These sources may indicate the flourishing of the medieval economy in the Kamakura era. Yoritomo redistributed between his warriors most of the estates confiscated from his defeated rivals.[42] He was always concerned with the economic status of his supporters. He rewarded not only his warriors but also his former enemies with estates and offices bringing in an appropriate income, thus making them his vassals and ensuring their loyalty and fidelity.[43] In this way, *shōgun* Yoritomo increased his control over the warriors and gained their allegiance. Binding the warriors to himself and his House, Yoritomo became the sole source of all their honours and appointments, as he forbade the warriors from having any contact with the court or accepting favours from the emperor.[44]

In 1185, while fighting the Taira clan, Yoritomo requested permission from the Court to appoint military governors (*shugo*), also called constables, and subordinated to them military land stewards (*jitō*) in both public and private estates in each province in the country. The purpose of this was to systematize land distribution. The *shugo* governed the provinces based on military instructions received from Kamakura, local customs, and the laws of the military House, rather than on the basis on centrally imposed codes of law as was the case in the *ritsuryō* system.

Shugo was appointed by the *shōgun*, and his duties were to oversee the stewards (*jitō*), assign vassals to guard duty, recruit metropolitan guards, keep strict control over subversives and criminals, and command the local retainers in wartime. They maintained public order and peace on their property, performed the various functions of local government and acted as magistrates.[45] They were the self-supporting personal retainers of Yoritomo, directly responsible to him. The *shugo* controlled the *jitō* and was the marshal of all of them in the province, combining a decentralized system of governors.[46] *Shugo* held regional political power while *jitō* were primarily responsible for collecting taxes on behalf of the *bakufu*.[47] Under military jurisdiction, *jitō* was not a vassal of the *shugo*.

The *jitō* remained direct vassals of the Kamakura *Shōgunate* and were subordinated to the *shugo* only in terms of military organization. Both, stewards and constables, controlled the provinces tightly and loyally. The *shugo–jitō* system worked well in terms of controlling the villages, increasing income for the *bakufu*, and combined with the idea of vassalage, it created clear structure of loyalty and financial reward.[48] Meyer argues that this system was similar to the feudal system in the sense that hereditary military groups swore personal allegiance and loyalty to the lord from whom they received lands as fiefs. In this way, the steward emerged as an important figure in late 12th-century provincial society. The *shōgun* could appoint any *jitō* as *shugo* of any province, without fear of disrupting the personal relationship between him and his retainers in that province. The offices of steward (*jitō*) and constable (*shugo*) over time became hereditary lucrative positions combining civil and military power. Their holders sometimes doubled up as the civil governors of the province, but this was more a matter of honour than of substantive power. Yoritomo designated himself the Steward General[49] and in this way, he was able to govern (and spread his power throughout Japan) without replacing the administration set up during the Heian period.[50] The system worked well for a long time.

Mass writes that the *jitō* supervised the management of the estates and held regional political power. They collected taxes on all estates because Yoritomo liquidated the tax-free *shōen* (no tax exemptions). They were also in charge of collecting and forwarding to Kamakura the special military rice tax (Yoritomo convinced Emperor Go-Shirakawa of it) necessary to finance the suppression of rebellions. It amounted to approximately 2% of the harvest and was collected from public and private lands without any exception. The steward (*jitō*) was supported by a share of the yield of the estate assigned to him. He was supported by *shiki* formalized by *appointment* and sanctioned by the authority of the central government. Their authority was based on this *shiki* right, but they did not have complete control over the *shōen* or *kokugaryō* to which they were appointed.[51] The lands in Japan consisted of small, scattered, irrigated rice fields, resembling the agrarian farms of earlier *uji*, but differed from them in that the communities of these estates were united not by blood or common descent but by *shiki* bonds, feudal rights and privileges.

The *daimyō*, or great lords, so important in the late feudal period and in the Tokugawa era, evolved from the ranks of the stewards, lesser gentry, and *samurai*. Yoritomo's vassals consisted of members of two categories: *samurai* with military rank and honorary *housemen* (*gokenin*). This small and privileged group included only people with the status of *samurai*. The Yoritomo housemen initially consisted only of minor nobility, Yoritomo's own retainers affiliated with Minamoto House, but soon he invited all of his allies and former enemies to join this group. Yoritomo's vassals gained positions of power throughout the country. The system he established to regulate and reward his own retainers (servants) and their subordinates became the effective government of Japan. The core of it was a group of vassal lords who, scattered throughout the country, took direct control over most of Japan. Yoritomo managed to significantly reduce the control of absentee *shōen* owners, which further contributed to lowering the revenues of noble court families and the central government. In the early years, the *shugo–jitō* system was not yet strong enough to ensure complete control, and therefore many aspects of the old administration persisted for some decades.

Japanese feudalism was distinctive because it operated through the traditional central civil administration and the personal relationship of lord–vassal (lord – parent and vassal child), although family bonds did not count much in the warrior's world. Personal loyalty was crucial in Yoritomo's control over his men.[52] The reciprocal obligation (loyalty/benevolence), underpinned by Confucianism, over time, became an established pattern of vassalage and the hallmark of Japanese feudalism.[53] As noted earlier, Japanese family organization was characterized by the strong concept of *house* (*ie*) in which a main family (*honke*) exerted primacy over its branch families (*bunke*).[54] This social pattern was widespread among *buke* Houses and formed an underlying principle in the lord–vassal link. Vassals received land and the right to keep private soldiers. Japan thus became a patchwork of decentralized units that were controlled only by a combination of the *shōgun*'s strong rule and the loyalty of vassals (*gokenin*) to him. The Taika system continued to function, but in an increasingly weak and nominal way, and therefore the governance system established by Yoritomo was not entirely new, but proved to be durable and uniform.

The Kamakura *Bakufu* did not possess enough land to grant it to its vassals as fiefs in exchange for service. Warriors could only control traditional *shōen* or accept appointments in newly confiscated lands. Landlords, such as temples, shrines, aristocratic, and royal families, held large tracts of land which reduced the land that could be granted to Kamakura warriors. Hence, a conflict of interests arose between the owners (or their local representatives), who wanted to retain as much control and income from the land as possible, and the *jitō*, who were interested in increasing their share in it. Therefore, the fair administration of justice in legal matters related to land disputes became an important goal of the Kamakura *Bakufu*.[55]

There were also conflicts of interest between farmers and warriors, primarily between *jitō* and peasants, resulting from the former's desire to increase personal and economic autonomy and expand their holdings within *shōen*.[56]

The status of the peasantry varied, ranging from wealthy farmers with large taxable named fields, small farmers with uncertain and changing tenures, peasants who only worked for landlords or *jitō*, and peasants of the lowest category known as low persons, that is, servants of the house without rights to the land.[57]

The central organs of the Kamakura government were simple and practical as local arrangements. In 1180, Yoritomo created at Kamakura three central boards.[58] The Administrative Board (*mandokoro*) acted as a central policymaking body at the highest level. This was analogous to the previously established secretariat managing the affairs of a large family such as the Fujiwara. It was headed by a *shikken* (director or regent) and after 1203, when Hōjō Tokimasa was appointed to this post, it became hereditary in the Hōjō family.[59] The second office was the Board of Retainers (*samurai-dokoro*), which regulated the affairs of the *shōgun*'s subordinates. It dealt with the assignment of military duties and the rewards and punishments given to warriors. Its regulations covered many aspects of *samurai*'s private lives, such as marriages, families, friends, recreation, and anything that might influence their loyalty to their superiors. During the war, the Board of Retainers served as the headquarters staff. The third body was the Board of Inquiry (*monchujo*), which acted as the court of appeal with final jurisdiction over the application of customary family law. It provided a link between Kamakura and the Court in Kyōto. Yoritomo invited the most experienced nobility and legal experts from Kyōto to help develop the rules for the operation of *monchujo*. In this way, cooperation between the two power centres was initiated.[60] These courts developed thorough judicial procedures, and judges administered justice in an impartial manner. The *bakufu* based its decisions on the evidence, examined it properly, and expedited judgment quickly.[61] Initially, this law only applied to the Minamoto House and its retainers, but since there was no other law legally binding throughout the country, litigants from all over Japan travelled to Kamakura for justice. The Board of Inquiry earned a reputation for administering just sentences which strengthened the reputation of the Kamakura *Bakufu*. Imposition of the Minamoto family system on traditional political norms led to the development of complex administrative laws during the Kamakura period. By consensus, all boards made unanimous decisions, reflecting the Japanese preference for collective responsibility and collective decision-making.[62] Kamakura's boards operated as committees, making unanimous public decisions and bearing collective responsibility, and this continues to be the principle of decision-making.[63]

Yoritomo's family governance rules and structures were followed throughout the country by his military retainers. Arbitration rather than resort to force was one of the enduring features of the Kamakura era. The *samurai*'s acceptance of this state distinguished them from later warriors, while emphasizing the central, stabilizing role of justice in the *bakufu*.[64] The political system built by Yoritomo was not intended to bring about changes but to consolidate his rule and promote himself and his retainers, but his actions led to the destruction of the *ritsuryō* system.

However, the very complex system of governing the state (the existence of emperors, cloistered emperors, regents, *shōguns* and *shōgun* regents) only worked effectively, when it was led by strong people in the highest positions. Minamoto Yoritomo was such a person, but after his death, the well-organized system started to break down. This governing system included the phenomenon of *kuromaku* (black curtain) referring to the powerbrokers that operate invisibly behind the scenes, a practice established early in Japanese history and continues today. After Yoritomo's death in 1199, a struggle for supremacy began between the Kamakura *Bakufu* and the Kyōto imperial court. The *shōgunate* and Hōjō (Yoritomo's wife's family) survived a challenge to their authority from the retired emperor Go-Toba (reigned 1183–1198) who attempted to regain political power. In 1221, he started the *Jokyu* riots against the Hōjō, who had taken control of the *shōgunate*. But the *bakufu* suppressed the rebellion within a month, defeating the imperial army in Kyōto. After the *Jokyu* Incident, the emperor and other government offices in Kyōto lost virtually all effective power.[65] The Hōjō took control and maintained authority over the *shōgunate* under the hereditary title of regent to the *shōgun* (*shikken*), an office held by nine successive members of this family until 1333.[66] The *shōgunate*, and the Hōjō *shōgun* regents, achieved complete control over Japan. The rebellious monarch was sent into exile, and the feudal system was cemented. A deputy *shōgun* was placed in Kyōto to oversee the court and determine the succession to the positions of titular and cloistered emperors. Thanks to the redistribution of land gained during the *Jokyu* riots (3,000 *shōen* were confiscated from the losing side and distributed to loyal *bakufu* vassals), the *shōgun* managed to gain the loyalty of all influential people in the country and strengthen the *bakufu's* power. The *shōgunate* continued to show the traditional respect for the imperial position (sacred prerogatives of the Throne).[67]

Three successive generations of Hōjō consolidated Kamakura's strong rule, but after 1252 they began to appoint court nobility and imperial princes as *shōguns*. This reduced the position of *shōgun* to a nominal one. With the progressive decentralization of central government power, the importance of regional forces, that is, constables, stewards, and warriors, grew.[68] The creator of the Kamakura *Bakufu*, Minamoto no Yoritomo, in 1185 usurped the right to approve or dismiss provincial warriors as estate managers (*jitō*). He wanted to restore peace after the five-year civil war that had brought him to power, so he ordered stewards to follow local precedents and comply with the demands of civilian landowners. Therefore, warriors were not placed on estates that did not have a resident warrior prior to 1185. However, the situation changed in 1221, when Kamakura officials began to place their appointees in the provinces, mainly in estates confiscated from the rebels, and to appoint *jitō* without following the accepted rules. The terms for the appointment of these stewards varied. To avoid legal (or other) disputes over the warriors' rights to income, the *bakufu* decided that the income of the new stewards would be one-eleventh of the estate's product (or its equivalent).[69] Many *jitō* found these terms too restrictive as they faced great financial pressures and many of them suffered from the commercialization of the economy, which grew faster than their income.

The first written Japanese feudal laws, the Legal *Jōei* Code (named after the period), were published in Kamakura in 1232 as the Hōjō Institutes of Judicature, also called the *Jōei* Formulary (*Jōei Shikimoku*), by the *shōgun* regent Hōjō Yasutoki. It was the earliest codification of warrior rights, based on the customary law of the House of Minamoto and the regulations of the *shōgun*'s court for the upper classes in matters of religion, land disputes, and crime. It was moderate and conciliatory in nature, especially towards former enemies of the *shōgunate*, and recognized the distinctiveness of the administrative system headed by the emperor, and formulated moral guidelines for feudal officials, which were not intended to replace customary law.[70] Its 51 articles were the first pragmatic laws established by the *bakufu* for the proper conduct of warriors in administering justice.[71] It defined practical rules for the conduct of vassals, regulations governing land tenure and penalties for various crimes and exhibited Confucian values, such as loyalty to the master, suppressing the decline of morality and discipline. The first few articles dealt with the proper maintenance of Shinto and Buddhist sites and the observance of religious rituals. The next ten articles outlined the duties of stewards and constables. Several articles were related to the tenure of fiefs and rights of succession.

The property was to remain in the hands of the owner, which in practice meant that the land was retained by the army, which occupied most of it. To establish clear ownership rights, a person had to have owned the land for at least 20 years. It enabled the *shōgunate*'s vassals or housemen (*gokenin*) to reclaim lands taken from them less than 20 years before. Only hereditary (family) holdings could be bought and sold. The lands granted to the *gokenin* by the Kamakura *Shōgunate* could not be transferred without the consent of the *bakufu*, because they were expected to render service to the *shōgun* in exchange for possession of them.[72] The status of women in warrior families continued to be comparatively high. Women were granted the rights to manage estates while their husbands were at war, to adopt heirs, to hold fiefs, and to obtain divorces, like their Heian predecessors, they could inherit a portion of the estate and even *jitō* posts, but this practice gradually was restricted.

The *Jōei* Formulary described contractual relations, regulated personal relationships, and outlined legal processes and penalties for breach of the peace. Lawsuits were also addressed in it. It discouraged land disputes, which placed unnecessary burdens on the judicial system.[73] The Kamakura *Shōgunate* created its own legal court, and its judgements followed the Common Law of *samurai*, codified in the *Jōei Shikimoku* mentioned earlier. It strengthened the *samurai* position but not their territories and rents. Unlike earlier imperial codes, it was not an import from China, but a pragmatic response to the existing situation.[74]

It was written in a complex Chinese form and contained a solemn oath by the *shōgun* and all his advisers to be just and uniform in the administration of justice. This code was so well constructed that it was incorporated into the legal system that survived until the end of the 19th century. These rules were not intended for all people but only for the *shōgun's* vassals. The rest of the population continued to be governed by either customary law or remnants of the older, more general Taihō Code.[75]

The Kamakura period was a relatively peaceful time, despite ongoing intrigues among the elites. However, during the period of Hōjō dominance, Japan had to face two extremely dangerous Mongol invasions. The first took place in 1274 (25,000 Mongols and Koreans, 900 ships) and the second in 1281 (troops of 150,000 and 4,000 ships). In both cases, very strong typhoons helped the warriors to defeat the invaders and forced them to retreat. For the Japanese, these victories were miracles, which they attributed to the protection of the gods (*shinkoku*) and to a divine wind destroying enemies called *kamikaze*.[76] The Mongol invasions united the Japanese and helped the Hōjō maintain power in the country introducing a state of emergency that ensured internal peace for 30 years. These events began a long period of isolation from China that lasted until the 14th century.

Although the defeat of the Mongol invasions strengthened the *bakufu* and its position relative to the Kyoto court, it placed a new, heavy burden on its finances and manpower. The *shōgunate* needed more and more resources to cover the rising costs of defence as the threat of Mongol invasion continued into the early 14th century.[77] The *bakufu* was given the rights to collect dues and recruit troops in Western Japan, which expanded its reach, as well as the right to refuse tributes to courtiers and religious institutions, which they desperately needed. This in turn caused increased dissatisfaction with the Hōjō *Shōgunate*. The invasions halted the internal fighting, but the enormous costs of financing the military alert, which lasted 20 years, severely strained the *shōgunate*'s finances, causing the Kamakura *Bakufu* to survive only another half-century.

The Mongol invasions directly cost the *samurai* many lives and wealth, but they cost the reputation of their leaders. During this dangerous period, the Hōjō assigned key command positions to family members and rewarded them very highly. But they did not reward the warriors who sacrificed blood, fortunes, and years of their lives defending Japan, as well as the religious institutions that protected the nation with prayers and material assistance. Military expenditures on preparation, fighting, and constant vigilance resulted in the insolvency of many direct retainers (*gokenin*) of the *bakufu*, significantly weakening the bonds between the *shōgun* and his vassals. Their dissatisfaction exacerbated rivalries and disputes concerning land, income, and perquisites of office and status.[78] The *bakufu* was unable to pay loyal warrior families the promised rewards (salaries) or compensate the incurred costs of their contributions to the nation's defense, as there were no newly acquired territories or spoils of war that could be used to compensate for their sacrifices. Therefore, in 1297, the weakened but still active imperial court ordered the *bakufu* to use the *concept of virtue* to reduce the debts incurred by the *samurai*. The law forbade creditors to go to the courts to enforce their loan agreements, and the *bakufu* judiciary refused to hear lawsuits brought by non-retainers over cases of debt default. *Tokuseirei* (ordering the return of sold land and the cancellation of debts) was the only way to reward warriors and protect retainers from moneylenders (usurers), enabling them to reclaim their lost land holdings. This law provided temporary financial relief but did not solve the *samurai*'s long-term solvency problems.[79] However, warriors' bonds with the *bakufu*, built on a system of gifts and exchange, were increasingly difficult to maintain in an expanding profit-driven money economy. The breakdown of personal, mutual relationships continued throughout the Middle Ages, long after 1333. The legislation from the mid-to-late 13th century was the combination of vice, virtue, and self-interest.[80]

Stewards (jitō) in the provinces became increasingly poor, while the property of senior officials such as constables (*shugo*) increased. *Shugo*, having the right to recruit soldiers, turned resident landlords into their vassals. This social change caused the rise of the great territorial lords known as *daimyō*, or *great names*.[81] The structure of the Kamakura *Shōgunate* began to unravel, and powerful local magnates and the *shōgun*'s vassals began to challenge the authority of the Hōjō regents, and the *bakufu's* system of governance. The situation was worsened by the lack of strong leadership of later Hōjō regents, which resulted in warriors becoming much less attached to their figurehead *shōguns*. As long as the hereditary *shōguns* were descended from Yoritomo, the *bakufu* could rely on the loyalty of the *jitō*, who were vassals of the Minamoto family, and this personal bond maintained the political unity of the country. After the extinction of the Minamoto line (1219), the successor *shōguns* had no hereditary or personal connection to the *jitō*, and the prestige of the *shōgun* alone was not sufficient to replace them. The Hôjô family, which had real power over the *shōgunate*, originally had no higher rank than *jitō* and could not demand obedience from any of the *shōgun's* retainers on its own behalf.[82] A strange pattern of political power continued throughout the remainder of the Kamakura period. In Kyōto, the titular emperor transferred power to the Fujiwara regent, who in turn submitted to the authority of a retired or cloistered emperor. All royal factions in Kyōto were controlled by the titular *shōgun* who was replaced by the Hōjō regent residing in Kamakura. Although Japan was at the height of indirect rule in the 13th century, the Hōjō regents were able to maintain internal peace until the following century. They ruled Japan efficiently and ably, setting an example of frugal living and faithfulness to duty. The structure created by Yoritomo turned out to be durable, and the vassals were assured reasonable justice and security in their holdings.[83] The regents and the Hōjō clan maintained tight control over the country, and any sign of rebellion was immediately suppressed. In this way, realizing the primary goal of the *bakufu*, which was to maintain peace in the provinces, they provided the country with several dozen years of peace and economic expansion. Overall, the country's economic situation improved during the Kamakura period due to relative peace, stability, and good administration under the *jitō-shugo* system.

During the Kamakura period, trade and crafts developed. Many merchants and artisans formed strong guilds, called *za* which were organized under the auspices of temples, shrines, or civil aristocrats, from whom they gained special monopoly privileges and exemptions from customs duties. The *za* played an important role in developing commerce and industry throughout the early feudal ages.[84] Changes in agricultural production and the spread of regional markets stimulated regional trade, changing the system of estate management.[85] But peasant life and status had not changed much. They farmed the land and worked for *za* corporations, and guilds. During the war, they had to become foot soldiers. But due to the economic and military needs, the lower classes were incorporated into the society more than before.[86]

Important changes occurred in warrior houses in the late Kamakura period. There was no law of primogeniture, so in times of peace, when the number of warrior families increased, the area of land allocated to each of them decreased as a result of constant divisions.[87] To solve this problem, inheritance by primogeniture was adopted, and the right of the eldest son to inherit land became customary throughout the country.[88] This enabled the concentration of power by the head of the house, to whom other members of the family were subordinated.

The urban lifestyle began to be imitated in the provinces. Bathing became a popular treatment for illnesses. Tea brought from China in the 8th century (by monk Eisei) was popularized, its healing properties were appreciated, and it soon became the national drink, and a tea ceremony was introduced.[89] Japanese influence could be seen in painting, architecture, and the production of high-quality ceramics. Sword-making reached high level of sophistication and formed a principal export to China. This was a time of significant cultural advancement, art and literature enjoyed the support of the feudal warriors, even though many had come from humble backgrounds and had little education.[90] All this created the early medieval culture and influenced everyday life in Japan.

The Kamakura era was characterized by the development of Japanese religion. Buddhism, initially limited to the aristocrats in the capital and monastic monks, soon spread to the provinces and lower classes, becoming a popular religion that took distinctly Japanese form. More and more schools of Buddhism were established. Buddhist leaders were mostly of humble origin, and they wrote in simple Japanese and therefore, most of its doctrines became understandable to ordinary people.[91] It flourished, partly because of the widespread suffering of the population from civil unrest and natural disasters, and partly because of the development of foreign trade links with China, favouring the influx of Zen Buddhism and Neo-Confucianism. According to Hara, the worst evil was the gradual transformation of the *shōgunate* into a princely court. Over time, the Kamakura warriors turned into pseudo-courtiers, and the Kyōto court nobility took on the militaristic temperament of the Kamakura warriors.[92] The increasing weaknesses of the *bakufu* enabled the Kyōto nobility to regain political power from the military. Some *samurai* stopped following military codes and ethics and became disloyal to their families. They were mainly warriors sent by the head of the family to oversee distant landholdings, who often broke away from their own family to become vassals of the local *shugo*. Some frustrated warriors broke the law by appropriating crops or disrupting local order.

Although the *gokenin* were in a difficult financial situation, the Hōjō continued to concentrate positions within their own family. For this reason, the dissatisfied *jitō* began to take steps to change the traditional owner–property relationship.[93] This further weakened their ties with the Kamakura *Bakufu* and the *shōgunate* began to gradually lose control and power in the 13th century. The highly valued justice in the Kamakura Courts deteriorated, slowing down legal processes and breaking the standards of fairness, efficiency, and timeliness of the early days. Influenced by the patterns of luxurious court life, *samurai* simplicity and frugality began to fade. Quarrels between the Hōjō themselves weakened their position, causing the joint rule of the Minamoto and Hōjō families to lose trust and support after almost a century.

Dissatisfaction towards the Hōjō *shōgunal* regents culminated under the emperor Go-Daigo (1288–1339). Upon ascending the throne in 1318, he was determined to overthrow the *shōgunate*, re-establish direct imperial rule, and restore power to the civilian government under the Heian Imperial House.[94] He wanted to strengthen his position by restoring the *ritsuryō* system, under which all land belonged to the imperial family. He was powerful because the current Hōjō regent was weak. Go-Daigo, in 1321, ended the time-honoured custom of cloistered emperors ruling behind the scenes, reverting to the system of centralized civilian government established in 645. He convinced part of the court and the army to become independent from Kamakura.[95] The *bakufu* opposed these attempts, and internal turmoil started which finally led to the overthrow of the Kamakura *Shōgunate*.

Emperor Go-Daigo challenged the *shōgunate* twice (Genko War, 1331–1333), the first time in 1331 when he failed to forcibly overthrow the *bakufu* and the Hōjō regency and was exiled to a remote island. However, he managed to escape and with the support of some leaders and militant Buddhist monks, he built an army and in 1333 he started a rebellion for the second time. The *shōgunate* sent general Ashikaga Takauji, to deal with him. But Takauji (a young head of a branch of the Minamoto family) decided to change loyalty from the *bakufu* to Go-Daigo, pledged allegiance to the emperor, defeated the government, and took over Kyōto for the monarch.[96] In consequence, Kamakura was captured and burned by forces opposing the *shōgunate*. The last Hōjō regent, his family and some 800 retainers, were killed or committed suicide. The Kamakura *Shōgunate* fell in 1334, and true state power was restored to Kyōto and Emperor Go-Daigo.[97] After 140 years, the Kamakura period was over and the *bakufu* destroyed.[98]

After returning to Kyōto in 1333, the victorious Emperor Go-Daigo began the Kemmu Restoration, intended to restore direct imperial rule. He abolished the powerful office of *kampaku* and put into operation a central bureaucracy reviving all the former ministries and official positions.[99] He revived the Records Office (*Kirokusho*) to settle lawsuits in the provinces, established the Court of Miscellaneous Claims (*Zassho Ketsudansho*) to handle minor suits, and a guard station (*musha-dokoro*) to keep order among the warriors in Kyōto.

However, many warriors who joined the imperial forces in overthrowing the *bakufu* were disillusioned with the distribution of the spoils and the direction of the emperor's reforms. Emperor Go-Daigo cared most for strengthening the imperial family and made members of it provincial leaders in the north and east of the country. The emperor's actions were doomed to failure, because the power of disappointed *samurai* and landowners was greater than support for him.[100] The only positive effect of the Restoration was re-establishment of contacts with Mongol China no longer seen as a threat.

In 1335, Ashikaga Takauji proclaimed himself *shōgun* at Kamakura, but Emperor Go-Daigo refused to recognize his usurped title. Therefore, Takauji turned against Go-Daigo, sparking a revolt. The emperor sent Nitta Yoshisada to reclaim Kamakura, but Takauji defeated him and forced Go-Daigo to leave Kyōto. Following his victory, the Ashikaga dethroned Go-Daigo and placed a rival branch of the imperial line on the throne. The new Emperor Kōmyō (1336–1348) confirmed Takauji as *shōgun* in 1336. Go-Daigo fled to a place called Yoshino (in the mountains near Nara), where his followers made him emperor of the southern line. Ashikaga unsuccessfully tried to compromise with the monarchy and seize power.[101] For the next 56 years (1336 to 1392), in the period called *Wars Between the Courts*, two emperors reigned simultaneously claiming legitimacy, and political power was divided between the Southern Court at Yoshino Mountains near Nara and the Northern Court at Kyōto.[102] The War of the Two Dynasties was an external form of combat, as the real issue was which group of warriors would dominate the court and take control over the country, as the Hōjō regents did. In this way, Go-Daigo's intention to restore ruling power to the imperial house destroyed the court-*bakufu* dyarchy and initiated decades of violence and disorder. Ashikaga Takauji, who overthrew the Kamakura *Bakufu*, created the Ashikaga or Muromachi *Shōgunate* and started the Muromachi era lasting from 1336 to 1573, a new political and military period of two-and-a-half centuries of feudalism.[103]

Notes

1 H. G. Wren, The Legal System of Pre-Western Japan. *Hastings Law Journal* 1968, Vol. 20, No. 1, pp. 217–244.

2 R. H. P. Mason, J. G. Caiger, A History of Japan. *TUTTLE Publishing* 1997, p. 122. file:///D:/Users/wzr/Downloads/A_History_of_Japan_Mason_Caiger%20(5).pdf.

3 C. Andressen, A Short History of Japan: From Samurai to Sony. *Allen & Unvin*, Canberra 2002, pp. 38, 53.
4 G. B. Sansom, A History of Japan to 1334, Vol. 1. *Stanford University Press*, Stanford 1958, p. 239.
5 M. P. Culeddu, The Evolution of the Ancient Way of the Warrior: From the Ancient Chronicles to the Tokugawa Period. *Asian Studies* 2018, Vol. 6, No. 2, pp. 87–109.
6 K. G. Henshall, A History of Japan: From Stone Age to Superpower. *Palgrave Macmillan,* London 2012, p. 28. www.gutenberg.org/files/37186/37186-h/37186-h.htm.
7 C. Andressen, A Short History of Japan . . . op. cit., p. 45.
8 Ibidem, p. 49.
9 R. H. P. Mason, J. G. Caiger, A History of Japan . . . op. cit., pp. 121–122.
10 W. S. Morton, J. K. Olenik, Japan: Its History and Culture. *McGraw-Hill Companies Inc.*, New York 2005, p. 69.
11 C. Andressen, A Short History of Japan . . . op. cit., p. 49.
12 M. W. Meyer, Japan: A Concise History. *Rowman & Littlefield Publishers Inc.*, Plymouth 2009, pp. 75–76.
13 www.britannica.com/topic/samurai.
14 W. S. Morton, J. K. Olenik, Japan: Its History and Culture . . . op. cit., pp. 62–65.
15 R. H. P. Mason, J. G. Caiger, A History of Japan . . . op. cit., p. 148.
16 W. S. Morton, J. K. Olenik, Japan: Its History and Culture . . . op. cit., pp. 66–67.
17 M. P. Culeddu, The Evolution of the Ancient Way of the Warrior . . . op. cit.
18 www.japanese-wiki-corpus.org/history/Myoden.html.
19 G. B. Sansom, A History of Japan to 1334 . . . op. cit., pp. 236–237.
20 M. P. Culeddu, The Evolution of the Ancient Way of the Warrior . . . op. cit.
21 W. S. Morton, J. K. Olenik, Japan: Its History and Culture . . . op. cit., p. 69.
22 G. B. Sansom, A History of Japan to 1334 . . . op. cit., p. 237.
23 C. Andressen, A Short History of Japan . . . op. cit., pp. 44–46.
24 K. Hara, An Introduction to the History of Japan. *Yamato Society Publication, G. P. Putnam's & Sons, The Knickerbocker Press*, New York and London 1920, pp. 162–164.
25 J. P. Mass, The Kamakura *bakufu*. In: The Cambridge History of Japan: Medieval Japan. Vol. 3. *Cambridge University Press*, Cambridge 2008, p. 46.
26 W. S. Morton, J. K. Olenik, Japan: Its History and Culture . . . op. cit., pp. 52–53.
27 G. B. Sansom, A History of Japan to 1334 . . . op. cit., p. 234.
28 W. S. Morton, J. K. Olenik, Japan: Its History and Culture . . . op. cit., p. 52.
29 Ibidem, p. 72.
30 M. W. Meyer, Japan: A Concise History . . . op. cit., p. 63.
31 K. Hara, An Introduction to the History of Japan . . . op. cit., p. 176.
32 W. S. Morton, J. K. Olenik, Japan: Its History and Culture . . . op. cit., p. 68.
33 M. W. Meyer, Japan: A Concise History . . . op. cit., p. 71.
34 D. H. Shively, W. H. McCullough, Introduction. In: The Cambridge History of Japan: Heian Japan. Vol. 2. *Cambridge University Press*, Cambridge 2008, p. 1.
35 M. W. Meyer, Japan: A Concise History . . . op. cit., p. 73; C. Andressen, A Short History of Japan . . . op. cit., p. 48.
36 W. S. Morton, J. K. Olenik, Japan: Its History and Culture . . . op. cit., pp. 70–72.
37 K. G. Henshall, A History of Japan . . . op. cit., pp. 35–37.
38 J. P. Mass, The Kamakura *bakufu*. In: The Cambridge History of Japan . . . op. cit., p. 46.
39 M. W. Meyer, Japan: A Concise History . . . op. cit., p. 73.
40 G. B. Sansom, A History of Japan to 1334 . . . op. cit., p. 239.
41 K. G. Henshall, A History of Japan . . . op. cit., p. 34.

42 C. Andressen, A Short History of Japan . . . op. cit., p. 50.
43 K. Asakawa, Some of the Contributions of Feudal Japan to the New Japan. *The Journal of Race Development* 1912, Vol. 3, No. 1, pp. 1–32.
44 K. G. Henshall, A History of Japan . . . op. cit., p. 35.
45 M. W. Meyer, Japan: A Concise History . . . op. cit., p. 72.
46 K. G. Henshall, A History of Japan . . . op. cit., pp. 17, 35–36.
47 C. Andressen, A Short History of Japan . . . op. cit., p. 49.
48 J. P. Mass, The Kamakura *bakufu*. In: The Cambridge History of Japan . . . op. cit., p. 61.
49 M. W. Meyer, Japan: A Concise History . . . op. cit., p. 74.
50 J. W. Hall, Feudalism in Japan: A Reassessment. *Comparative Studies in Society and History* 1962, Vol. 5, No. 1, pp. 15–51.
51 J. P. Mass, The Kamakura *bakufu*. In: The Cambridge History of Japan . . . op. cit., pp. 61, 266.
52 K. G. Henshall, A History of Japan . . . op. cit., pp. 17, 35–36.
53 C. Andressen, A Short History of Japan . . . op. cit., p. 50.
54 J. W. Hall, Feudalism in Japan: A Reassessment . . . op. cit.
55 J. Nagle (ed.), Feudalism, Monarchies, and Nobility. *Britannica Educational Publishing and The Rosen Publishing Group, Inc.*, New York 2015, p. 115.
56 I. Susumu, The Decline of the Kamakura *bakufu*. In: The Cambridge History of Japan: Medieval Japan. Vol. 3. *Cambridge University Press*, Cambridge 2008, p. 129.
57 J. Nagle, Feudalism, Monarchies, and Nobility . . . op. cit., p. 116.
58 W. S. Morton, J. K. Olenik, Japan: Its History and Culture . . . op. cit., pp. 70–72.
59 K. G. Henshall, A History of Japan . . . op. cit., p. 132.
60 W. S. Morton, J. K. Olenik, Japan: Its History and Culture . . . op. cit., pp. 70–72.
61 J. P. Mass, The Origins of Kamakura Justice. *Journal of Japanese Studies* 1977, Vol. 3, No. 2, pp. 299–322.
62 R. C. Marshall, Collective Decision Making in Rural Japan. Vol. 11. *University of Michigan, Centre for Japanese Studies* 1984. https://expeditiorepositorio.utadeo.edu.co/bitstream/handle/20.500.12010/18289/9780472901999.pdf?sequence=1.
63 M. W. Meyer, Japan: A Concise History . . . op. cit., pp. 74–75.
64 J. P. Mass, The Origins of Kamakura Justice . . . op. cit.
65 www.japan-guide.com/e/e2133.html.
66 J. Clements, A Brief History of the Samurai: The Way of Japan's Elite Warriors. *Running Press Book Publishers*, Philadelphia 2010, p. 22.
67 J. P. Mass, The Origins of Kamakura Justice . . . op. cit.
68 M. W. Meyer, Japan: A Concise History . . . op. cit., p. 84.
69 E. IE. Segal, Coins, Trade, and the State Economic Growth in Early Medieval Japan. Harvard East Asian Monographs. *Harvard University Press*, Cambridge, MA and London 2011, p. 86.
70 H. G. Wren, The Legal System of Pre-Western Japan . . . op. cit.; www.britannica.com/topic/Joei-Shikimoku.
71 www.britannica.com/place/Japan/Medieval-Japan#ref319299.
72 E. I. Segal, Coins, Trade, and the State Economic Growth in Early Medieval Japan . . . op. cit., p. 108.
73 Ibidem, pp. 108, 118–119.
74 M. W. Meyer, Japan: A Concise History . . . op. cit., p. 77.
75 C. Andersson, A Short History of Japan . . . op. cit., p. 52.
76 W. S. Morton, J. K. Olenik, Japan: Its History and Culture . . . op. cit., pp. 74–76; K. G. Henshall, A History of Japan . . . op. cit., pp. 36–37.
77 W. W. Farris, Japan to 1600: A Social and Economic History. *University of Hawai'i Press* 2009, pp. 136–163. www.jstor.org/stable/j.ctt6wqt09.12.

78 C. D. Totman, A History of Japan. *Blackwell Publishing*, Malden; Oxford; Carlton 2014, p. 162. www.perlego.com/book/1006239/a-history-of-japan-pdf.
79 E. I. Segal, Coins, Trade, and the State Economic Growth in Early Medieval Japan . . . op. cit., pp. 110–118.
80 Ibidem, pp. 108, 146, 147.
81 W. S. Morton, J. K. Olenik, Japan: Its History and Culture . . . op. cit., p. 79.
82 K. Hara, An Introduction to the History of Japan . . . op. cit., pp. 213–214.
83 W. S. Morton, J. K. Olenik, Japan: Its History and Culture . . . op. cit., p. 76.
84 K. G. Henshall, A History of Japan . . . op. cit., pp. 17, 38.
85 E. I. Segal, Coins, Trade, and the State Economic Growth in Early Medieval Japan . . . op. cit., pp. 146–147.
86 M. W. Meyer, Japan: A Concise History . . . op. cit., pp. 77–78.
87 K. G. Henshall, A History of Japan . . . op. cit., pp. 17, 52.
88 H. G. Wren, The Legal System of Pre-Western Japan . . . op. cit.
89 M. W. Meyer, Japan: A Concise History . . . op. cit., p. 80.
90 C. Andressen, A Short History of Japan . . . op. cit., p. 53.
91 M. W. Meyer, Japan: A Concise History . . . op. cit., p. 78.
92 K. Hara, An Introduction to the History of Japan . . . op. cit., p. 205.
93 E. I. Segal, Coins, Trade, and the State Economic Growth in Early Medieval Japan . . . op. cit. p. 88.
94 K. G. Henshall, A History of Japan . . . op. cit., p. 40.
95 M. W. Meyer, Japan: A Concise History . . . op. cit., pp. 83–84.
96 F. Brinkley, D. Kikuchi, A History of the Japanese People from the Earliest Times to the End of the Meiji Era. *The Encyclopaedia Britannica Co.*, New York and London 1912, pp. 382–384.
97 K. Hara, An Introduction to the History of Japan . . . op. cit., pp. 204–205.
98 K. G. Henshall, A History of Japan . . . op. cit., pp. 17, 39; W. S. Morton, J. K. Olenik, Japan: Its History and Culture . . . op. cit., p. 79.
99 E. I. Segal, Coins, Trade, and the State Economic Growth in Early Medieval Japan . . . op. cit., p. 188.
100 C. Andressen, A Short History of Japan . . . op. cit., p. 54.
101 K. Asakawa, Japan: From the Japanese Government History. In: H. C. Lodge (ed.), The History of Nations. Vol. 7. *The Collier Press,* New York 1906. www.gutenberg.org/ebooks/45645.
102 K. G. Henshall, A History of Japan . . . op. cit., pp. 17, 39–40.
103 W. S. Morton, J. K. Olenik, Japan: Its History and Culture . . . op. cit., p. 80.

Bibliography

Andressen, C., A Short History of Japan: From Samurai to Sony. *Allen & Unvin*, Canberra 2002.

Asakawa, K., Some of the Contributions of Feudal Japan to the New Japan. *The Journal of Race Development* 1912, Vol. 3, No. 1, pp. 1–32. *JSTOR*. https://doi.org/10.2307/29737937.

Brinkley, F., Kikuchi, D., A History of the Japanese People from the Earliest Times to the End of the Meiji Era. *The Encyclopaedia Britannica Co*, New York and London 1912. https://archive.org/details/historyofjapanes00briniala/page/n5/mode/2up.

www.britannica.com/place/Japan/Medieval-Japan#ref319299.

www.britannica.com/topic/Joei-Shikimoku.

www.britannica.com/topic/samurai.

Clements, J., A Brief History of the Samurai: The Way of Japan's Elite Warriors. *Running Press Book Publishers*, Philadelphia 2010.

Culeddu, M. P., The Evolution of the Ancient Way of the Warrior: From the Ancient Chronicles to the Tokugawa Period. *Asian Studies* 2018, Vol. 6, No. 2, pp. 87–109. https://doi.org/10.4312/as.2018.6.2.87-109.

Farris, W. W., Japan to 1600: A Social and Economic History. *University of Hawai'i Press* 2009, pp. 164–194. *JSTOR*. www.jstor.org/stable/j.ctt6wqt09.12.

Hall, J. W., Feudalism in Japan: A Reassessment. *Comparative Studies in Society and History* 1962, Vol. 5, No. 1, pp. 15–51. *JSTOR*. www.jstor.org/stable/177767.

Hall, J. W., Jansen, M. B., Kanai, M., Twitchett, D. (eds.), The Cambridge History of Japan. In: D. H. Shively, W. H. McCollough (eds.), Heian Japan, Vol. 2. *Cambridge University Press*, Cambridge 2008.

Hara, K., An Introduction to the History of Japan. *Yamato Society Publication, G. P. Putnam's & Sons, The Knickerbocker Press*, New York and London 1920. www.gutenberg.org/files/37186/37186-h/37186-h.htm.

Henshall, K. G., A History of Japan: From Stone Age to Superpower. *Palgrave Macmillan* 2012. www.gutenberg.org/files/37186/37186-h/37186-h.htm.

www.japan-guide.com/e/e2133.html.

www.japanese-wiki-corpus.org/history/Myoden.html.

Marshall, R. C., Collective Decision Making in Rural Japan, Vol. 11. *University of Michigan, Centre for Japanese Studies* 1984. https://expeditiorepositorio.utadeo.edu.co/bitstream/handle/20.500.12010/18289/9780472901999.pdf?sequence=1.

Mason, R. H. P., Caiger, J. G., A History of Japan. *TUTTLE Publishing* 1997. file:///D:/Users/wzr/Downloads/A_History_of_Japan_Mason_Caiger%20(5).pdf.

Mass, J. P., The Origins of Kamakura Justice. *Journal of Japanese Studies* 1977, Vol. 3, No. 2, pp. 299–322. *JSTOR*. www.jstor.org/stable/132114.

Meyer, M. W., Japan a Concise History. *Rowman & Littlefield Publishers Inc*, Plymouth 2009. file:///D:/Users/wzr/Downloads/epdf.pub_japan-a-concise-history-4th-edition.pdf.

Morton, W. S., Olenik, J. K., Japan: Its History and Culture. *McGraw-Hill Companies Inc.*, New York 2005. https://vdocuments.mx/japan-its-history-and-culture-56811b380a71d.html.

Nagle, J. (ed.), Feudalism, Monarchies, and Nobility. *Britannica Educational Publishing and The Rosen Publishing Group, Inc.*, New York 2014.

Sansom, G. B., A History of Japan to 1334, Vol. 1. *Stanford University Press*, Stanford 1958.

Sato, E., Ōyama Estate and Insei Land Policies. *Monumenta Nipponica* 1979, Vol. 34, No. 1, pp. 73–99. *JSTOR*. https://doi.org/10.2307/2384282.

Segal, E. I., Coins, Trade, and the State Economic Growth in Early Medieval Japan. Harvard East Asian Monographs. *Harvard University Press*, Cambridge, MA and London 2011. file:///D:/Users/wzr/Downloads/coins-trade-and-the-state-economic-growth-in-early-medieval-japan-illustrated-0674060687-9780674060685_compress.pdf.

Totman, C. D., A History of Japan. *Wiley* 2014. www.perlego.com/book/1006239/a-history-of-japan-pdf.

Wren, H. G., The Legal System of Pre-Western Japan. *Hastings Law Journal* 1968, Vol. 20, No. 1, pp. 217–244. https://repository.uchastings.edu/hastings_law_journal/vol20/iss1/5.

Yamamura, K. (ed.), The Cambridge History of Japan. In: Medieval Japan, Vol. 3. *Cambridge University Press*, Cambridge 2008.

8 An introduction to the Kamakura *Shōgunate* economy

During the Kamakura era, the *ritsuryō* system decayed and was abolished despite the attempt to re-establish it in 1333. The *bakufu*, as the military arm of the imperial central government, began a new era in which the independent government of the warriors opposed the political power of the civil aristocracy. Because of the relative peace, stability, and good administration and governance under the *jitō-shugo* system the nation's economic situation improved. The political and economic changes of the period enabled and motivated *samurai* to increase their economic power and legitimized their authority.[1] The emerging system was a combination of the complex administrative system of China and the clan communities indigenous to Japan, providing an excellent example of successful hybridization. The government became a mixture of old and new because of the need for legitimacy and the will to continue ancient traditions during the changes.

The economy of the Kamakura *Bakufu* was based almost entirely on agriculture. The economic changes resulted from a slow but steady rise in agricultural productivity which had a great impact on people and social organizations, including the expansion of commerce. Rice was the basis of trade, so landowners who were able to produce the most rice quickly gained political and social power. After the middle of the Kamakura period, the farming villages in which the warriors lived changed, mainly through improved seeds, irrigation, better management, improved technology, and double crops.[2] The cultivation of lacquer and mulberry trees and the raising of silkworms were encouraged and extended during that time.[3] Peasants began to feel the need to improve management, which resulted in the creation of self-government organizations. The social, economic, and technological changes influenced the *shōen* flourishing since the 11th century.[4] The *shōen* system was built on mutual benefits and on respect for power and rank. They were well managed, controlled, and oriented towards maximization of revenues for the stakeholders. They had dual structure of power, one subjected to *jitō* and immune to the owner, the other controlled by the owner's agents. These agents were either long-time residents of the area and probably the original commanders of some of the *shōen*-forming lands, or centrally dispatched professional managers.[5]

DOI: 10.4324/9781003497936-11

Intensification of agriculture in the 14th century, especially the rise of the *myoden* (a paddy named after a *myoshu*), became an important step towards the private ownership of land. In Kamakura days, manors rarely exceeded 500 acres of good rice land in extent, and only a proportion of them were held by men in military service. The *myoshu* shared any increases in production, so they were motivated to raise productivity levels. This in turn increased the economic power of the *samurai* class, as many of them were originally *myoshu* who later became *myoshu*-turned warriors or *shōen* administrators. They participated in the increasing agricultural output at the expense of the *shōen* owners in Kyōto.[6] In the modernized economy, tax optimization was applied; productivity and market surpluses were increased. Innovation was the driving force of Japan's medieval economy.

The expansion of villages and their status as economic centres facilitated contacts with strangers. Competition over natural resources increased as commerce grew throughout Japan. Increased productivity contributed to the prosperity of traders who distributed rice and other goods throughout the country. Artisans, often associated with *shōen*, gradually specialized to meet the growing demands of consumers. The peasants produced various handicrafts for sale at the markets.[7] The surplus of provincial production gave estates the opportunity to sell their products on external markets and participate in the growing commercial economy. Urban commercial centres began to be established near villages or along important communication routes. The rural markets were no longer places of barter but started to use money, which facilitated exchange across the whole country.[8] The cash economy began to spread even though real money was not minted in Japan, but large amounts of coins were imported from China, giving rise to financial intermediaries and the payment of *shōen* taxes in cash.[9] Chinese copper coins circulated in the markets, and bills of exchange were used for payments to distant localities (to deliver *nengu* from the provinces to the centre) by merchants and estate managers. *Kawase* were used, which circulated like paper money but without government backing, so it was no longer necessary to transport cash to the capital. The sale of valid bills of exchange (promissory notes) was the key to the long-term prosperity of merchants who, taking care of their customers, did not sell them bad bills of exchange. They wanted to gain the trust of the estate managers, take advantage of the exchange system, and get more profit from the sale of agricultural products (one promissory note was usually worth 10,000 Chinese coins). This proves how creative merchants and managers of provincial estates were in solving financial problems in the 15th century.[10]

The activity of traveling merchants increased and specialized wholesale merchants appeared in large ports. In various provinces, centres for metal casting, metalworking, paper manufacture, and other skills appeared.[11] Many consumer items such as fish, rice, silk, lacquer, and paper became a means of accumulating wealth and of payment. The exchange of agricultural products and manufactured goods prospered and local markets, held on three fixed days a month, became common. Some merchants got rich by trading coins, which had important advantages in terms of durability and ease of transport. Bills of exchange provided more significant advantages over payment of receivables in goods or coins, because they drastically reduced the risks and costs of shipping them over long distances.[12] The craftsmen and merchants, connected to powerful religious houses or having special authorization from the court or the *bakufu,* were allowed to move freely across political borders and pass-through tolls without paying fees. Many merchants and artisans formed strong guilds known as *za*, which were organized under the auspices of temples, shrines, or civil aristocrats, from whom they gained special monopoly privileges and exemptions from customs duties.[13]

In the early modern economy, commodity and financial markets were well integrated, while land and labour markets were segregated and managed by local communities in a personal way and using long-term relationships.[14] Therefore, the economic growth proved damaging to traditional economic relations within the framework of the old imperial tax system. The weakening of the economy in the late Heian period resulted from reliance on private contributions rather than redistribution of state taxes through the official market. In the provinces, farming communities found an advantage in trading in markets that were not dependent on central landlords. The warriors disrupted the tribute economy by taxing property residents in cash. The result was a shift of power in the provinces from civilian landowners, based in temples or capital, to local warriors. Many of the landowners found themselves in a difficult financial situation (some out of greed) and demanded more and more cash from the peasants.

In 1263, the *Golden Period* characterized by the regency *(shikken)* system ended. Changes in the social, economic, and technological spheres shook the *shōen* system that had been flourishing since the 11th century. According to Seagal, already in 1239 the financial situation of many of warriors became desperate. Some insolvent warriors tried to get out of debt by appointing their creditors to local positions and allowing them to receive income directly from the residents of provincial estates; therefore, the *bakufu* banned, in 1239, the appointment of money-lending dealers and monks as *jitō* deputies. In 1240, the *bakufu* decreed that, if *gokenin* paid more than half of his debt by the due date of the loan, his properties would not be confiscated, but the loan would be adjusted to give him more time to repay the remaining balance. The need or desire of retainers to purchase manufactured goods for money led them to seek larger amounts of cash. Unable to obtain the necessary funds from their regular estate income, they tried to increase the available cash by taking away income rights from civilian estate owners, allying with the *bakufu* against other warriors to receive their estates in exchange for military service, raising taxes in their own villages, or turning to usurers. The *bakufu* knew about the abuses of its agents, but called them *cash greedy* and tried to prevent the warriors from going into further debt. This showed that the *shōgunate* was unaware of the desperate financial difficulties its warriors found themselves in.

Since 1255 usury had been spreading in Kamakura and Kyōto. The decree banned such activities, comparing usurers to thieves.[15] Because the Kamakura *Bakufu* was concerned about improving the financial situation of its retainers, in 1260, it established standard rates for *gokenin* on watch and then renewed the issuance of the *virtuous government edicts* (*tokuseir*ei). In 1267, the *bakufu* enacted a four-clause decree that allowed *gokenin* to keep their lands even, if they defaulted on loans, banned land management contracts (*wayo*) under which the warriors managing the land, paid a fixed fee to the civilian owner of the land, suspended *non-gokenin* appeals against court decisions regarding retainers, and forbade women who were remarrying from giving land to their new husbands unless they were related to the warrior government. The first three clauses concerned the *bakufu's* efforts to help its financially distressed retainers, while the fourth clause prevented the transfer of service land to persons unrelated to the *shōgunate*.[16] However, the following years brought even greater problems. The costs of defending against Mongol invasions caused many *samurai* to fall into debt and lose estates to moneylenders. In order to save the indebted *gokenin* and prevent them from losing their lands, an economic relief policy was implemented in form of another edict on *virtuous administration* (*tokusei*) in 1297. It stipulated (1) abolition of the appeal suit system (*osso*), (2) prohibition of further pawning or sale of *gokenin* property and a guaranteed return of previously sold property to the original owner at no cost, and (3) refusal by the *bakufu* to accept any litigation involving the collection of loans, in order to curtail excessive usury practices.[17] According to Segal, announcing the cancellation of all mortgage debts should be considered as a combination of vice, virtue, and self-interest.[18] It turned out to be a disaster which sent the economy into downturn. Money became tighter and loans harder to obtain by the warriors who still needed cash. The new loan agreements began to include a clause excluding cancellation by future acts of *tokusei*.[19] The *gokenin* unable or unwilling to obey the *bakufu*'s prohibition against selling their land or using it as collateral, committed crimes, such as gambling, dealing with moneylenders, oppressing peasants, or breaking laws. During the Kamakura period, no more *tokuseirei* were issued, not because the need for cash had declined, but because by the end of the 13th century the *bakufu* was too weak to resist the dictates of a monetary economy.[20]

The governance system of the *bakufu* began to be challenged. Changes in agricultural production and the spread of regional markets contributed to the development of regional trade, which disrupted the classical system of estates (land) management and ultimately led to the collapse of the Kamakura *Bakufu*.[21]

Notes

1 K. Yamamura, The Development of Za in Medieval Japan. *Business History Review* December 1973, Vol. 47, No. 4, pp. 438–465.
2 K. G. Henshall, A History of Japan: From Stone Age to Superpower. *Palgrave Macmillan* 2012, pp. 17, 38. www.gutenberg.org/files/37186/37186-h/37186-h.htm.
3 W. S. Morton, J. K. Olenik, Japan: Its History and Culture. *McGraw-Hill Companies Inc.*, New York 2005, p. 21.
4 I. Susumu, The Decline of the Kamakura *bakufu*. In: K. Yamamura (ed.), The Cambridge History of Japan: Medieval Japan. Vol. 3. *Cambridge University Press*, Cambridge 2008, p. 129.
5 J. P. Mass, The Kamakura *bakufu*. In: The Cambridge History of Japan: Medieval Japan. Vol. 3. *Cambridge University Press*, Cambridge 2008, p. 84.
6 K. Yamamura, The Development of Za in Medieval Japan . . . op. cit.
7 I. Susumu, The Decline of the Kamakura *bakufu*. In: The Cambridge History of Japan . . . op. cit., p. 129.
8 E. I. Segal, Coins, Trade, and the State Economic Growth in Early Medieval Japan. Harvard East Asian Monographs. *Harvard University Press*, Cambridge, MA and London 2011, pp. 80–82.
9 I. Susumu, The Decline of the Kamakura *bakufu* . . . op. cit., p. 129.
10 E. I. Segal, Coins, Trade, and the State Economic Growth in Early Medieval Japan . . . op. cit., pp. 180–183.
11 www.britannica.com/place/Japan/Samurai-groups-and-farming-villages.
12 E. I. Segal, Coins, Trade, and the State Economic Growth in Early Medieval Japan . . . op. cit., pp. 83, 150.
13 K. G. Henshall, A History of Japan: From Stone Age to Superpower . . . op. cit., pp. 17, 38.
14 M. Nakabayashi, Institutions and Economic Development of Early Modern Japan. *ISS Discussion Paper Series F-146* August 2009, pp. 1–26. https://www.iss.u-tokyo.ac.jp/publishments/dpf/pdf/f-146.pdf.
15 E. I. Segal, Coins, Trade, and the State Economic Growth in Early Medieval Japan . . . op. cit., p. 121.
16 Ibidem, pp. 108, 122.
17 I. Susumu, The Decline of the Kamakura *bakufu* . . . op. cit., p. 157.
18 E. I. Segal, Coins, Trade, and the State Economic Growth in Early Medieval Japan . . . op. cit., pp. 146–147.
19 K. Yamamura, The Growth of Commerce in Medieval Japan. In: The Cambridge History of Japan: Medieval Japan. Vol. 3. *Cambridge University Press*, Cambridge 2008, p. 375; E. I. Segal, Coins, Trade, and the State Economic Growth in Early Medieval Japan . . . op. cit., pp. 146–147.
20 K. Yamamura, The Growth of Commerce in Medieval Japan. In: The Cambridge History of Japan . . . op. cit., p. 375.
21 E. I. Segal, Coins, Trade, and the State Economic Growth in Early Medieval Japan . . . op. cit., p. 147.

Bibliography

www.britannica.com/place/Japan/Samurai-groups-and-farming-villages.
Henshall, K. G., A History of Japan: From Stone Age to Superpower. *Palgrave Macmillan* 2012. www.gutenberg.org/files/37186/37186-h/37186-h.htm.

Morton, W. S., Olenik, J. K., Japan: Its History and Culture. *McGraw-Hill Companies Inc.*, New York 2005. https://vdocuments.mx/japan-its-history-and-culture-56811b380a71d.html.

Nakabayashi, M., Institutions and Economic Development of Early Modern Japan. *ISS Discussion Paper Series F-146* August 2009, pp. 1–26. https://www.iss.u-tokyo.ac.jp/publishments/dpf/pdf/f-146.pdf.

Segal, E. I., Coins, Trade, and the State Economic Growth in Early Medieval Japan. Harvard East Asian Monographs. *Harvard University Press*, Cambridge, MA and London 2011. file:///D:/Users/wzr/Downloads/coins-trade-and-the-state-economic-growth-in-early-medieval-japan-illustrated-0674060687-9780674060685_compress.pdf.

Yamamura, K., The Development of Za in Medieval Japan. *Business History Review* December 1973, Vol. 47, No. 4, pp. 438–465. www.jstor.org/stable/3113366?seq=1&cid=pdf-reference#references_tab_contents.

Yamamura, K. (ed.), The Cambridge History of Japan. In: Medieval Japan, Vol. 3. *Cambridge University Press*, Cambridge 2008.

9 Shaping corporate governance in the Kamakura era

Application of selected theories of corporate governance in the Kamakura *Shōgunate*

It is believed that the system of government established by Yoritomo was not new, but durable and uniform, and vassals were assured of reasonable justice and security in their domains. The rights and obligation of each loop of the hierarchical system *shōgun–shugo–jitō* were clear, strict, and obeyed. The Hōjō regents, propagated frugal living and faithfulness to duty, maintained tight control and immediately dealt with any sign of rebellion. The clear division of power was bringing benefits and order to the country. However, the selfish policy of the *shōgunate* (of Hōjō), as well as the growing economic problems it caused, and the lack of innovative methods to comprehensively solve them, led to the collapse of the Kamakura *Bakufu*.

During the Kamakura period, the possibility of applying previously selected corporate governance theories can be considered. The Resource Dependency Theory (RDT) emphasizes the strength and tactics available to organizations. As noted earlier, the state built internal and external social, institutional, and industrial environment networks to obtain synergy effects, influencing its solidarity, relationships, and integrity. During the Kamakura era, there was a diarchy as there were two centres of power in the country – Kyōto where the emperor and the court resided, and Kamakura, where the *shōgun* and his government was based. The administration headed by the emperor and his court followed the *ritsuryō* regulations, while the *shōgun* and his government used the *bakufu* laws. Emperors and *shōguns* sought to gain greater power in the dyarchy, but *shōguns* also had to take care of increasing their legitimacy, respect, and cooperation with the emperor. Power conditioned the acquisition of wealth, which is why the aristocracy, headed by the emperor, strived for development and implementation of strategies that would ensure synergy effects and maximize their income. The warrior government had the same goals. Thus, both parties were striving for the resources. Strong and well-organized governance was essential for achieving that purpose. The interests of the court and *bakufu* were initially

DOI: 10.4324/9781003497936-12

compatible. The emperor and *shōgun* were the sources of titles, positions, and associated income for the aristocracy and *samurai* who served them, so opposing them could result, as previously stated, in the loss of all these privileges, and therefore resources for which all classes competed. The imperial court and the *bakufu* competed against each other in many respects but they acted jointly in maintaining the *shiki* structure. In the manorial system, this meant privileges to acquire rents, accompanied by specific delegated duties. Relational (friendly) capital was important in the Kamakura period. However, it turned out that the resources the state had were not sufficient to meet the needs of the *samurai*, which were seriously undermined by the costs incurred in repelling the Mongol invasion and the subsequent long period of maintaining defensive readiness. The ruling elites were not ready to introduce new solutions in the economy, driven by selfish motives and fear of changing social relations established for centuries. Counteracting the reduction of their resources by those in power was the cause of the collapse not only of the *ritsuryō* system but also of the governance system created by the Kamakura *Bakufu*. The struggle for power turned into a rivalry between the aristocracy, which brought about war within the state and a dual monarchy. The courts were reintegrated after evaluating the total benefits and costs of the duality and enabled the equal access to the resources by both sides of the conflict. This led finally to the recreation of a strong military supervisory and control system in Japan.

The Managerial and Class Hegemony Theory (MCHT) also concerns the Kamakura period. It sees corporate governance as a political process. The Kamakura *Shōgunate* was organized in accordance with the earlier practice of glorifying the imperial family, being the symbol of supreme power in the country, while the real power was exercised from behind the throne. This was the specificity of mutually beneficial relations between the developing feudal system and the old monarchical system, defined in written legal codes. The Kamakura period shows that the monarch's self-perception varied over time, affecting the government (board) and the court behaviour and performance. The very complicated governance system at this time (the existence of emperors, cloistered and retired emperors, regents, *shōguns*, and *shōgunal* regents) could operate effectively only when exercised by strong men in top posts. Minamoto Yoritomo was such a person, but after his death, the system was fluctuating depending on its main actors. Therefore, the relationship between the court and the *bakufu* changed over time, ultimately leading to wars for hegemony (Wars between the Courts). Some monarchs wanted to gain real power and become hegemons (Go-Daigo and the short Kenmu Restoration), while others had no such ambitions. The rivalry for power with the Ashikaga *Shōguns* finally turned into a disaster for the country. Appointments at the highest level had to be in line with the requirements of the elite or class. Weak *shōguns*, unable to maintain powerful administration, could be blamed for the fall of the Kamakura *Bakufu*. *Shōguns* took on great responsibilities, perhaps too great, but because of the existing system of wealth division, the *bakufu* lost hegemony and failed.

In the Kamakura period, as in the *Ritsuryō* State, religion was an important factor in gaining hegemony and political consolidation. Monasteries became important centres, much involved in power struggles, politics, and wars. The aristocracy still perceived itself as an elite group with divine roots, to whom all privileges, the highest positions, and honours were due. They confirmed it by law, which together with intrigues, and the use of force, allowed for their domination in the organization and rule of the state. The nobility was determined not only to sustain their position and rights to preferences but also to ensure that they stayed with the strict class structure. This was done by the methods best adapted to the state of the economy and external and internal political pressures, in order to assert their dominance and gain wealth. An effective system of motivation was retained and exercised by the emperor (source of titles and positions), stimulating struggles for power and personal benefits within the court aristocracy. To dominate the court and the emperor was most important for powerful families and their heads. They sought to dominate the government (board), weak emperors, and *shōguns*, and were ready to achieve their goals through agreements (contracts) or force. Their ambitions and jealousies sparked bloody wars. Their disappointment often dictated the policy of the country. The main aim of their activity was maximization of benefits, based on birth privileges, which in turn were inevitable in gaining state positions and estates. The fierce competition for hegemony existed between the powerful families for centuries, on macro and micro levels; however, the families changed.

During the Kamakura period, the state was under a well-organized system of vertical governance and control by the *bakufu*. The *shugo–jitō* system worked well, and was efficient and effective in keeping peace in the country. A new police carefully watched all events and activities, especially those of land ownership and tax avoidance. It had the right to deal with the security matters and investigate crimes and arrest suspects. This system was very efficient in preserving the hegemony of the ruling person – *shōgun*.

As noted earlier, according to the Theory of Social Networks (TSN), those involved in corporate governance processes are linked through networks. Maximizing position and interests of the members of the networks are the main reasons for creating them. This was also the goal of the networks created within the Kamakura *Bakufu*. They were invaluable in achieving the group's strategic aims. Social networks and their subnetworks had a significant impact on the goals and independence of its governance system. Their identification and monitoring enabled insight into the essence and quality of various aspects of the governance system and the most important bodies and factors influencing it. Leaders played a key role in the networks, especially those who were able to successfully connect them with the strategic environment of the state and province. Network leaders should also ensure that networks are kept united, rich and content, able to compete and defend their own interests, and placed in appropriate network structures.

There were two main networks in the Kamakura *Bakufu* – the network organized by *shōgun* and the network headed by the emperor. The power of emperor was supported by the system of granting titles and rewards. As far as the network of aristocracy is concerned, its political power was ambiguous. In Kyōto, a titular emperor handed over power to regent, who often yielded to the authority of the cloistered emperor. All royal factions in Kyōto were controlled by the *shōgun*, who together with his network ruled Japan. Thus, the two networks coexisted well until Yoritomo's death in 1199 when the fight for supremacy started between the Kamakura *Bakufu* and the imperial court in Kyōto. In consequence, the military network proved to be more powerful and *shōgunate* achieved complete control over Japan and determined the succession to the positions of titular and cloistered emperor. However, after Yoritomo's death, *shōguns* became dominated by the Hōjō regents.

Under the *shōen–kokugaryō* system of landholding, the central civil aristocracy, temples, and shrines held huge public lands (*kokugaryō*) and private estates (*shōen*) in various provinces and wielded power comparable to that of the *bakufu*. They organized their own networks and determined relations between them, both internally and externally. Under this system, the multi-layered *shiki* formed the basis of positions and of rights for the higher-level and the lower-level proprietary lords in *shōen* and in *kokugaryō*. Among the highest-level proprietary lords, there was one who held the most important rights of proprietary lordship. The absentee owners were dependent on managers eager to maximize their own interests. The *shōen–kokugaryō* estates were managed by influential resident landlords, officials of the provincial government, or agents of the *shōen* who often were or became warriors. This pattern of governance, in which each level of administration of these agriculture enterprises was oriented towards maximization of own benefits, was responsible for the failure of the *shōen* system.

Under the *shōen–kokugaryō* system, persons receiving *shiki* had an obligation to provide a fixed amount of rice tax and *corvée* to the upper-level nobles who granted the *shiki*. Although the *shiki* did not claim ownership of the land, certain rights were transferred from the superior to the subordinate. The holder of the *shiki* did not directly exercise military and police power over the population, but relied on the central authority, that is, the imperial court in Kyōto or the Kamakura *Bakufu*.

A very effective network and a governance structure was created by *shōgun* Yoritomo called *shugo–jitō* system, subordinated to the *bakufu*. The *shōgun* nominated *shugo* or constables (the estate managers had been appointees of the owners) and subordinated to them military land stewards (*jitō*) in both public and private estates in each province in the country. They were self-supporting personal retainers of the *shōgun*, directly responsible to him. They sometimes doubled as the civil governors of the province. To control the system, Yoritomo appointed himself the Constable General. In this way, he was able to govern (and spread his power throughout Japan) without replacing the *ritsuryō* administration set up during the Heian period. The *shugo–jitō* network was not to replace imperial local administration but to supplement it. It was important, because it provided the *shōgun with* a network of provincial connections which stretched across the country and gave it national character.[1] For years, the *bakufu* ruled Japan efficiently and ably and was able to keep peace in provinces and Kyōto, bringing several decades of peace and economic expansion to Japan.

The *samurai* formed their own solid multifunctional network. The offices of steward (*jitō*) and constable (*shugo*) soon became hereditary, lucrative posts, combining both civil and military authorities. *Shugo* administered the provinces under their charge on the basis of local custom and the military House laws. He held regional political power, maintained public order and peace, while on their property, they performed functions of the local government and magistrate. The duties of these constables (*shugo*) included supervising stewards, appointing vassals to guard service, recruiting metropolitan guards, keeping strict control over subversives and criminals, keeping law and order in their provinces, and commanding the local retainers in wartime. They supervised collection of dues for the *bakufu* and were entitled to keep a part of produce for themselves. Initially, the legal remuneration of the *jitō* along with other privileges was defined as 1/11 of the income from the land under their jurisdiction, but it was later increased.[2]

Shugo passed on to *jitō* the military instructions he received from Kamakura. He was a marshal of all the *jitō* within the province and unified the decentralized system of governors. They were loyal agents of the *shōgun* and an important link in the governance system created by the *bakufu*. *Jitō*, the second link of the governance system, was responsible for supervision of individual estates collecting taxes on behalf of the *bakufu*. There was no vassalage relationship between *shugo* and the *jitō* under the military jurisdiction. The *jitō* remained the direct vassals of the Kamakura *Shōgunate* and were subordinated to the *shugo* only regarding the military organization. Stewards became important in provincial society in the late 12th century, rewarded with *shiki*, formalized through an appointment sanctioned by the central government.[3] They supervised the proper distribution of the shares of the crop, including those belonging to the owner. Warrior landlords lived in farming villages and supervised peasant labour or carried out agricultural tasks themselves. The *shōgun*'s vassals gained positions of authority all over the country. Constables and stewards controlled the provinces and public and private estates tightly and loyally and the *shugo–jitō* system worked well for a long time, not only to control the countryside and raise revenue for the *bakufu* but, in combination with the idea of vassalage, also to form the military network of *shōgun* and his retainers.[4] The presented network structures allow to appreciate the rationality of governance and the advancement of the implemented control instruments and supervisory mechanisms. Three more networks can be distinguished in the Kamakura period, the network of merchants and artisans, the village network, and the network of powerful temples and shrines.

The relationship between emperor and *shōgun* may also be considered in the light of the Stewardship Theory. The *shōgun* took responsibility for the security and prosperity of the country, which he ruled in the emperor's name. The duties of the divine emperor were limited to performing the religious ceremonies and rituals, nominating *shōgun*, and to granting titles and offices. The *shōgun* still derived his authority from the emperor, and the *bakufu* was the military force of the imperial government. The emperor's authority remained supreme because it was necessary for establishing the position of *shōgun*, who by such nomination was acquiring the divine-given legitimacy of his authority. However, in Kamakura period, the leaders of the diarchy became rivals changing the stewardship relation into a rivalry for hegemony.

Shugo as well as *jitō* can be regarded as stewards of the *shōgun*. They owed loyalty to the *shōgun*, for whom they performed public service. In return, the *shōgun* not only guaranteed them security of tenure in their landholdings but rewarded them with new lands and privileges. Loyalty supported by mutual benefits underpinned by the Confucian ideology was the basis for creating the stewardship relations and the feudal system during the Kamakura period. The relationships between social classes and their leaders can be considered in the light of not only Network and Stewardship Theories but also Agency Theory.

The Agency Theory may be used to characterize the principal–agent relations in the Kamakura period. This relatively peaceful period was full of intrigues (conflicts of interest) among the elites, especially during the time of indirect rule of both, the emperor and the *shōgun*. The conflicts of interest had a national, local, and family dimension.

The first group of agency conflicts can be considered in three aspects: the relationship between the emperor and the *shōgun*, the relations between the emperor and the court, and the relationship between the *shōgun* and his subordinates. The main conflict was between the emperor (principal) and the *shōgun* (agent) and had its basis in the struggle for power. The intensity of the agency conflict between these two principals varied throughout the Kamakura era and depended on their personality and power of the networks organized by them. Conflicts were resolved by agreeing on contracts reconciling the interests of both networks, but sometimes broken agreements were resolved through armed fighting. The war between the two dynasties was an example of the impossibility of solving a serious problem peacefully, which ultimately ended in an agreement. It gave victory to warriors who again dominated the court and took control of the country.

The second conflict of interests existed within the court headed by the emperor. As before, this balance of power depended on the personality of the emperor. Strong emperors could manage the court effectively and solve ably emerging conflicts. But rarely they were. Conflicts of interests existed between emperors having nominal power, and the cloistered emperors having real power, their henchmen, as well as between powerful regents, spouses, and families influencing decisions and authority of the emperor. The emperor's power, except divinity, was based on granting titles and rewards; thus, insubordination towards a powerful or dominated monarch could be very costly for the offender. But only an emperor (or his *guardian*) having a strong personality and independence was likely to run into conflicts with aristocrats or members of his own family. Court aristocrats functioned in a very competitive environment, requiring high diplomatic skills, gaining strong partners, and using the weaknesses of opponents, and were able to use own position, power, and influence. Conflicts within this group were sometimes resolved by military actions.

The emperor was the owner of the land that was under strict control. Land, at first, was governed, and then owned by officials nominated by emperor (principal), so there existed separation of ownership and control. The separation concerned also the lower tiers in the hierarchy structure. Under the *shōen* and *shōen-koguaro* systems, the absentee owners–aristocrats had to rely on their agents to manage their propriety and get benefits. These agents were high status and qualified managers, responsible for the production process, who wanted to maximize their own interests. The aristocrats, to secure and increase their revenues, had to establish a proper governance and incentive systems, put their interests in line with the interests of the managers of their lands; however, this turned out to be impossible in practice. There were also serious conflicts of interest between the courtiers and the religious institutions, competing for the revenues and privileges. They competed for top positions, expanding their estates by opening new rice fields, obtaining tax exemptions, and strengthening the power of their institutions. The monks formed strong military groups that expanded their wealth and protected their interests through connections at court or armed fighting. In addition to great wealth, they possessed great political power which enabled them to interfere in the affairs of the state.

Another conflict of interest emerged between the Kamakura appointees and nobles residing in provinces and districts, who had managed to build up their power and wealth by using knowledge of agriculture, good management, financial planning, loopholes in law, as well as nepotism. It became the most heated conflict in the economic realm. The power and prestige of the provincial and local landowners increased, because growing wealthier, they were more capable of defending their property and privileges by force. The rule of internalizing problems in organization was still used, and local separatism started to be promoted, causing that the authority of central government declined, the strong, unified state started to shatter, and the wars for power began.

The third area of conflicts of interest concerned *bakufu*, in which the power of the *shōgun* began to be limited by his regent. The system *shugo–jitō* worked well enabling keeping Japan in peace. Initially, there was no conflict of interest between the *shōgun* and his retainers, as their relationship was based on loyalty (father–sons), and the *shōgun*'s authority built on leadership skills and, above all, military experience gained in wars and battles. Then, military rulers who did not meet high standards in the art of war lost prestige. Over time, the conflict between the *bakufu* and its subordinates increased. Its main source was the disappointment of the *samurai*, who not only suffered from low incomes but also did not receive adequate financial compensation for their expenses and war service during the period of the Mongol invasion and the alert years. The *Shōgunate* could not meet their expectations because there were no new lands and war gains to divide among the warriors. To mollify this conflict of interest, and *to* improve the financial situation of *shōgun's* direct retainers (*gokenin*) the *bakufu* passed the law of *virtuous administration* (*tokusei*), a general cancellation of debts and mortgages owed by the retainers to those outside their class. This caused another conflict of interest, between the *samurai* and merchants.

There were conflicts between central proprietors (usually a local representative of the proprietor) and the *jitō*. The *shōgunate* officials interfered with the collection of taxes, claimed larger portions of private estate produce than they were entitled to, and disrupted the flow of tribute from the provinces to centrally based nobles and temples. Landowners also wanted to retain as much control and income as possible, which led to conflicts of interest with the *jitō*. Both sides, to achieve their aims, had to employ loyal agents, able to guard their interests, and maximize their revenues, tradition, and law guarded their activities.

It is also worth paying attention to the conflicts between *samurai* and peasants. They occurred primarily between managers at various levels (*jitō, mioshu, tato*) and peasants and resulted mainly from the desire to increase their position and economic autonomy, as well as to enlarge their farms. The victims of the selfish behaviour of state and local officials were usually taxpayers, peasants cultivating fields, and craftsmen.

Characteristics of corporate governance in Kamakura *Bakufu*

Literature analysis can be helpful in identifying factors that may be responsible for the specificity of current Japanese corporate governance. Some of them may be traced back to the Kamakura period. They can be divided into factors occurring at the macro and micro levels.[5]

As far as the macro dimension is concerned, an important driving force for corporate governance development was entrepreneurship. The development of entrepreneurship resulted from the increase in land productivity, the implementation of innovations, and the ability to produce high-quality products, which enabled farmers to obtain additional income, motivating them to take up new challenges. It required diligence (lack of it was punished), ingenuity, and courage to undertake new, difficult tasks, as well as the ability to take advantage of opportunities. Subject to thorough control, taxpayers, peasants cultivating fields, craftsmen, merchants, and *shōen* managers were able to use the tax optimization methods available to them. Everyone was expected to respect superiors, the law, and fulfil professional, personal, and family responsibilities to the best of their ability. This resulted in the development of specific character traits of the Japanese that have survived to this day, also shaping relationships in the area of corporate governance.

An important feature of the Japanese is respect for the law. The Kamakura *Bakufu* placed great importance on administering justice in court cases and gained a reputation for honesty.

Conflicts of interest were resolved by law, which defined contractual relationships, personal relationships, and obligations to the state and its officials, and vice versa. During the Kamakura period, the nobles and temples could appeal to the *bakufu*, if their rights were violated by *samurai*, or to the emperor, if the offenders were aristocrats or temples. Those entitled to receive *shiki* had the opportunity to seek redress in court and to ask the *bakufu* to enforce their rights if they were violated. The Board of Inquiry (*monchujo*) served as an appellate court of final jurisdiction in the administration of customary family law, providing a link between Kamakura and the court in Kyōto. It took care of documentary evidence and earned a reputation for administering just sentences. Courts functioned as committees, giving unanimous public decisions, and bearing the responsibility collectively. Unanimity is the rule in decision-making, as the Japanese still prefer anonymity and demonstrate the ability to make collective decisions. The system of severe punishments was also important for keeping order and rule of law. All were aware that breaking the law incurred severe penalties. The old practice of mutual responsibility of the family and the village for its members was reinforced. This contributed to the expansion of cooperation, self-governance, and control in social groups, as well as joint solving of internal problems and aversion to outsiders. These features are reflected to some extent in contemporary Japanese corporate governance.

Other factors responsible for the specificity of the current Japanese corporate governance include a strong group identity – with family and community, the ability to cooperate and organize teamwork, self-sacrifice, respect for superiors, and education. Loyalty, duty of care, submission, responsibility, obedience, respect for elders, and preventing the decline of morality and discipline have been important to the Japanese for centuries, since before the introduction of Confucianism. Other characteristics are internalization of problems, unity against outsiders, respect for law and recognition of social differences, and social-class separation. The analysis of the literature allows us to conclude that many customs and rules developed during the *Ritsuryō* State were preserved and developed in the regulations and practices of the Kamakura *Bakufu*. Thus, values derived from the Yamato period, confirmed or developed over subsequent eras, continue to be important features of Japanese corporate governance.

It can be assumed that during the Kamakura period, the concept of family functioned at different levels, since the state, *shōen*, village, city, and its lower structures can be treated as families of different sizes and powers. Power was concentrated in the head of the house to whom other family members were subordinated. Families were run as businesses (corporations) having own aims, assets, and obligations. Families competed with each other to acquire more property, titles, positions, rights, power, and other privileges. If inappropriate decisions were made, family members were punished, excluded, or deprived of certain benefits by the head of the family or the family council. Any actions detrimental to the family were severely punished. A poorly governed family (business) went bankrupt, which meant loss of property, position, demotion, or even liquidation. Family was, and still is, very important in Japan, in both macro and micro aspects. Its concept still operates in Japanese corporations, influencing the shape of Japanese corporate governance.

The Japanese have developed a great ability to hybridize at both the state (macro) and individual (farm) levels. The foreign ideas that were similar, understandable, or useful to Japanese society persisted, those not suitable or impractical, lost their importance and ceased to exist. Hybridization built Japanese civilization and continued to be a very important feature of corporate governance in the *Ritsuryō* State and in all subsequent eras, despite the exceptional respect of the Japanese for their own tradition and culture, especially shown in the Heian period. It was successfully used in creating the political system of the feudal Japan, in establishing administrative structures of the central government, and a strict governance system which acquired distinctively Japanese form. The centuries-old ability to adopt innovations, legal principles, and apply procedures and processes in unique ways[6] continues to play a very important role in shaping Japanese corporate governance.

It should be noted that from the very beginning of their existence, Japanese governments, leaders, and landowners were guided by the ideas of social responsibility, particularly appreciating the importance of ethical principles. At least since the 6th century, values such as obedience, stewardship, and responsibility for the proper use of resources were implemented. There was even a type of whistle-blowing in the form of a *complaint box*, which was installed at the palace gate to give people the opportunity to complain or report irregularities directly to the emperor. Perhaps, shared responsibility for breaking the law can be treated as an inspiration for the whistle-blowing.

At the micro level of governance, *shōen* played a key role in the economy and society of medieval Japan. They were not controlled politically and economically, closed and independent entities that existed within the framework of the national political authority which empowered the *shiki* structure.[7] They produced much of the material wealth that sustained all levels and groups of society and satisfied even the refined needs of consumers of their goods. They were created to organize, protect, and expand property and highly specialized production, but above all,. to increase efficiency and profitability in order to enrich their stakeholders. An important tool for achieving benefits was tax exemptions, the scope of which depended on the strength and attitude of the person heading the *shōen*. Even in ancient times, Japanese were good at economizing and calculating costs and benefits. They constantly improved efficiency of their corporations (*be*, families, *shōen*) and understood importance of learning to become best. *Shōen* functioned as large corporations that were *the nexus of contracts*. They were well managed, specialized, and efficient. In the 12th century, they were centres of production, headquarters of managers and trade networks, places of development of agricultural technology, and centres of religious practices and rituals, influencing all institutions and social classes throughout Japan.[8] It can be assumed that *shōen* provided evidence of the existence of corporate governance in the Nara, Heian, and Kamakura periods. During the Kamakura period, villages became self-governing units, with their own headmen and subordinate officials, subject to the supervision of owners and civil and military officials. Villages, functioning as well-organized corporations, gained a new awareness as unified communities, to which social and economic changes have contributed.

During the Kamakura period, there was a well-organized dual system of supervision consisting of a civilian and military component. Hérail writes that a system of strict governance was established and strengthened by provincial governors (*kokushi*), who managed local affairs as they saw fit, but under state supervision. As noted earlier, the governor's mission was to supervise the cult of deities, register the population, act as a father to the people, foster agriculture and sericulture, rectify wrongs, supervise the police and hear grievances, register households and rice fields, impose taxes and corvée labour, maintain irrigation systems, public buildings, and pastures, and ensure that the province was able to defend itself by means of militias, arms, and signal fires. They were obliged to control all aspect of life of the population under their control. In the mid-to-late Heian period, *zuryō* were appointed to perform administrative functions in the provinces, while their governors (*kokushi*) remained in the capital. Thus, the separation of ownership and control was sanctioned. He took over the management of the province, its people and public goods from his predecessor. Only *zuryō* was responsible for managing the province, its property and taxes.[9] Using his influence, *zuryō* was able to amass great wealth. Many of the successful *zuryō* settled in their designated province after their term ended. It was found that they were more law-abiding than the wealthy *fumyo tato*, who kept many servants, managed large farms, and had many private warriors and pursued their own interests.[10] Hérail writes that

> the . . . formal duties performed by a zuryō on arrival in his province were listed in forty-two articles written prior to 1132. The duties were grouped into three sections. The first concerned the journey, arrival in the province, the choice of auspicious days for leaving the capital, crossing the border, moving into the residence, and beginning work. The second section concerned the transfer of powers as the outgoing governor had waited for his successor. The new governor had to check the records, inspect the storehouses to confirm that their contents was compatible with the registers, and make a general assessment of his predecessor's management to avoid being held responsible for any of . . . shortages. The third section described conduct befitting a good governor: he should be knowledgeable of his subordinates' abilities, keep

distance, be frugal, and make a good choice for his *mokudai* (his right-hand man and replacement during his absences); he should not use *rōdō* of the fifth rank, but should have on his staff men who write a good hand, an efficacious monk, and one or two good warriors – this last in spite of the fact that a good governor (ryōri) ordinarily need not resort to force.[11]

These recommendations were rather general and did not specify provincial governance. According to Hérail, the *zuryō*'s duties included responding to the situation, maintaining order, and satisfying the court with submitted taxes, reports, and records. He was obliged to avoid conflicts with the population of his own province, neighbouring provinces, with other governors and local elites, as well as with religious institutions. When leaving office, the governor, in order to avoid future disputes, had to agree with his successor on the possible financing of necessary repairs of damaged property and outstanding arrears. In case of difficulties in completing the administrative formalities related to the transition, such as disagreement, the death of the predecessor, his renunciation of Buddhism, or his premature return to the capital, the new governor called the inspector responsible for the transition (*kōtaishi*), who prepared a record of the process. A discharge document (*geyujō*) had to be signed by the departing and the incoming *zuryō*. This document could not be drafted unless the public and religious buildings were in satisfactory condition, the permanent rice reserves were full, receipts were presented to show that all fiscal obligations had been met, and the attesting registers had been audited and approved. Only then, the outgoing governor could return to the capital. This situation never occurred because the outgoing governor was not able to settle all matters within 120 days, after which he could not remain in the province. Therefore, both of them confirmed the debt of the outgoing governor and signed a document in which they stated the reasons for not delivering the discharge document (*fuyogeyujō*). In urgent cases, the new governor granted his predecessor a pro forma discharge, so that he could return to the capital before assessing the situation in the province. This was performed later in the capital, using written documents. An outgoing *zuryō* was able to return to Heiankyō by means of a document in lieu of discharge.[12] The second area of implementation of good governance and supervision was the previously described system that could be called military, namely the *shugo–jitō* system built and supervised by the *bakufu*.

This short summary indicates that the state and its matters were formally under a highly sophisticated, well-organized system of vertical governance and control in the Kamakura *Bakufu*. The existing tax system was undergoing changes in line with the situation of the social groups, and tax optimization was used, as well as strict control and external and internal audits. It can therefore be concluded that internal and external corporate governance mechanisms were used during this period. Despite this, the Kamakura *Bakufu* fell. The reasons for this failure can be found in weak leaders who were unable to effectively manage the state and achieve hegemony, but above all, in the weaknesses of the economic and social system, which rejected new solutions and strived to preserve old customs and principles (the predominance of conservatism over innovation).

Notes

1 J. W. Hall, Feudalism in Japan: A Reassessment. *Comparative Studies in Society and History* 1962, Vol. 5, No. 1, pp. 15–51.
2 J. Tubilewicz, Historia Japonii. *Zakład Narodowy Imienia Ossolińskich*, Wrocław 1984, p. 16.
3 J. W. Hall, Feudalism in Japan: A Reassessment . . . op. cit.
4 J. P. Mass, The Kamakura *bakufu*. In: K. Yamamura (ed.), The Cambridge History of Japan: Medieval Japan. Vol. 3. *Cambridge University Press*, Cambridge 2008, pp. 80–87.
5 K. Rost, Introduction to the Corporate Governance of Religion. The Zurich Open Repository and Archive. *University of Zurich*, Zurich 2017.
6 J. McEldowney, Hybridization: A Study in Comparative Constitutional Law. *Penn State International Law Review* 2010, Vol. 28, No. 3, Article 5, pp. 355–376.
7 K. Nagahara, Landownership Under the Shōen-Kokugaryō System. *Journal of Japanese Studies* 1975, Vol. 1, No. 2, pp. 269–296. *JSTOR*. www.jstor.org/stable/132127.
8 J. R. Goodwin, J. N. Piggott (eds.), Land, Power, and the Sacred: The Estate System in Medieval Japan. *University of Hawaii Press*, Honolulu 2018, p. 446.
9 F. Hérail, The Position and Role of Provincial Governors at the Height of the Heian Period. *French Journal of Japanese Studies* 2014, No. 3.
10 www.japanesewiki.com/history/Zuryo%20(The%20Head%20of%20The%20Provincial%20Governors).
11 F. Hérail, The Position and Role of Provincial Governors . . . op. cit.
12 Ibidem.

Bibliography

Goodwin, J. R., Piggott, J. N. (eds.), Land, Power, and the Sacred: The Estate System in Medieval Japan, *University of Hawaii Press*, Honolulu 2018.

Hall, J. W., Feudalism in Japan: A Reassessment. *Comparative Studies in Society and History* 1962, Vol. 5, No. 1, pp. 15–51. *JSTOR*. www.jstor.org/stable/177767.

Hérail, F., The Position and Role of Provincial Governors at the Height of the Heian Period. *French Journal of Japanese Studies* 2014, No. 3. https://journals.openedition.org/cjs/658.

www.japanesewiki.com/history/Zuryo%20(The%20Head%20of%20The%20Provincial%20Governors).

McEldowney, J., Hybridization: A Study in Comparative Constitutional Law. *Penn State International Law Review* 2010, Vol. 28, No. 3, Article 5, pp. 355–376. http://elibrary.law.psu.edu/psilr/vol28/iss3/5.

Nagahara, K., Landownership Under the Shōen-Kokugaryō System. *Journal of Japanese Studies* 1975, Vol. 1, No. 2, pp. 269–296. *JSTOR*. www.jstor.org/stable/132127.

www.researchgate.net/deref/https%3A%2F%2Fdoi.org%2F10.5167%2Fuzh-133251?_tp=eyJjb250ZXh0Ijp7ImZpcnN0UGFnZSI6InB1YmxpY2F0aW9uIiwicGFnZSI6InB1YmxpY2F0aW9uIiwicG9zaXRpb24iOiJwYWdlQ29udGVudCJ9fQ.
Rost, K., Introduction to the Corporate Governance of Religion. The Zurich Open Repository and Archive. *University of Zurich*, Zurich 2017.
Tubilewicz, J., Historia Japonii. *Zakład Narodowy Imienia Ossolińskich*, Wrocław 1984.
Yamamura, K. (ed.), The Cambridge History of Japan. In: Medieval Japan, Vol. 3. *Cambridge University Press*, Cambridge 2008.

Part 4

Corporate governance developments in the Ashikaga *Shōgunate* (1338–1573) and the Azuchi–Momoyama era (1573–1603)

10 Characteristics of the Muromachi (the Ashikaga *Shōgunate*) era and the Azuchi–Momoyama era (1573–1603)

The most important events in the Muromachi era (1336–1573)

The Kamakura *Shōgunate* broke down in the year 1334 after 140 years of rule. After a three-year interregnum known as the Kemmu Restoration (1333–1336), during which Emperor Go-Daigo unsuccessfully attempted to restore imperial power, the Ashikaga period of Japanese history began. Another name for this era is the Muromachi Period (1338–1573), named after the Kyōto district where Yoshimitsu, the best Ashikaga *Shōgun*, had his residence. This period ends with the Sengoku or Warring States era, a 100-year period of constant civil wars and turmoil, that began with the Ōnin War (1467–1477). The war originated in the quarrel about the succession to the *Shōgunate* between the son and the adopted son (the younger brother) of the *shōgun* Yoshimasa.[1] The Sengoku period was a long and devastating struggle for the *daimyō* for their own interests and domination in the country. Japan was divided into several semi-independent territories, each of which had a *shugo* at its head. The Ōnin War ended Ashikaga rule, although the Ashikaga *Shōgunate* formally existed until 1573, when the powerful *daimyō* Oda Nobunaga overthrew Yoshaki, the 15th and last Ashikaga *Shōgun*.[2] In this way, the Azuchi–Momoyama period, also called the Momoyama period (1574–1600) began and lasted until Tokugawa Ieyasu's victory at the Battle of Sekigahara in 1600. It took its name from the castles (headquarters) of Nobunaga and Hideyoshi, both located near Kyōto. The Azuchi–Momoyama era is a period of difficult unification of Japan, which led to the re-emergence of a centralized and strong state.

The Muromachi Period began when there were two competing Imperial courts – the Southern Court of Go-Daigo at the Yoshino Mountains, and the Northern Court in Kyōto.[3] From 1336 to 1392, the Ashikaga *Shōgunate* representing the Northern Imperial Court fought against the Southern Imperial Court and won. The winner, Ashikaga Takayuki, established a *bakufu* in Kyōto. His grandson, *shōgun* Yoshimitsu, moved its headquarters to the Muromachi district in Kyōto (1378), where the *shōgunate* took its final shape. The Muromachi district where the government buildings were located gave the government and

DOI: 10.4324/9781003497936-14

the historical period their names. According to Hara, the greatest advantages of moving the seat of the *shōgunate* to Kyōto were the proximity of the centre of civilization and the seat of the southern dynasty, the political concentration of the empire, and the fact that Kyōto was closer to the main supporters of Ashikaga than Kamakura.[4] At that time, the political situation in Japan was unstable as warriors who had pledged loyalty to the Southern Court wanted to retake Kyōto and install Go-Daigo as emperor. Ashikaga *Shōguns* sought to eliminate the risk of a coup by attack and were determined to defend Kyōto, which had become a trading city by the 1330s.[5] This situation existed for many decades in the Muromachi *Bakufu*. The Muromachi period is one of the most difficult eras in Japanese history, which can be called a period of opposites. As usual, strong and weak *shōguns* ruled the country, but in the Muromachi *Bakufu*, the latter dominated. They were unable to gain authority because neither their family's martial traditions, nor war gains, nor personal advantages, nor did they have the means to buy loyalty of the *samurai*. It was a period when the country suffered from internal wars, plagues, natural disasters, and the greed of the rulers, but it was also a time of construction of the greatest architectural monuments, cultural development, and luxurious life for the elite. It was a period of destruction of weaker families and building of power by the most ambitious and cunning clan leaders. It was a period of economic development and limiting the factors of its development, creating and enforcing state law, but also bypassing it and introducing their own law by the most powerful families and classes. However, the ambitions of great families (clans) led to the creation of the Ashikaga Shōgunate and also caused its fall.

The Ashikaga *Shōguns* exercised politically legitimized power derived from the bureaucratic authority of the *ritsuryō* agrarian model, the patrimonial authority of the Kamakura feudal model, and the aristocratic power of the imperial *kuge* tradition. Thus, these three elements, bureaucratic, feudal, and aristocratic, formed the basis for the *bakufu* founded by Ashikaga Takauji in 1336.[6]

The most successful of all the Ashikaga *Shōguns* was Yoshimitsu (*shōgun* – 1368–94 and prime minister (chancellor) – 1394–1408) who was able to introduce some order in the country devastated by civil war fought between the two courts. He managed to unite these two courts in 1392, ending the conflict that had lasted for over 50 years (1336–1392). The Southern line was promised an alternating succession with the Northern line. Therefore, in 1393, the southern ruler Gokameyama voluntarily renounced his claim to the throne and handed over the insignia to his northern rival, uniting the two dynasties and agreeing that Gokomatsu would be the 100th Emperor of Japan.[7] During the rule of *shōgun* Yoshimitsu, and his four strong and able successors, there was relative peace in the Empire, and the Muromachi *Bakufu* they governed ran well and smoothly.[8]

The real winners of the unification were the courtiers. The long civil war made them realize that they were unable to overthrow the military regime, already well established, and that it was more beneficial for them to make use of this military power, than to act against it. Accordingly, courtiers obtaining income from their manors freed themselves from all problems related to maintaining real state power. They transferred all problems related to state and military affairs to the *shōgunate*, which believed that it was its duty to take care of the interests of the courtiers with all its military power. Therefore, the grateful court awarded subsequent Ashikaga *Shōguns* honorary titles, much higher than those held by the Kamakura *shōguns*, and they were given special respect in the imperial palace. Personal ambition and individual aggrandizement were the ruling motives of the time.[9] The increase in the rank of *shōgun's* court meant that his subordinates began to compete for official ranks and distinctions in the hierarchical scale of courtiers.[10]

The Ashikaga *Shōguns* adopted the proven structure of the Kamakura *Bakufu* with only minor changes. In 1336, Ashikaga Takauji, after overthrowing the Kamakura (Hojo) *shōgunate*, issued the Kenmu Code (*Kenmu Shikimoku*) to supplement the Hōjō Code, considered the basic law of warriors. It contained the governing philosophy of the warrior government and became an important feudal legislation. *Kenmu Shikimoku*, based on 17 articles of the constitution of Prince Shōtoku, together with the code of conduct of *samurai* from the Kamakura era (*Gosseibai-shikimoku*) were called the Joken Codes. Murdoch writes that it also included 17 articles. The first four stated that

> Economy must be universally practised; Drinking parties and wanton frolics must be suppressed; Crimes of violence and outrage must be quelled; The practice of entering the private dwellings of the people and making inquisitions into their affairs must be given up.

Articles 5 and 6 dealt with the ownership of vacant plots and the re-building of houses and fire-proof godowns in the devastated sections of the capital. The following paragraphs provide that

> (7) Men of special ability for government work should be chosen for the office of shugo; (8) A stop must be put to the practice of influential nobles and women of all sorts and Buddhist ecclesiastics making their interested recommendations (to the sovereign); (9) Persons holding public posts must be liable to reprimand for negligence and idleness; (10) Bribery must be firmly put down; (11) Presents made from all quarters to those attached to the Palace whether of the Inside or Outside services must be sent back; and (12) Those who are to be in personal attendance on the rulers must be selected for that duty. Ceremonial etiquette to be the predominant principle; Men noted for probity and adherence to high principle to be rewarded by more than ordinary distinction; The petitions and complaints of the poor and lowly to be heard and redress granted; The petitions of Temples and Shrines to be dealt with on

their merits; Certain fixed days to be appointed for the rendering of decisions and the issue of government orders.[11]

This Feudal Code was the last of the important written documents that preceded the Tokugawa law.[12] By 1430, some 208 articles had been added to this by the Ashikaga *Shōguns* or their ministers. However, the great difference between the Kyoto and Kamakura legislation was that the Kamakura *Shōgunate* issued relatively few laws, but these were rigorously enforced in *bakufu* domains. However, the Kyoto *Shōgunate* issued many laws, most of which were violated more often than obeyed. Actions taken in the 1370s to enforce the law strictly, rigorously, and impartially were met with great reluctance by individuals and classes who had no interest in following it.[13] This was a consequence of the difficult situation of the *shōgun*, who for many years fought with great difficulty and consistency against the selfish actions of large clans, building his authority and the position of *bakufu*.

The Ashikaga clan, during the first hundred years of rule, maintained control of the country by developing alliances with *daimyō* families. The agreements were respected because of the personal skills of the *shōguns*.[14] The whole empire came again under one military regime, and for about two centuries, the Ashikaga family continued as the heads of the new *bakufu*.[15] *Shōgun* Yoshimitsu, to strengthen his personal power, created the position of *retired shōgun*, which he himself occupied after abdicating in favour of his nine-year-old son in 1395.[16]

The position of the *shugo* changed during the Ashikaga period. It was not an ordinary office like in the Kamakura *Bakufu*, but the legal status of a warrior ranking next to the *shōgun*. As a result, each province under the *shugo* became a political unit, whereas in the Kamakura era it was only a military unit.[17] During the Ashikaga *Shōgunate*, *shugo*, who were the heads of powerful families, were made responsible for large areas of the country. The land that the *shugo* held directly became his own property, not the land that he had the right to use as a retainer of the *shōgun*. The land, therefore, ceased to be associated with the *shugo* office.[18] Their power increased significantly during the war of dual courts, and they became well-connected, wealthy leaders of their provinces. To limit their power *shōgun* Yoshimitsu used the old Yamato practice and made the 12 most powerful *shugo* establish primary residences in Kyōto, where they ruled in council with the *shōgun* (the three most prominent families rotated as deputies to the *shōgun*), and could be watched. This limited their abilities to develop stronger ties with local warriors in their provinces, because they had to send out deputies to manage their provincial areas in their absence. They entrusted the care of their provinces to *jitō*, who soon made themselves independent of their patrons, and later, many *shugo* were overthrown by their own deputies.[19]

According to Hara, *shugo* were happy to spend time at Kyōto where they led lavish, aristocratic life, on account of holding some civil offices in the *bakufu*. An intimate relationship between the *shugo* and the courtiers was maintained and cemented. There were frequent marriages between members of both groups, thanks to which the courtiers gained materially, and the soldiers were able to acquire good manners and customs. Hara writes that, in time, the high-ranking warriors of Kamakura lost their military character and were turned into pseudo-courtiers. In turn, the court nobles of Kyōto were fascinated by the militaristic temperament of the Kamakura warriors. Thus, the *shōgunate* (an office for household affairs and the camp of the *shōgun*) was gradually turning into a princely court.[20] The highest court elite and *bakufu* leaders quarrelled over titles, income, and inheritance rights. Conflicts occurred at lower levels as the number of farmers grew faster than the area of rice fields. Moreover, taxes were constantly increasing, and more and more peasants had difficulty in paying them. The situation was made worse by the increasingly frequent use of money, causing unpredictability of collecting tributes, the possibility of fraud by collectors, and imprudent borrowing, which gave rise to conflicts between debtors and creditors.[21]

Hara writes that in the Ashikaga period the relation of *shugo* and *jitō* in the provinces changed to the relation of vassalage, a legal status which had not existed in the Kamakura period.[22] Kamakura *shugo* were military governors of the provinces nominated by *shōgun*, often appointed from the *jitō*. They held positions of civilian and military supervisors in the provinces. Their duties were to maintain peace, supervise the guard service, command local retainers in battles, and were empowered to investigate and judge cases from treason to robbery. S*hugo* stood in the position of protectors to all the *jitō* of the province he governed. They formed an administrative system, which gradually eroded the civil administrative structure of the emperor.[23] This office became hereditary in some privileged families high in the warrior hierarchy.

From the early 12th century, the *bakufu* appointed *jitō* (land stewards) whose duties included supervising the management of landed estates, maintaining public order, collecting taxes, maintaining peace in the manor, enforcing the edicts of the *shōgunate*, ensuring the proper distribution of taxes, and serving as local judges. In return for their services, the *jitō*'s position was made hereditary, and they received a share of the produce of the estate in form of a special *commissariat-rice* (*hyōrō-mai*) tax for their own use.[24] In any emergency, the *jitō* were expected to provide military service to the *shōgun*. They had immunity from the disciplinary authority of their absentee landlords. The *jitō's* obligation to manage land on behalf of an owner who had no direct control over him made this position revolutionary. This also created a great need to provide the *bakufu* with judicial authority.[25] By the 14th century, the power of the *shugo* had increased significantly, while the *jitō* had merged with the landowning class. During the Ashikaga period, *shugo* were the overlords of the *jitō* and also owned some land in the provinces they oversaw. Another difference was that in the Kamakura era the *shōgun's* retainer was first installed as a *jitō* in the estate and then appointed *shugo*. The relation of vassalage arose between the *shugo* and the *jitō* in the same province, causing that the direct relationship between the common *jitō* and the *shōgun*, which was the basis of the political system of the Kamakura era, came to an end.[26]

The Muromachi *Bakufu* was one of the country's most important political and economic institutions in crafting new policies and seeking new sources of income. The Kamakura *Bakufu* relied primarily on landed estates for its income, but the Ashikaga *Shōguns* fully embraced monetization and urban taxation as sources of revenue.[27] Success or failure depended on military power, which relied on income; therefore, great incentive existed to promote economic expansion. There was significant growth in the economy, which resulted in the development of markets, towns, and new social classes. In villages, in addition to conducting detailed land surveys, the *daimyō* also built irrigation systems and opened new rice fields to stimulate production. Agricultural productivity increased due to improvements in tools and techniques (use of the water wheel), fertilizers, more intensive use of the land (double cropping), and new types of rice. Those *daimyō* who exploited mineral wealth of their territories (gold, silver, copper) were particularly powerful, and because miners proved useful as sappers in attacks on enemy fortifications. In general, the wealth of the domains was drawn from the hard work and enterprise of farmers, merchants, and artisans. A significant improvement was the use of bills of exchange to deliver *nengu* from the provinces to the centre. This, together with importation of cash, improved the traditional tribute payment system, despite the opposition of the nobles. Already in the 14th century, the value of most goods was estimated in coins, which made it easier to exchange one product for another. Merchants and provincial estate managers were very creative in solving financial problems in the 15th century.[28]

Under *shōgun* Yoshimitsu foreign relations again became important. A letter to the Ming court (1403) he signed *the king of Japan* which meant that *shōgunate* had power to deal with foreign countries independently of the imperial court. The *shōgunate* was anxious to establish commercial relations with Ming China (Yoshimitsu's son showed no interest in maintaining them), and influential Zen advisors encouraged them to expand contacts with the Middle Kingdom.[29] The profits from the Chinese trade were great and vital for Yoshimitsu's enormous investments. They stimulated the growth and development of the economy and supplemented financial deficiencies. Zen Buddhism was getting increasingly popular among the warriors.[30] Its ideas of simplicity, restraint, discipline, and meditation were very attractive in times of chaos and war, and became so important and popular that they characterize Japanese culture to this day.[31]

After Yoshimitsu's death (1408), *shōgunal* power started to decline. *Shōgun*'s orders were often ignored and disregarded by the court that was weak itself.[32] The Ashikaga *Shōgunate* was unable to gain the unconditional obedience of all the higher military officials (*shugo)* because the family, though an offshoot of the Minamoto, had nothing in its history to attract warriors to serve under its banner. Subsequent *shōguns* had neither land nor money to buy themselves retainers.

The *bakufu* was able to control the central provinces, but gradually lost influence over outer regions as provincial families became powerful. Local warriors attached themselves to *shugo* who were increasingly independent of the central authority. The position of deputy shugo appointed not by the immediate superior (shugo), but by the central authorities, gained importance. This office became hereditary in the family of its holder. They became great vassals in the provinces they controlled and administered, often more influential than their lords.[33]

Till the middle Muromachi period, many powerful *shugo* were overthrown by their own deputies because the *shōgunate's* control over the nation was very weak. Foundations of the *bakufu* were shaken by the increasing power of the *daimyō* and by the frequent uprisings of local *samurai* and farmers. In 1441, the despotic *shōgun* Ashikaga Yoshinori (1394–1441) was assassinated by Akamatsu Noriyasu. The assassin was captured and executed, but not by the *shōgun's* army, but by a rival warlord wanting the assassin's territory. Yoshinori's death effectively ended the period of assertive *bakufu* leadership and *shōgunal* autocracy that had begun under Yoshimitsu.[34] The time from 1443 to 1454 was especially restless and unhappy for Japan.[35] The Ashikaga *Shōguns* were perpetually confronted by disturbances and disaffections, mainly because they made immense grants of land to their supporters without developing some effective system of control of territorial magnates thus created. Many nobles developed such strong position and wealth, that they were not concerned about Kyōto or Muromachi government, siding instead with the party most convenient for them.[36]

The lack of control of the *shōgun* meant that the provincial families increasingly fought against each other, and alliances were made and broken to achieve wealth, especially land. With the growing insecurity, lords and warriors assumed more duties and powers in their domains.[37] Over time, *shugo* extended their power beyond their military duties, acting as civil rulers and taking an ever-greater share of taxes from estates. They were called *shugo-daimyō* because they not only were officials appointed by the *shōgun* but became territorial lords. They were building castles, strong military bases, in various localities until the first half of the 16th century. The source of their power was control over retainers and over land as the provinces held by them were almost completely free of *bakufu* control. The *daimyō* turned local leaders into retainers and took away their independence by enforcing land surveys and directly controlling the farming villages. *Daimyō* created their own council board (a supervisory board) in which the heads of the most influential among them sat. Its creation was an important step in the development of the feudal system in Japan. They issued their own laws (*bunkoku-hō*) to govern their territories. These provincial laws, based on the warrior code, the *Joei* Formulary, also included regulations for farmers and applied strict controls over retainers.[38] In principle, the lord's permission was necessary for his vassals to inherit property (restricted to the main heir and clan chief) and to marry, as well as female fiefs and female inheritance of real estate were abolished.[39] *Daimyō* tried to maintain direct control of his warrior vassals and potential rivals by bringing them near the main castle of the domain. The only non-military manors that survived belonged to the shrines and temples because the warrior class was afraid of the wrath of the gods. They had a superstitious reverence for the three sacred things, Buddha, Law, and Priesthood.[40]

Because the *daimyō* (territorial lords) diverted to themselves the traditional taxes and *shōen* dues from the rural districts, the *shōgun's* revenue had significantly declined, causing increasing dissatisfaction among his generals and *samurai*.[41] The *shōgunate* became unable to cope with the care of the state and military affairs on its own. The weakness of the central government caused unrest in Kyoto and the provinces, which led to the political dissolution of the entire empire, resulting in Japan transforming into several semi-independent bodies, each with a *shugo* at its head.[42] In this way, the state became decentralized.

As noted earlier, each province under a *shugo* became a political entity, while it had been a military entity in the Kamakura era. The manors became integral parts of great fiefs. *Samurai* swore allegiance to his *daimyō* and in return were granted fiefs, in which each *samurai* had control over both land and people. However, none of these *shugo-daimyō* was strong enough to keep order even within his own military jurisdiction. They needed wealth as well as military strength to maintain themselves as independent rulers. In this way, Japan, which was a conglomeration of political units of various sizes, with rulers and borders changing without reference to the historical background of families, legal and administrative rules, old patterns, and traditions, fell into a state of chaos. This period completed the total disintegration of the empire and the disappearance of the manorial system initiated by the Taika reform.[43] The old *shōen* system of estates disappeared together with many other features of the centralized Japanese state.

The Ashikaga fiscal and financial administration was one of the very worst that Japan ever had.[44] The expenditures of the Muromachi *Bakufu* were not met from its revenues from the land under its direct control, despite the *mandokoro* control of the finances of the *bakufu*. The difficult financial situation *forced shōgun* to impose heavy burdens on the provinces. The *shugo* and *jitō* of each province were ordered to impose monetary taxes on each unit of land or each household, but this was not enough to meet the financial needs of the *bakufu*. Peasants suffered from high taxes and debts, as well as diseases and natural disasters. The Muromachi *Bakufu* also embraced the cash economy and saw trade and moneylenders as part of the solution to its financial needs.[45] For the first time, the *shōgunate* imposed taxes on the richest merchants (pawnbrokers, sake brewers, transport). Merchants in Kyōto were taxed five or six times in a year.[46]

After the fall of Ashikaga and *shugo* rule and the obliteration of *shōen*, agriculture began to develop intensively, as did trade and small-scale manufacturing, which prospered in the villages around Kyōto. Peasants, dissatisfied with their poor financial situation, were able to mobilize themselves to fight to secure and improve their position. Led by local men, they defended themselves against warring armies and high-taxing authorities. They were afraid not so much of war as of hunger, plague, and above all, of tax collectors, who in the days of Ashikaga collected about 70% of the crops of their fields. During the years of ineffective central governments, they managed to organize themselves, formed a united front against powerful military men, and gained the ability to govern themselves. Smaller landowners defended their local interests by forming trade unions to jointly manage forests and carry out irrigation works. Villages in the country became self-governing, and, if they paid taxes, *daimyō* left them to manage their own affairs. As previously, an elected leader, called the elder (*otona*), headed village government, members of which regularly held assemblies at the village shrine or temple, during which rules of social life were drawn up. According to Murdoch, a self-government became strong in the communities and the resistance of farmers increased significantly. They were using technological advances, gained thanks to their experience, ingenuity, and relative independence in managing their land.[47] Therefore, the peasants' dignity and self-esteem increased.

Many taxes were levied on farmers, artisans, and merchants – house tax, door tax, cart tax, rice-shop tax, taxes on pawnshops, on sake, on sake warehouses (there were 327 in the capital alone), and on fire-proof *godowns*. But the most burdensome was the *dansen*, an emergency tax levied initially every six or seven years to cover coronation expenses or palace reconstruction, which was later required several times a year. *Shugo* and *daimyō* in their provinces, districts, and fiefdoms began to imitate the actions of the central administration, erecting barriers on highways and on waterways, where high tolls were collected from all passengers and goods passing through them. They needed money for their luxurious lifestyles in Kyōto and in their fiefs. Lawlessness was growing in central Japan and the seas. The old problem of regionalism resurfaced as land passed into the hands of local leaders and out of the control of the *bakufu*.[48]

In the 15th century, control of the central administration over the provinces was very weak, and the fading power of the *shōen* system and the *bakufu* was revealed.[49] Peasants, craftsmen, traders, and the travellers were heavily taxed, but this revenue was rarely paid to the *shōgun* because the great military families made themselves independent of the *bakufu*.[50] The court had lost power, courtiers, and *shōen* holders were impoverished and desperate, the *bakufu* was unsafe in its own city and had almost no control over *daimyō*, major *daimyō* domains were threatened by lesser warriors, and other well-organized social groups were ready to use force.[51] From 1447, there was a series of well-organized rebellions of peasants against the *shōgunate* and the great *shugo*.[52] They demanded that landowners reduce their annual taxes and establish a moratorium on their debts to moneylenders.[53] The leaders of these uprisings were local *samurai* with village roots who often established themselves as domain lords (*daimyō*) during the riots. The armed uprisings were depriving the absentee landlords of much needed income (taxes) from the land they owned. Responding to the great riots (1447, 1451, 1457, and 1461), the government declared that debts were to be liquidated by the payment of one-tenth of the principal, except obligations to shrines and temples. During his tenure as *shōgun* Yoshimasa issued 13 edicts for the cancellation of debts known as *tokuseirei* or *acts of grace*. The results of the *tokusei* proved to be a disaster for industry and commerce because they made it impossible to obtain any credit, which, together with the *dansen*, meant that merchants and producers were unable to raise sufficient capital to expand their businesses.[54] Around 1454, some of the great provincial lords began to employ landless men without any occupation, what in few years, ended slavery in Japan. At that time, an insolvent debtor usually became the slave of his creditor, but service under a great feudal lord meant, that warrior debtors did not have to worry about creditors and the courts.[55] By the 1460s, the *kenmon system* (*system of ruling elites*) began to fall apart.[56]

Economic difficulties, mismanagement and the Ashikaga personal ambitions culminated in the Onin Civil War of 1467–77 which began with the controversy over the succession of the *shōgun* (in 1464, a dispute arose between the two Ashikaga brothers over which of them would succeed as *shōgun*, and *daimyō* clans declared allegiance to one of them).[57] Then, the system of alternate succession agreed between the two emperor lines that restored peace in 1393 was disregarded by the Ashikaga family who twice secured the succession to a prince of the Northern dynasty. According to Asakawa, this started the darkest age of Japan's history.[58] The inconclusive Ōnin War began a long conflagration that effectively ended Ashikaga influence and rule.[59] It devastated Kyōto which was a battleground for more than decade, revealing the inability of the *shōgunate* to quell civil unrest. Kyōto had been looted, ruined, and abandoned, and the fighting spread to the provinces. The Ōnin War, a ten-year battle for Kyōto and power, exposed and reinforced the nationwide struggle for control over land production and the need for mechanisms to control and redistribute wealth and power. By the late 16th century, the most powerful people developed mechanisms of control enabling them to dominate the others and restore order.[60]

The reasons for the turmoil in medieval Japan were the increase in agricultural and artisanal productivity, allowing demographic growth, acceleration of consumption, development of larger, cohesive, and internally managed and directed villages, able to be more involved in political life. Other factors concerned handling of goods and services, and commercialization that made the rural output more accessible to the society.[61] The growth in agricultural production and distribution, supplemented by the changes in political and religious life, speeded up the development of towns, which in turn fostered the diffusion of power, wealth, and sharing of the higher culture.[62] However, the ruling elites did not want to allow changes that would allow the political and social system to be adapted to the needs of the emerging market economy.

The blackest era of Japanese history, as far as the preservation of public peace, order, security of life, and property was concerned, became a time of high artistic development.[63] *Shōguns*, aristocrats, and generals led the most luxurious and refined lifestyles. The culture they were fascinated by illustrates the delicate, subtle and more austere flavour of the period, characteristics that remain evident even in Japanese culture today.[64] Many of Kyōto's most iconic buildings were created during this period (Golden Pavilion, Silver Pavilion), and cultural arts such as *noh* plays, ikebana flower arrangements, tea ceremonies, linked verses, *sansui* paintings, *shoin*-style architecture, and landscaped gardens also come from this era. It was the golden age of Japanese pictorial art. Thus, many elements seen today as Japanese culture have their roots in medieval Japan, despite the rise and fall of the two *bakufu*, all the political turmoil, and wars that entailed the political events of that period.[65] This process began in the golden age of *shōgun* Ashikaga Yoshimitsu, at the end of the 14th century, when science and art flourished in Zen monasteries of Kyōto under *shōgunal* patronage, as most of the greatest artists of this age were monks.[66] Although the older schools were not neglected, the new schools based on Chinese traditions (Sung and Mongol), ran mainly by the Zen priests, became most popular and financed. The new Buddhist sects and Zen Buddhism became an integral part of Japanese society and culture during the Kamakura and Muromachi periods.

Until the War of Succession in the years 1337–1392, the great patron of painting was the imperial court, which did a lot for the development of native Japanese art schools. However, the war impoverished the court, so the Ashikaga *Shōguns* (Yoshimitsu and his grandson Yoshimasa) became patrons of the arts. Their artistic fantasies were very refined and expensive.[67] Migration of aristocrats and priests disseminated the higher culture of the capital to the provinces. The local *daimyō* absorbed and promoted it in their domains, seeking to raise their dignity as lords by building temples and shrines in their castle towns. The artists and scholars employed helped spread the traditional culture of the Kyōto civil aristocracy as well as Chinese culture, especially that associated with Zen Buddhism.

Despite the wars and disturbances, the Muromachi epoch offered more peace and stability in comparison to other periods in the history of Japan.[68] It was a period of transition from the old centralized system to feudalism, where power was regionally based.[69] Elements of both systems operated throughout this period, but the country gradually transformed into a feudal state.[70] So, after centuries of efforts to build a centralized and unified state, Japan became decentralized again in the early 16th century.

Characteristics of the *Azuchi–Momoyama* era (1573–1603)

The *Azuchi–Momoyama* period (1573–1603) is included in the Age of Warring States or the *Sengoku* period (1467–1615). It was a very dark period in history of Japan, full of conflicts terribly wasteful of lives and money. The country suffered from a moral and political crisis.[71] It was broken into many, mostly small, and strong principalities. Powerful and conflicted *daimyō* and Buddhist monasteries protected by warrior monks fought each other for land and power. Neither the emperor nor the *shōgun* could stop the war because neither of them had the power to do so. Peace was not restored till the fall of the Ashikaga *Shōgunate*. After the Ōnin War, the military and civilian classes were plunged into poverty, the laws were discarded, and the administration of justice was in disorder. The territorial magnates in the provinces discontinued the payment of taxes, closed their domains to communication from the outside, and governed as they wished.[72] Thus, the court and the *shōgunate* lost power, control over most sources of income, and the ability to maintain order in the capital city.[73] According to Segal, the Ashikaga directly controlled only 300,000 *koku* of land, far less than the Tokugawa shōguns who succeeded them (who controlled some 4 million koku of land).[74] Imperial decrees and instructions from the *shōgun* were disregarded. Every 16th-century Ashikaga *Shōgun* had to flee Kyōto at least once during his tenure, the only one who died in Kyōto was assassinated there. Real power was exercised by regional commanders, who were consolidating their holdings and followers.[75]

During the Muromachi period, the power of independent local leaders increased greatly. The nominees appointed by the Ashikaga disappeared from Kyōto and its surroundings. Many aristocratic families, to earn their living, returned to their lands, taking up residences in the castle towns, under the protection of local *daimyō*.[76] Returning to their provinces, they found that the *shōgunate* was unable to support them in any way. Thus, after 1477, few of them were able to maintain their position and property, which they lost to new families, who were often their subordinate relatives or vassals. Many deputies of great *shugo* Houses usurped the domains of their superiors, retainers overthrew their overlords, and branch families seized power from main families (inferiors overcame superiors). The nobility who had served the court for almost a thousand years were left without income, and administrative officials were deprived of their salaries. The *shiki* rights to income from the *shōen*, which had sustained court life for so long, ceased to exist. In consequence, in a short time, many aristocratic families lost their identity as courtiers.[77] The previous *shugo* disappeared and a new type of domain lord, the *daimyō*, took their place.[78]

The Sengoku *daimyō* represented the apex of the feudal power structure that was based on the strength of local powers.[79] The new local rulers, *daimyō*, were self-reliant and usually had no contacts with the capital, as neither the emperor nor the *shōgun* were powerful. They made and enforced their own laws and rules to govern the land they controlled and protected, and exercised unlimited judicial power in their domains. They declared wars, made peace without any authorization, and acted in the name of the *shōgun* only when it served their private aims. They taxed their subjects as much as they wanted and stopped paying taxes to the central government and their overlords.

Daimyō domains were usually smaller than the lands assigned to the *shugo* but compact, easy to defend, and under strict control.[80] As noted already, they closed them against outside communication and governed them according to their own will.[81] The *daimyō* transferred lands or income to their retainers, who in return had to perform military service and swore allegiance to them. In the fiefs granted, each *samurai* exercised control over the land and people.[82] They built huge castles for use and showing wealth rather than for defence. They were built of stones and surrounded by moats and castle towns.[83] *Daimyō* castle towns were governed by the laws of the House, which defined the rights and responsibilities of those who served them. The emphasis was on a highly personal relationship between lord and servant, based on the loyalty of vassals. The retainers were loyal to the regional lord, not to the *shōgunate*. Loyal service to the overlord became the fundamental ethic and bond that existed between *samurai* and their masters. Actions of incredible courage and endurance were motivated by personal pride, honour, and loyalty to the lord, and took precedence over loyalty to the emperor, religion, and family. However, loyalty was sometimes betrayed in power struggles and to prevent this, the old practice of family and village mutual responsibility for its members was reinforced.[84] Thus, the Japanese family organization based on the concept of the house (*ie*), and the domination of the head of the house, was the basic principle in the lord–vassal relationship.[85]

After the *Ōnin* War, the imperial household was in ruin losing its *shōen* and support from *shōgun* and *daimyō*. The mandate of the emperor did not arouse due respect, ordinary court ceremonies were abandoned, and the court experienced extreme poverty. Asakawa writes that such was the poverty in Kyōto that the emperor Gotsuchimikado was unable to perform the customary ceremony on his accession to the throne, and at the time of his death, his funeral rites could not be performed because of lack of funds. With great difficulty, the needed sum was collected and the burial rites were performed. For the same reason, the coronation ceremony of his successor Gokashiwabara was not performed. It took place only 22 years later, when lord abbot Hongwan-ji donated the sum of 10,000 gold pieces for this purpose.[86]

According to Murdoch, satisfying everyday life needs became a problem in the imperial court, the damaged palace buildings could not be repaired either. The surroundings of the imperial pavilion were used for selling tea, a playground for children, and for peeping into the imperial apartments. The sovereign himself lived chiefly on money gained by selling his autographs to any citizen who deposited a few coins with a written request. During the War of *Onin*, the emperor had to spend some 13 years within the *bakufu* buildings in Muromachi, all the court functions were abandoned, and later resumed only in the form of Abridged Ceremonies. But between 1465 and 1585, there was no incidence of an emperor's abdication, and the succession passed without any dispute, because the throne had lost importance and even when the sovereigns wished to abdicate, there were no funds to cover the costs of such a ceremony. The position of the retired emperor ceased to exist in the century after the *Ōnin* War because no one had any reason to manipulate the imperial position.[87]

The Age of Warring States is marked by social upheaval, political intrigues, constant military conflicts, and by earthquakes and famines.[88] For almost a century and a half, Japan was suffering from constant internal conflicts. In such turbulent times, some powerful *daimyō* realized that if Japan wanted to remain an independent state, it was necessary to reunify the nation and return to the political stability of the earlier Muromachi period. To achieve stability and strength in the face of growing external and internal threats, it was necessary to centralize the state and power.[89] This goal was achieved by the cumulative efforts of three successive powerful and determined military leaders – Oda Nobunaga (1534–82), Toyotomi Hideyoshi (1536–98), and Tokugawa Ieyasu (1542–1616),[90] who one after another ruled over feudal Japan. Each of them, in turn, enacted a series of social, economic, and political regulations to pacify society long accustomed to war and instability and created the institutions necessary for lasting central rule. Each brought characteristics, methods, and talents reflecting their different personalities. The results of their actions were the unification of Japan under strong feudal leadership. It is said that Nobunaga mixed the dough, Hideyoshi baked the cake, and Ieyasu ate it.[91]

The first *Great Unifier* was Oda Nobunaga, the head of the powerful Oda clan and a deputy *shugo*, known as a military genius who used innovative military tactics, and was the first to use firearms in Japanese warfare. In the 1560s, he started a war to unify the country under his leadership and soon became the most powerful *daimyō* in Japan. He was powerful enough to gradually impose his will on rival *daimyo* clans being determined to *rule the Empire by force*. In 1560, Nobunaga had proved his brilliant strategic skills by subduing all of Owari. In the same year, he defeated the major *daimyō* (Imagawa Yoshimoto) and entered into an alliance with one of the latter's vassals, Matsudaira Motoyasu (the future Tokugawa Ieyasu). Nobunaga captured Kyōto in 1568 (responding to requests from the emperor Ogimachi and Ashikaga Yoshiaki, who was shortly confirmed as 15th and last Ashikaga *Shōgun*) and gained control of the city. But in 1573, he overthrew the nominally ruling last *shōgun* of the Ashikaga line and the Muromachi *Bakufu*.[92] It was the first major step towards the unification of Japan, ending a century of feudal wars and lawlessness.[93] By the 1580s, Nobunaga managed to subdue his immediate enemies and turned against militant Buddhist sects with serious political and military power.

During his rule, Nobunaga eagerly promoted trade and industry, encouraged free trade between *daimyō*-controlled domains, abolished customs duties, standardized the currency, weights and measures, built roads, kept highways in a proper state, reformed Japanese civil administration, encouraged Christianity to balance the power of the Buddhist sects, and started the *Momoyama* (peach mountain) historical art period.[94] In the three decades of his military career, he subordinated himself half of the whole country and contemplated the conquest of Shikoku, Chugoku, and Kyushu. His ambition was self-aggrandizement in the first place, but the peace of the empire, the welfare of the people, and the stability of the throne was his second purpose. His first actions, after taking control of Kyōto, were appointing officials who would impartially administer justice, reducing taxes for citizens; helping widows and orphans and ensuring safety and peace for all. In 1572, he ordered the provinces to build roads 21 to 12 feet wide, erect milestones and plant trees along these roads, build bridges, remove barriers, and facilitate communication.[95] In the same year, Nobunaga ordered the court to name the new era *Tensho*, meaning the era of Heavenly Righteousness. Thus, the Muromachi *Bakufu*, which had lasted over 230 years, ceased to exist, as well as the political system of which it was the centre.[96]

Nobunaga promoted himself as a divine ruler. He managed to defeat and displace the militant Buddhism, which never again regained a strong position in Japan.[97] He demanded worship from *samurai*, claiming that it would help them to gain wealth and happiness.[98] In exchange for worship, he offered them military and divine protection. He argued that the services rendered by a loyal vassal in this life would benefit him in the next. But unlike earlier military hegemons, he rejected the position of the *shōgun* because accepting nomination from the emperor would make him his subordinate. Nobunaga hosted the emperor as an equal at his palace in Kyōto. His spouse was made equal in status to the emperor's mother, and the status of his son was the same as the emperor's son. He arranged for the construction of a shrine dedicated to himself as the Great August Deity with nationwide recognition.[99]

Nobunaga was known for the brutal suppression of opponents, eliminating those who refused to cooperate or yield to his demands. He gave the acquired land to his vassals and initiated a policy of territorial redistribution, which was developed by his successors. In 1571, following the Taika reforms of a thousand years earlier, he began surveying the agricultural lands under his control. Nobunaga's brilliance brought half of Japan's provinces under his control by 1582, with powerful *daimyō* in the outer provinces. However, the basic factor that contributed to Oda's hegemony was his monetary and free market policy.[100]

On the other hand, a new warrior culture was created under Nobunaga rule. The construction of magnificent castles resulted in a flourishing of artists and craftsmen involved in decoration and entertainment. Western culture was smoothly absorbed into life. Its influence was revealed in the language, architecture, weapons, dressing, religion, and lifestyle. Artists produced colourful pictures of animals and landscapes. Because of rich colours and great reliance on gold, Momoyama paintings provided a vivid contrast to the sombre tones of the monochrome paintings of the Muromachi era. Therefore, they were often referred to as *southern barbarian* pictures, because they presented the European priests and traders who had entered Japan.[101] The powerful *daimyō* wanted to get the latest technology available in the world.[102] Oda Nobunaga supported for political reasons, the development of Christianity brought to Japan by Jesuits in 1549. He did this not only because of his interest in European culture but also because he saw the spread of Christianity as another way to limit the influence of Buddhist temples. Therefore, he extended his protection to the Jesuit missionaries and assisted them in building a church in the capital and a seminary in Azuchi. However, his great unification achievements came to an abrupt halt because he was betrayed by his officer (Akechi Mitsuhide), and, wounded during the attack, with no chance of escape, he committed *seppuku* at the age of 49 in 1582.[103]

Nobunaga's killer was pursued and defeated at the Battle of Yamazaki, by Toyotomi Hideyoshi, retainer who had served in Nobunaga forces since 1558 and fought in many important battles. His courage and brilliance caused him to rise from a humble foot soldier to a general, highly appreciated (best) by his commander. In September 1573, by overthrowing two powerful *daimyō*, Hideyoshi became a lord of Nagahama, Ōmi province, and subsequently took the name of Hashiba, Lord of Chikuzen. In 1583, he built a magnificent castle in Osaka and received the family name Toyotomi from the emperor, henceforth calling himself Toyotomi Hideyoshi.[104] He became the most powerful person in the country, extremely shrewd, capable, a brilliant leader, able to win friends, but also a ruthless fighter, when it was needed.[105]

Hideyoshi continued Nobunaga's policy of uniting the state, seeking alliances to avoid unnecessary bloodshed, but also through successful battles, when necessary. He never became *shōgun*, partly because he had left alive Yoshiaki, the last of the Ashikaga *shōguns*, and partly because of his humble beginnings. In 1585, he was adopted by Konoe Sakihisa of the Fujiwara family who monopolized the position of imperial regent (*kampaku*) established in the Heian era, the highest position after the emperor in the court system of the empire, which was always held by Fujiwara. Unlike Nobunaga, he assumed several legitimizing high titles,[106] such as *kampaku* (civil dictator or chancellor to the emperor) in 1591, *dajō-daijin* (chief minister) and the retired regent (*taikō*').[107] In 1590, Hideyoshi became the head of the *daimyō* alliance, which established a government of national unification. Toyotomi managed to unify the empire by force just eight years after Nobunaga's death. To calm the country, he demanded absolute submission from every class of society. Foreign merchants and missionaries interfered with this submission, so Hideyoshi expelled the foreigners, persecuted those who remained, and finally brutally killed them. Initially, he followed Nobunaga's policy of accepting Christianity (increasing trade) but later became afraid of a religion that was not related to Japanese tradition and posed a threat to his legitimization. Christianity as a religion of technologically advanced foreigners was also a colonization threat. Missionaries provided contacts with the outside world, traded with China and Europe, and in particular, they traded weapons, which were so important to the Japanese and useful in the fight against the power of militarized Buddhist temples. Despite these benefits, in 1587, Hideyoshi issued an edict expelling Christian missionaries, viewing Christianity as a potential threat to Japan's political and social institutions. According to him Shintoism, Buddhism and Confucianism were *different aspects of a sole reality, praised for their functions as warrants of social order and peace.*[108] Morck and Nakamura argue that by prohibiting Europeans from trading and propagating religion, he caused Japan to escape colonization.[109]

Hideyoshi continued the Nobunaga's policy of redistributing the fiefs of defeated enemies to faithful followers (used later by Tokugawa) known as *province changing*. This had a double strategic advantage as he placed loyal vassals among the less loyal ones and separated the less loyal vassals from the people who formed their traditional power base.[110] This allowed Hideyoshi to control both the regional *daimyō* and his powerful allies. Knowing Tokugawa Ieyasu great ambitions, he forced him, by the means of a *reward* for distinguished service, to move from his power base in Chūbu region to the undeveloped distant Edo (now Tokyo), to the Kantō domain, formerly controlled by the Hōjō family.[111] He also began several practices (or continued those of Nobunaga), later used by Ieyasu, to consolidate his power. He implemented the practice of keeping the families of *daimyō* visiting their fiefs as hostages at his headquarters in Momoyama (near Kyōto). This helped to suppress the opposition, although family ties were not always most important to warlords.

Toyotomi continued the policy of governing through the authority of the emperor.[112] He sought to restore the prestige of the throne by covering all the expenses of the imperial household and requiring the nobility to swear to honour the monarch and not to encroach on the imperial estates. He was generous to the court but stripped the nobility of power.[113] His policy differed from Nobunaga's only with respect to the land and the military obligation within the lord–vassal relationship. Nobunaga based vassal's military obligation on agreements between lord and vassal or on the vassal's voluntary tribute. Hideyoshi established rules regarding military duties based on *kokudaka*, so tied military duties to the actual product of the land. *Koku* (a Japanese unit of dry measure equivalent to 5.12 bushels or 1.8 hectolitres) was the metric by which a domain size was evaluated. A feudal lord was only considered *daimyō* class when his domain amounted to at least 10,000 *koku*.[114] Another difference in his policy concerned commerce. Nobunaga implemented the policy of *free trade with no guilds* (*rakuichi-rakuza*) but actively protected the privileges of the *za* (guilds) in Kyōto, Nara, and other parts of Japan. He used the guilds for his own benefit, while Hideyoshi abolished them completely in about 1590, promoting free trade. In this way, he destroyed the medieval commercial practices and privileges.[115] The basic philosophy of the Kamakura and Murochomachi *Bakufu* was to levy various taxes on commercial goods but leave untouched the *nengu* tax that provincial estates owed to their patrons and owners. The Muromachi warrior government was actively promoting and taxing commerce and directly controlled toll stations.[116]

Hideyoshi also continued Nobunaga's policy of confiscating weapons from peasants during the so-called *sword hunting* (1588). The confiscated arms were melted and transformed into an enormous statue of the Kyōto's Buddha. The *sword hunt* substantially reduced the threat of peasant uprisings and the use of peasants by rival warlords.[117] This also helped to separate peasants and warriors in terms of class. This separation was further enforced by the *Freezing Class Regulations* issued by Hideyoshi in 1591, which severely limited opportunities for social advancement until the late 19th century.[118] This document introduced a social-class system known as *shi-nō-kō-shō* – meaning *warrior-peasant-artisan-merchant*. The inspiration was the Chinese Confucian hierarchical social system, systematized according to moral virtues and secular power in descending order of status (from top to bottom).[119] Peasants ranked higher than artisans and merchants because, in Confucian terms, they were essential producers. Within each class, particularly the *samurai* class, there were numerous sub-rankings. Court nobles *(kuge)*, priests, and monks were outside the classes, while below the classes were two *outcast* sub-classes, *eta* (great filth or hamlet people), and *hinin* (non-persons) who were engaged either in despised 'impure' activities such as butchering, leatherwork, and burial, or in 'suspicious' activities such as peddling, acting beggars, guards in jails, executioners, police informants and road cleaners. McGinty writes that these two groups are today called *burakumin* and continue to fight for equal treatment as they are still isolated from mainstream society.[120] Distinctions between the statuses of warriors, farmers, artisans, and merchants were strictly enforced, but especially strict was the distinction between the *samurai* and the other three classes. Class was determined by birth, and movement between them was difficult, though, in practice, not impossible.[121] This system was an essential ideological basis for the establishment of Japanese political power. Titles and higher offices were always exclusive to civil and military nobles.[122] Rigidly segregated warriors, farmers, craftsmen, and merchants were ordered to live in different areas of the city or countryside to promote the orderliness of feudal society. A clear distinction between the social classes increased the government's control over people. *Samurai* were forced to move into the castle towns. The Social Status Control order promulgated in 1591 prohibited warriors from engaging in agriculture and prohibited *daimyō* from employing a *samurai* who had deserted his master. Only *samurai* were allowed to have swords.

Peasants had rights as cultivators only if their land was duly registered. They were bound to pay land tax in rice and forbidden to neglect the cultivation of their fields, to move elsewhere, and to take any other profession. Hideyoshi revived and expanded the practice of collective responsibility, threatening entire villages and towns with punishment for the individual transgressions of their inhabitants. The class separation and collective responsibility were aimed at increasing control, preventing instability, and eliminating threats of rebellion.[123] Hideyoshi continued the land survey commenced by Nobunaga, which played crucial role in the separation process between warriors and peasants.[124] It was conducted throughout the country from 1583 to 1598 in order to clarify the complicated relations of land ownership rights that had existed since the Kamakura period. Hideyoshi sent inspectors to all provinces who made thorough land surveys and assessed returns to be made to the state, inflicting severe penalties on all officials accused of accepting bribes in the exercise of their office. As a result, large tracts of land previously improperly exempt from taxation were included in the tax system.[125]

The former *shōen* system of complex landholding had been obliterated and the feudal system, based on the *kokudaka* assessment, was established in the country. According to Osamu, the policies that characterized the *Kinsei* era (17th century to the first half of the 19th) were the separation of classes, the *kokudaka* system, and, for the Tokugawa period, *sakoku*. *Kinsei* society had feudal features such as a fief system and an imposed class structure. The *kokudaka* landholding system was expressed by the *principle* of *one land, one cultivator*.[126] Land taxes were collected from the village as a unit. A radical change was introduced in registering land that has so far been classified according to the monetary income obtained from it. From then on, it was valued according to products in kind and taxes were calculated on the basis of this new valuation. In place of previous land taxes in rice (*nengu*) assessed as so many hundred *kan* of silver per person, an assessment of *kokudaka* was made as so many hundred *koku* of rice (the amount of rice consumed by one person (about 5 bushels) in one year, or a measure by which the size of the feudal domain (*han*) was estimated). It was used as standard on which military services were levied in proportion. About two-thirds of the produce went to the state, the remainder to the cultivators of the land.[127] This also applied to the *daimyō*'s landholdings, the revenues from which were collected by the central government with great accuracy and honesty.[128] The establishment of the *kokudaka* system was the final blow to the *shōen*, which were already disappearing due to the actions taken by the Sengoku *daimyō*.[129] Hideyoshi (*taikō*') also decided that the *tan* unit was 300 *tsubo* of 360, leaving the taxable amount unchanged what significantly increased (about five times) revenue derived from the land[130] throughout the empire. All these measures were strengthened under the Ieyasu's rule and, to some extent, have been influencing Japanese society to this day.

Brinkley and Kikuchi write that Hideyoshi also issued supplementary regulations (six points), such as instructions called the *Osaka Castle Wall Writings*, which stated that intermarriages between *daimyō*'s families required the consent of the *taikō*' (retired regent); neither *daimyō* nor *shomyo* (smaller holder) was permitted to enter into secret engagements or to exchange written oaths, or to give or take hostages; in a quarrel the one who forebears should be recognized as having reason; no man, whatever his income, should keep a large number of concubines; the amount of sake imbibed should be limited to one's capacity; and the use of sedan-chairs shall be confined to Ieyasu, Toshiie, Kagekatsu, Terumoto, Takakage, the court nobles, and high priests. A young *daimyo* should ride on horseback. Those over 50 years of age may use a sedan-chair when they have to travel a distance of over one *ri* (two-and-a-half miles). Priests were exempted from this veto. According to these authors, another important legislation in force was the *Taikō*' *Shikimoku* consisting of 73 articles of which 13 are translated as follows: (1) free yourself from the thraldom of passion, (2) avoid heavy drinking, (3) be on your guard against women, (4) be not contentious or disputatious; (5) rise early, (6) beware of practical jokes, (7) think of your own future, (8) do not tire of things, (9) beware of thoughtless people, (10) beware of fire, (11) stand in awe of the law, (12) set up fences in your hearts against wandering or extravagant thoughts, and (13) hold nobody in contempt.[131]

Hideyoshi's administrative organization was remarkable. He created the positions of five *bugyō* in 1585, namely mayor of Kyōto city, tax administrator, court administrator, superintendent of public works, and supreme judge of civil affairs.[132] A year later he issued regulations that were to guide them, stating that (1) no subordinate shall leave his liege lord without the latter's permission, nor shall anyone give employment to a violator of this rule. (2) Farmers must remain on the land assigned to them and must never leave it untilled. Landowners should visit their tenants and should investigate in company with the latter the actual amount of the harvest reaped. One-third of this should be left to the farmer, and two-thirds should go to the owner of the land. (3) If owing to natural calamity the harvest be less than two bushels per acre, the whole of the yield shall go to the farmer. But if the harvest exceeds that figure, it shall be divided in the proportions indicated in (2). (4) No farmer shall move away from his holding to avoid the land tax or to escape forced labour. Anyone harbouring a violator of this rule shall expose to punishment not only himself but also the inhabitants of the entire village where he resides. (5) The lord of a fief must issue such instructions as shall guarantee his agricultural vassals against trouble or annoyance and shall himself investigate local affairs instead of entrusting that duty to a substitute. Landowners who issue unreasonable orders to farmers shall be punished. (6) In calculating cubic contents, the regulated unit of measure shall be used, and 2% shall be the maximum allowance for shortage. (7) Embankments injured by floods and other mischief wrought by natural calamities must be repaired during the first month of the year when agriculturists are at leisure. In the case, however, of damage which exceeds the farmers' capacity to repair, the facts should be reported to the taiko who will grant necessary assistance.[133] This legislation illustrates the ethics of the time.

In 1585, Toyotomi established a council of state (*gotairō*), or the Council of the Five Great Elders, consisting of the five greatest *daimyō* (one of them was Tokugawa Ieyasu) to consider all important national affairs.[134] All its elected members (regents) enjoyed the trust of Hideyoshi, who considered them competent administrators.[135] The second board consisted of three lower-ranking nobles, called middle ministers (*churo*), whose task was to arbitrate between a council of senior ministers and a third council of five administrators (*bugyo*). As noted earlier, this third board was originally organized by Hideyoshi in 1585, but it had not been associated with the other two boards, which came into existence after Hideyoshi's death

Aristocracy that traditionally relied on income in form of goods paid as taxes by the provinces, gradually found itself in increasing financial difficulties in the Muromachi period. Other groups were adapting well to a growing and changing economy by agreeing to receive converted cash payments. *Daimyō* created toll collection points to tax commercial goods, were protectors of medieval guilds (*za*), which paid them for protection and monopoly rights, and engaged in pawnbroking and money lending. They spent the money they obtained on purchasing goods at urban markets.

Warrior institutions also changed as the economy matured. The Kamakura *Bakufu* did not impose taxes directly on trade and was mainly concerned with economic matters in terms of maintaining peace and order. The Muromachi *Bakufu* imposed taxes on trading posts in Kyōto, accepted cash donations in exchange for help with debt relief (or debt collection), and sent diplomatic missions to China to obtain large amounts of copper currency.[136] Hideyoshi needed revenue for his vassals and to support his army. He, therefore, placed key trading cities, such as Osaka and Nagasaki, under his direct control, fostered profitable international trade, and controlled gold and silver mines. To improve the condition of the currency, Hideyoshi ordered the minting of gold coins of two denominations – *ōban* and *koban* – as well as silver bars and silver and copper coins (*tenshō tsūhō-sen*).[137] During the Warring States period, he strengthened government control over economic activity, standardized its measurements, and conducted a census (1590). In 1591, the provinces in the far north came under his control.[138]

Hideyoshi intended to establish a pan-Asian empire and, therefore, invaded Korea in 1592, but Japanese troops were defeated by combined Korean and Chinese forces. Japan was not yet strong enough to achieve that goal. Hideyoshi was of different opinions and tried again in 1597, but this campaign was abandoned, because he died from illness in 1598.

During his terminal illness, Hideyoshi tasked all 13 members of the councils with protecting his minor son Hideyori and ensuring that he would inherit his father's great fortune. He asked the Council of the Five Great Elders, to rule Japan until Hideyori's adolescence. Each of them was obliged to sign a written oath consisting of following eight articles: (1) that they would serve Hideyori with the same single-minded loyalty they had shown to his father; (2) that the rules of Hideyoshi's house were not to be altered; and that if, in the administration of public affairs, the five *bugyo* were unable to determine a course of action, they should consult Hideyori through Ieyasu and Toshiie; or, if necessary before taking action, the Emperor was to be consulted; (3) that there were to be no factions among them, personal considerations and partiality of every kind being excluded from their councils; (4) that they must endeavour to work together in the discharge of their duties, suppressing all petty jealousies and differences; (5) that, in settling matters, the opinion of the majority was usually to be followed, but, at the same time, if the opinion of the minority showed no sign of being dictated by personal interests, it should be duly considered. That without permission from Hideyori no administrator should dispose of any of his (the administrator's) territory to another person; (6) that all accounts were to be kept in a manner above suspicion; that there were to be no irregularities and no pursuing of personal interests; that no questions concerning landed estates should be dealt with during the minority of Hideyori; that no petitions should be presented to him, and that Ieyasu himself would neither ask for changes to be made in the matter of land ownership nor accept any gift of land from Hideyori during the latter's minority; (7) that whatever Hideyori desired to have kept secret, whether connected with his private life or with the Government, must on no account be allowed to leak out; and (8) that if any of the administrators or their subordinates found that they had unwittingly acted contrary to orders, they should at once report the fact to their superiors, who would then deal leniently with them.[139] It should be noted that in 1591, childless Hideyoshi adopted his nephew Toyotomi Hidetsugu as his heir. But, after the birth of his son Hideyori, he ordered Hidetsugu to commit *harakiri*, because he wanted Hideyori to be the only possible heir. Hidetsugu's family and retainers were also killed. Execution of family members was one of the reasons for questioning Hideyoshi's sanity.

However, the five trusted greatest *daimyō* broke their oath to Hideysoshi. They did not trust each other and closely monitored each other's actions. The council's only success before its dissolution was the recall of Japanese troops from Korea in 1598. An old rivalry arose between these feudal chiefs and they began to fight each other for supremacy. After Hideyoshi's death, Tokugawa Ieyasu (1543–1616) realized that he had to gain dominance at all costs; otherwise, he would be eliminated by jealous rivals.[140] Ultimately, the great *daimyō* formed two parties, one of which was led by the most powerful regent Ieyasu, a man of great ambition and ability, characterized by magnanimity, self-control, and strategic skills. Ieyasu spent his youth as a political hostage to the Imagawa family, and after release he started to fight to regain the position owed to him. At the age of 17, he became the head of the family. He laboured for the good of his household, retainers, and children, and refused to compete for purely personal glory. His keen observation showed him every aspect of the case, and he was extremely patient in resolving all difficulties. Ieyasu managed to survive many battles. He was not a family man, but always oriented towards regaining power by his clan and succession oriented, careful with money, of simple and frugal habits, and had only one entertainment hawking.[141] Asakawa calls him a self-made man. He showed great courage in war but used gentler methods than his predecessors.[142] The second party was nominally led by Hideyori (Hideyoshi's son), but the real leader was Ishida Mitsunari, a great enemy of leyasu. The struggle of both sides for supremacy ended in the greatest, bloodiest, *samurai* field battle in history, fought on 21 October 1600, on the Sekigahara plain (near Nagoya). An army, counting 130,000 men provided by a coalition of *western daimyō*, led by Ishida Mitsunari attacked the 80,000 *eastern* troops under the command of Ieyasu, and was defeated. After the battle, Hideyori, Hideyoshi's young son and successor, was replaced by Tokugawa. Leyasu was determined to build on his victory at Sekigahara and the achievements of Nobunaga and Hideyoshi that formed the basis of his power.[143] The conquest of those who fought for Hideyori's cause ended the civil war of the Sengoku period. Ieyasu completed the national reunification process by subordinating local *daimyō* to the hereditary *shōgunate* in 1603, when Emperor Go-Yozei granted him the title of *shōgun*. The winner of the Sekigahara battle was of the Minamoto family, a descendant of the founder of the Kamakura *Bakufu* Minamoto no Yoritomo; therefore, he had an adequate lineage required to take the title of *shōgun*. After the death of the titular Ashikaga *Shōgun* (Yoshiato), Ieyasu had no difficulty to take the title of *sei-i-tai-shōgun* for himself and his descendants. The court issued the formal letter of appointment at the end of 1603 and the Tokugawa *Shōgunate* was established, within which 15 Tokugawa *shōguns* (Ieyasu (1542–1616), *shōgun* 1603–1605; Hidetada (1579–1632), *shōgun* 1605–1623; Iemitsu (1604–1651), *shōgun* 1623–1651; Ietsuna (1641–1680), *shōgun* 1651–1680; Tsunayoshi (1646–1709), *shōgun* 1680–1709; Ienobu (1662–1712), *shōgun* 1709–1712; Ietsugu (1709–1716), *shōgun* 1713–1716; Yoshimune (1684–1751), *shōgun* 1716–1745; Ieshige (1711–1761), *shōgun* 1745–1760; Ieharu (1737–1786), *shōgun* 1760–1786; Ienari (1773–1841), *shōgun* 1787–1837; Ieyoshi (1793–1853), *shōgun* 1837–1853; Iesada (1824–1858), *shōgun* 1853–1858; Iemochi (1846–1866), *shōgun* 1858–1866; Yoshinobu (Keiki) (1837–1913), *shōgun* 1866–1867) ruled Japan till the 1868.[144] By taking the title, *shōgun* Ieyasu became the emperor's military deputy, head of the military class, and de facto ruler of Japan.[145] The Tokugawa became the most influential family. The administrative power of the empire came wholly to the *shōgun*, and the entire country accepted his control. Because of the security reasons, Ieyasu made his headquarters in a century-old castle at Edo (now Tōkyō), situated far away from Asian continent, turning this fishing village surrounded by marshland, into a metropolis.[146]

Ieyasu was *shōgun* for only two years, because he passed the title to his son Hidetada in 1605. The court's practice of appointing a successor while the *shōgun* was still in good health (Hidetada handed over the office of *shōgun* to his son Iemitsu in 1623) ensured continuity in their policy and strengthened the administrative system during the critical years of its founding. The consolidation was done so well that in 1651 the regime not only overcame the immediate problem of having a *shōgun* child but remained fully effective even when *shōgun* Ietsuna was too ill to rule. Ieyasu retired to ensure a smooth succession, but he continued to rule from behind the scenes. He was able to concentrate on increasing the family's hold on power by looking after the affairs of the nation and his family without dealing with the details of routine administration. Before his death in 1616, he managed to resolve the conflict with Hideyoshi's son. In order to ensure that the Tokugawa maintain power and control over the nation, he decided to get rid of his main rival in 1615. Therefore, he besieged and destroyed the headquarters of Hideyori (Hideyoshi's son), killing him and his family (*seppuku*) in the attack on the Osaka castle. The two decisive Sekigahara and Osaka campaigns gave Ieyasu military control of the entire country and consolidated his power. He either killed the obstructing *daimyō*, especially those who had been faithful to the Toyotomi House to the last, confiscated (wholly or in part) the estates of the chiefs who had opposed him, or exiled them into distant parts of the country. The acquired land estates Ieyasu distributed among his supporters. It was his priority, because he was aware that the domain lords were able to resist him with force. The *samurai* of the defeated *daimyō* were disarmed, and the peasants involved in the revolt and their families bound to a specific area of land.[147] In this way, Ieyasu consolidated Hidetada position as the ruling *shōgun* of the Edo *Shōgunate*. Japan once again became a centralized, strong feudal state, based on powerful lord–vassal relations in the provinces. The central authority fell to the *shōgun* starting the long Tokugawa period, during which Japan lived at peace both with the outside world and within her own frontiers.[148] But, unlike the peaceful revolution of the 7th century, the 16th-century struggles to centralize Japan were long, bloody, and costly.

Notes

1 K. Hara, An Introduction to the History of Japan. *Yamato Society Publication, G. P. Putnam's & Sons, The Knickerbocker Press*, New York and London 1920, p. 216.
2 M. B. Jansen, The Making of Modern Japan. *The Belknap Press of Harvard University Press*, Cambridge, MA and London 2002, pp. 4–5.
3 K. G. Henshall, A History of Japan: From Stone Age to Superpower. *Palgrave Macmillan* 2012, pp. 17, 39–40. www.gutenberg.org/files/37186/37186-h/37186-h.htm.
4 K. Hara, An Introduction to the History of Japan . . . op. cit., pp. 208–210; K. G. Henshall, A History of Japan . . . op. cit., pp. 17, 41.
5 E. I. Segal, Coins, Trade, and the State Economic Growth in Early Medieval Japan. Harvard East Asian Monographs. *Harvard University Press*, Cambridge, MA and London 2011, p. 191.
6 K. A Grossberg, From Feudal Chieftain to Secular Monarch: The Development of *Shōgunal* Power in Early Muromachi Japan. *Monumenta Nipponica* 1976, Vol. 31, No. 1, pp. 29–49.
7 K. Asakawa, Japan: From the Japanese Government History. In: H. C. Lodge (ed.), The History of Nations. Vol. 7. *John D. Morris and Company* 1906, p. 91. www.gutenberg.org/ebooks/45645.
8 J. Murdoch, History of Japan, from the Origins to the Arrival of the Portuguese in 1542 A.D., Vol. I. *The Asiatic Society of Japan* 1910, p. 590. file:///D:/Users/wzr/Documents/Japonia%20Ks1/Ksi%C4%85%C5%BCki%20Hist/A%20history%20of%20Japan%20Volume%201%20(1903).pdf.
9 K. Asakawa, Japan: From the Japanese Government History. In: H. C. Lodge (ed.), The History of Nations . . . op. cit., p. 95.
10 K. Hara, An Introduction to the History of Japan . . . op. cit., p. 205.
11 J. Murdoch, History of Japan . . . op. cit., p. 570.
12 H. G. Wren, The Legal System of Pre-Western Japan. *Hastings Law Journal* 1968, Vol. 20, No. 1, pp. 217–244.

13 J. Murdoch, History of Japan . . . op. cit., p. 468.
14 Japan Under *Shōguns*. Chapter 15. *Oxford University Press*, pp. 263–264. www.oup.com.au/__data/assets/pdf_file/0026/58193/Chapter-15-Japan-under-the-shoguns.pdf.
15 K. Hara, An Introduction to the History of Japan . . . op. cit., p. 206.
16 K. G. Henshall, A History of Japan . . . op. cit., p. 41.
17 K. Hara, An Introduction to the History of Japan . . . op. cit., p. 215.
18 K. A. Grossberg, From Feudal Chieftain to Secular Monarch: The Development of *Shōgunal* Power in Early Muromachi Japan. *Monumenta Nipponica* 1976, Vol. 31, No. 1, pp. 29–49.
19 www.britannica.com/place/Japan/The-Muromachi-or-Ashikaga-period-1338-1573.
20 K. Hara, An Introduction to the History of Japan . . . op. cit., pp. 204–211.
21 C. D. Totman, A History of Japan. *Wiley,* Berkeley 2014, pp. 161–162. www.perlego.com/book/1006239/a-history-of-japan-pdf.
22 K. Hara, An Introduction to the History of Japan . . . op. cit., p. 215.
23 www.britannica.com/topic/shugo.
24 www.britannica.com/topic/jito.
25 J. P. Mass, The Kamakura *bakufu*. In: The Cambridge History of Japan: Medieval Japan. Vol. 3. *Cambridge University Press*, Cambridge 2008, p. 83.
26 K. Hara, An Introduction to the History of Japan . . . op. cit., p. 215.
27 E. I. Segal, Coins, Trade, and the State Economic Growth in Early Medieval Japan . . . op. cit., p. 191.
28 E. I. Segal, Coins, Trade, and the State Economic Growth in Early Medieval Japan . . . op. cit., pp. 180–183.
29 J. Murdoch, History of Japan, op. cit., p. 596.
30 T. Kuroda, J. C. Dobbins, The Development of the *Kenmitsu* System as Japan's Medieval Orthodoxy. *Japanese Journal of Religious Studies* 1996, Vol. 23, No. 3–4, pp. 233–269.
31 K. G. Henshall, A History of Japan . . . op. cit., pp. 41–42.
32 C. Andressen, A Short History of Japan . . . op. cit., p. 41.
33 J. Murdoch, History of Japan . . . op. cit., p. 608.
34 W. W. Farris, Japan to 1600: A Social and Economic History . . . op. cit.
35 J. Murdoch, History of Japan . . . op. cit., p. 601.
36 K. Asakawa, Japan: From the Japanese Government History. In: H. C. Lodge (ed.), The History of Nations . . . op. cit., p. 95.
37 M. W. Meyer, Japan: A Concise History . . . op. cit., pp. 81–84.
38 Ibidem, p. 77.
39 J. Murdoch, History of Japan . . . op. cit., p. 566.
40 Ibidem, p. 620.
41 R. H. P. Mason, J. G. Caiger, A History of Japan . . . op. cit., p. 140.
42 K. Hara, An Introduction to the History of Japan . . . op. cit., pp. 212, 216.
43 Ibidem, p. 217.
44 J. Murdoch, History of Japan . . . op. cit., p. 602.
45 E. I. Segal, Coins, Trade, and the State Economic Growth in Early Medieval Japan . . . op. cit., p. 192.
46 K. Asakawa, Japan from the Japanese Government History . . . op. cit.
47 T. Kuroda, S. Gay, Buddhism and Society in the Medieval Estate System. *Japanese Journal of Religious Studies* 1996, Vol. 23, No. 3–4, 1996, pp. 287–319.
48 C. D. Totman, A History of Japan . . . op. cit., p. 170.
49 C. Andressen, A Short History of Japan . . . op. cit., p. 55.
50 J. Murdoch, History of Japan . . . op. cit., p. 619.

51 C. D. Totman, A History of Japan . . . op. cit., p. 170.
52 K. Hara, An Introduction to the History of Japan . . . op. cit., pp. 213–215.
53 K. Asakawa, Japan: From the Japanese Government History. In: H. C. Lodge (ed.), The History of Nations . . . op. cit., p. 93.
54 J. Murdoch, History of Japan . . . op. cit., pp. 606–607.
55 Ibidem, pp. 603–605.
56 T. Kuroda, J. I. Stone, The Imperial Law and the Buddhist Law. *Japanese Journal of Religious Studies* 1996, Vol. 23, No. 3–4, pp. 271–285.
57 Japan Under *Shōguns* . . . op. cit., p. 264.
58 K. Asakawa, Japan: From the Japanese Government History. In: H. C. Lodge (ed.), The History of Nations . . . op. cit., pp. 94–97.
59 M. Jensen, Making a Modern Japan . . . op. cit., p. 5.
60 C. D. Totman, A History of Japan . . . op. cit., p. 146.
61 Ibidem, p. 147.
62 J. Murdoch, History of Japan . . . op. cit., p. 621.
63 K. Asakawa, Japan: From the Japanese Government History. In: H. C. Lodge (ed.), The History of Nations . . . op. cit., p. 108.
64 C. Andressen, A Short History of Japan . . . op. cit., p. 56.
65 K. Yamamura, Introduction. In: The Cambridge History of Japan: Medieval Japan. Vol. 3. *Cambridge University Press*, Cambridge 2008, p. 1.
66 www.britannica.com/place/Japan/The-establishment-of-warrior-culture.
67 J. Murdoch, History of Japan . . . op. cit., p. 634.
68 C. Andressen, A Short History of Japan . . . op. cit., pp. 59–60.
69 K. G. Henshall, A History of Japan . . . op. cit., p. 35.
70 T. Kuroda, J. C. Dobbins, The Development of the Kenmitsu System as Japan's Medieval . . . op. cit.
71 K. Hara, An Introduction to the History of Japan . . . op. cit., p. 262.
72 K. Asakawa, Japan: From the Japanese Government History. In: H. C. Lodge (ed.), The History of Nations . . . op. cit., p. 100.
73 C. D. Totman, A History of Japan . . . op. cit., p. 171.
74 E. I. Segal, Coins, Trade, and the State Economic Growth in Early Medieval Japan . . . op. cit., p. 196.
75 M. Jansen, Making a Modern Japan . . . op. cit., p. 5.
76 K. Asakawa, Japan: From the Japanese Government History. In: H. C. Lodge (ed.), The History of Nations . . . op. cit., p. 100.
77 R. H. P. Mason, J. G. Caiger, A History of Japan . . . op. cit., pp. 145–146.
78 www.britannica.com/place/Japan/The-Onin-War-1467-77.
79 W. Osamu, The Emergence of the State in Sixteenth-Century Japan: From Oda to Tokugawa. *Journal of Japanese Studies* 1982, Vol. 8, No. 2, pp. 343–367.
80 R. H. P. Mason, J. G. Caiger, A History of Japan . . . op. cit., p. 145.
81 K. Hara, An Introduction to the History of Japan . . . op. cit., p. 100.
82 C. Andressen, A Short History of Japan . . . op. cit., p. 58.
83 A. R. Leen, M. C. Huang, How a Free Market System Resulted in Hegemony and a Magnificent Era: The Case of Nobunga Oda, 16th Century, Japan. *Archives of Economic History* 2008, Vol. XIX, No. 1, pp. 5–16.
84 C. Andressen, A Short History of Japan . . . op. cit., p. 58.
85 J. W. Hall, Feudalism in Japan: A Reassessment . . . op. cit.
86 K. Asakawa, Japan: From the Japanese Government History. In: H. C. Lodge (ed.), The History of Nations . . . op. cit., p. 100.
87 J. Murdoch, History of Japan . . . op. cit., p. 633.

88 P. Streich, The Failure of the Balance of Power in Medieval Japan, 1568–1600 (2009). *APSA 2009 Toronto Meeting Paper* 2009. SSRN. https://ssrn.com/abstract=1451549.
89 F. Brinkley, D. Kikuchi, A History of the Japanese People . . . op. cit., p. 475.
90 K. G. Henshall, A History of Japan . . . op. cit., pp. 17, 44.
91 K. Asakawa, Japan: From the Japanese Government History. In: H. C. Lodge (ed.), The History of Nations . . . op. cit., p. 110; A. Gordon, A Modern History of Japan: From Tokugawa Times to Present, *Oxford University Press*, New York and Oxford 2003, p. 11.
92 M. B. Jensen, Making a Modern Japan . . . op. cit., pp. 12–14.
93 K. Asakawa, Japan: From the Japanese Government History. In: H. C. Lodge (ed.), The History of Nations . . . op. cit., p. 101.
94 M. W. Meyer, Japan: A Concise History . . . op. cit., p. 177.
95 F. Brinkley, D. Kikuchi, A History of the Japanese People . . . op. cit., p. 492.
96 A. Naohiro, The Sixteenth-Century Unification. In: J. W. Hall (ed.), The Cambridge History of Japan: Early Modern Japan. Vol. 4. *Cambridge University Press*, Cambridge 1991, p. 43.
97 M. W. Meyer, Japan: A Concise History . . . op. cit., p. 95.
98 A. Naohiro, The Sixteenth-Century Unification. In: J. W. Hall (ed.), The Cambridge History of Japan . . . op. cit., p. 44.
99 R. H. P. Mason, J. G. Caiger, A History of Japan . . . op. cit., pp. 174–176.
100 A. R. Leen, M. C. Huang, How a Free-Market System Resulted in Hegemony and . . . op. cit.
101 H. P. Varley, Cultural Life in Medieval Japan. In: The Cambridge History of Japan: Medieval Japan. Vol. 3. *Cambridge University Press*, Cambridge 2008, pp. 493–497.
102 A. R. Leen, M. C. Huang, How a Free-Market System Resulted in Hegemony . . . op. cit.
103 www.britannica.com/biography/Oda-Nobunaga.
104 www.britannica.com/biography/Toyotomi-Hideyoshi.
105 K. Asakawa, Japan: From the Japanese Government History. In: H. C. Lodge (ed.), The History of Nations . . . op. cit., p. 114; C. Andressen, A Short History of Japan . . . op. cit., p. 46.
106 A. Naohiro, The Sixteenth-Century Unification. In: J. W. Hall (ed.), The Cambridge History of Japan . . . op. cit., p. 47.
107 K. G. Henshall, A History of Japan . . . op. cit., p. 48.
108 A. Boscaro, Toyotomi Hideyoshi and the 1587 Edicts Against Christianity. *Oriens Extremus* 1973, Vol. 20, No. 2, pp. 219–241.
109 R. K. Morck, M. Nakamura, A Frog in a Well Knows Nothing of the Ocean: A History of Corporate Ownership in Japan. NBER Chapters. In: A History of Corporate Governance Around the World: Family Business Groups to Professional Managers, *University of Chicago Press*, Chicago 2005, pp. 367–466.
110 C. Andressen, A Short History of Japan . . . op. cit., pp. 61–62.
111 R. H. P. Mason, J. G. Caiger, A History of Japan . . . op. cit., p. 148.
112 W. Osamu, The Emergence of the State in Sixteenth-Century Japan . . . op. cit.
113 M. W. Meyer, Japan: A Concise History . . . op. cit., p. 97.
114 W. Osamu, The *kokudaka* System: A Device for Unification. *Journal of Japanese Studies* 1975, Vol. 1, No. 2, pp. 297–320.
115 Ibidem.
116 E. I. Segal, Coins, Trade, and the State Economic Growth in Early Medieval Japan . . . op. cit., p. 167.

117 R. H. P. Mason, J. G. Caiger, A History of Japan . . . op. cit., p. 179.
118 C. Andressen, A Short History of Japan . . . op. cit., p. 62.
119 S. McGinty, From Peasant to Shareholder: Divergent Paths of Group Litigation in Tokugawa Japan and England (January 21, 2012). Collective Actions: Enhancing Access to Justice and Reconciling Multilayer Interests. *Cambridge University Press* April 2012. SSRN. https://ssrn.com/abstract=3581528.
120 S. McGinty, From Peasant to Shareholder . . . op. cit.; C. Andressen, A Short History of Japan . . . op. cit., p. 68.
121 C. Andressen, A Short History of Japan . . . op. cit., p. 68.
122 M. P. Culeddu, The *Samurai* Bond of Loyalty: Transition from Blood Ties Through Self-Interested Allegiance to Absolute Devotion. *Journal of Cultural Interaction in East Asia* 2013, Vol. 4.
123 K. G. Henshall, A History of Japan . . . op. cit., p. 49.
124 C. Andressen, A Short History of Japan . . . op. cit., p. 46.
125 K. Asakawa, Japan: From the Japanese Government History. In: H. C. Lodge (ed.), The History of Nations . . . op. cit.
126 . W. Osamu, The *kokudaka* System: A Device for Unification . . . op. cit.
127 K. Asakawa, Japan: From the Japanese Government History. In: H. C. Lodge (ed.), The History of Nations . . . op. cit.
128 R. H. P. Mason, J. G. Caiger, A History of Japan . . . op. cit., p. 148.
129 W. Osamu, The *kokudaka* System: A Device for Unification . . . op. cit.
130 F. Brinkley, D. Kikuchi, A History of the Japanese People from the Earliest . . . op. cit., p. 526.
131 Ibidem, pp. 525, 526.
132 K. Asakawa, Japan: From the Japanese Government History. In: H. C. Lodge (ed.), The History of Nations . . . op. cit., p. 115.
133 F. Brinkley, D. Kikuchi, A History of the Japanese People from the Earliest . . . op. cit., p. 525.
134 K. Asakawa, Japan: From the Japanese Government History. In: H. C. Lodge (ed.), The History of Nations . . . op. cit.
135 F. Brinkley, D. Kikuchi, A History of the Japanese People from the Earliest . . . op. cit., pp. 523–524.
136 E. I. Segal, Coins, Trade, and the State Economic Growth in Early Medieval Japan . . . op. cit., pp. 180–181.
137 K. Asakawa, Japan: From the Japanese Government History. In: H. C. Lodge (ed.), The History of Nations . . . op. cit., p. 115.
138 C. Andressen, A Short History of Japan: From Samurai to Sony. *Allen & Unvin*, Canberra 2002, p. 46.
139 F. Brinkley, D. Kikuchi, A History of the Japanese People from the Earliest . . . op. cit., p. 523.
140 R. H. P. Mason, J. G. Caiger, A History of Japan . . . op. cit., pp. 190–191.
141 K. Asakawa, Japan: From the Japanese Government History. In: H. C. Lodge (ed.), The History of Nations . . . op. cit., p. 124.
142 Ibidem, p. 122.
143 K. G. Henshall, A History of Japan . . . op. cit., p. 53; K. Asakawa, Japan: From the Japanese Government History. In: H. C. Lodge (ed.), The History of Nations . . . op. cit., p. 125.
144 K. Asakawa, Japan: From the Japanese Government History. In: H. C. Lodge (ed.), The History of Nations . . . op. cit., p. 125.
145 W. G. Beasley, The Meiji Restoration. *Stanford University Press*, Stanford, CA 1972, p. 14.

146 S. McGinty, From Peasant to Shareholder . . . op. cit.
147 E. Ehrlich, Japan: A Case of Catching Up. *Akademiai Kiado*, Budapest 1984, p. 21.
148 C. Andressen, A Short History of Japan . . . op. cit., pp. 42–65.

Bibliography

Andressen, C., A Short History of Japan: From Samurai to Sony. *Allen & Unvin*, Canberra 2002.

Asakawa, K., Japan: From the Japanese Government History. In: H. C. Lodge (ed.), The History of Nations, Vol. 7. *John D. Morris and Company* 1906. www.gutenberg.org/ebooks/45645.

Beasley, W. G., The Meiji Restoration. *Stanford University Press*, Stanford, CA 1972.

Boscaro, A., Toyotomi Hideyoshi and the 1587 Edicts Against Christianity. *Oriens Extremus* 1973, Vol. 20, No. 2, pp. 219–241. *JSTOR*. www.jstor.org/stable/44001284.

Brinkley, F., Kikuchi, D., A History of the Japanese People from the Earliest Times to the End of the Meiji Era. *The Encyclopaedia Britannica Co.*, New York and London 1912. https://archive.org/details/historyofjapanes00briniala/page/n5/mode/2up.

www.britannica.com/biography/Oda-Nobunaga.

www.britannica.com/biography/Toyotomi-Hideyoshi.

www.britannica.com/place/Japan/The-establishment-of-warrior-culture.

www.britannica.com/place/Japan/The-Muromachi-or-Ashikaga-period-1338-1573.

www.britannica.com/place/Japan/The-Onin-War-1467-77.

www.britannica.com/topic/jito.

www.britannica.com/topic/shugo.

Culeddu, M. P., The Samurai Bond of Loyalty: Transition from Blood Ties Through Self-Interested Allegiance to Absolute Devotion. *Journal of Cultural Interaction in East Asia* 2013, Vol. 4. file:///D:/Users/wzr/Downloads/Samurai_Bond_of_Loyalty_Transition_from%20(2).pdf.

Ehrlich, E., Japan: A Case of Catching Up. *Akademiai Kiado*, Budapest 1984.

Farris, W. W., Japan to 1600: A Social and Economic History. *University of Hawai'i Press* 2009, pp. 164–194. *JSTOR*. www.jstor.org/stable/j.ctt6wqt09.12.

file:///D:/Users/wzr/Downloads/A_frog_in_a_well_knows_nothing_of_the_oc%20(1).pdf.

Gordon, A., Modern History of Japan: From Tokugawa Times to Present. *Oxford University Press*, New York and Oxford 2003.

Grossberg, K. A., From Feudal Chieftain to Secular Monarch: The Development of *Shōgunal* Power in Early Muromachi Japan. *Monumenta Nipponica* 1976, Vol. 31, No. 1, pp. 29–49. *JSTOR*. https://doi.org/10.2307/2384184.

Hall, J. W., Feudalism in Japan: A Reassessment. *Comparative Studies in Society and History* 1962, Vol. 5, No. 1, pp. 15–51. *JSTOR*. www.jstor.org/stable/177767.

Hall, J. W., McClain, J. L. (eds.), The Cambridge History of Japan. In: Early Modern Japan, Vol. 4. *Cambridge University Press*, Cambridge 2008.

Hara, K., An Introduction to the History of Japan. *Yamato Society Publication, G. P. Putnam's & Sons, The Knickerbocker Press*, New York and London 1920. www.gutenberg.org/files/37186/37186-h/37186-h.htm.

Henshall, K. G., A History of Japan: From Stone Age to Superpower. *Palgrave Macmillan* 2012. www.gutenberg.org/files/37186/37186-h/37186-h.htm.

Jansen, M. B., The Making of Modern Japan. *The Belknap Press of Harvard University Press*, Cambridge, MA and London 2002. *JSTOR*. https://doi.org/10.2307/j.ctvjf9vr7.

Japan Under *shōgun*. Chapter 15. *Oxford University Press*. www.oup.com.au/__data/assets/pdf_file/0026/58193/Chapter-15-Japan-under-the-shoguns.pdf.

Kuroda, T., Dobbins, J. C., The Development of the *Kenmitsu* System as Japan's Medieval Orthodoxy. *Japanese Journal of Religious Studies* 1996, Vol. 23, No. 3–4, pp. 233–269. *JSTOR*. www.jstor.org/stable/30233574.

Kuroda, T., Gay, S., Buddhism and Society in the Medieval Estate System. *Japanese Journal of Religious Studies* 1996, Vol. 23, No. 3–4, pp. 287–319. *JSTOR*. www.jstor.org/stable/30233576.

Kuroda, T., Stone, J. I., The Imperial Law and the Buddhist Law. *Japanese Journal of Religious Studies* 1996, Vol. 23, No. 3–4, pp. 271–285. *JSTOR*. www.jstor.org/stable/30233575.

Leen, A. R., Huang, M. C., How a Free Market System Resulted in Hegemony and a Magnificent Era: The Case of Nobunga Oda, 16th Century, Japan. *Archives of Economic History* 2008, Vol. XIX, No. 1, pp. 5–16, ISSN 1108-7005.

Mason, R. H. P., Caiger, J. G., A History of Japan. *TUTTLE Publishing* 1997. file:///D:/Users/wzr/Downloads/A_History_of_Japan_Mason_Caiger%20(5).pdf.

McGinty, S., From Peasant to Shareholder: Divergent Paths of Group Litigation in Tokugawa Japan and England (January 21, 2012). Collective Actions: Enhancing Access to Justice and Reconciling Multilayer Interests. *Cambridge University Press* 2012. SSRN. https://ssrn.com/abstract=3581528.

Meyer, M. W., Japan: A Concise History. *Rowman & Littlefield Publishers Inc*., Plymouth 2009. file:///D:/Users/wzr/Downloads/epdf.pub_japan-a-concise-history-4th-edition.pdf.

Morck, R. K. (ed.), A History of Corporate Governance Around the World: Family Business Groups to Professional Managers. *University of Chicago Press*, Chicago 2005.

Murdoch, J., History of Japan, from the Origins to the Arrival of the Portuguese in 1542 A.D., Vol. I. *The Asiatic Society of Japan* 1910. file:///D:/Users/wzr/Documents/Japonia%20Ks1/Ksi%C4%85%C5%BCki%20Hist/A%20history%20of%20Japan%20Volume%201%20(1903).pdf.

Osamu, W., The *kokudaka* System: A Device for Unification. *Journal of Japanese Studies* 1975, Vol. 1, No. 2, pp. 297–320. *JSTOR*. www.jstor.org/stable/132128.

Osamu, W., The Emergence of the State in Sixteenth-Century Japan: From Oda to Tokugawa. *Journal of Japanese Studies* 1982, Vol. 8, No. 2, pp. 343–367. *JSTOR*. https://doi.org/10.2307/132343.

Segal, E. I., Coins, Trade, and the State Economic Growth in Early Medieval Japan. Harvard East Asian Monographs. *Harvard University Press*, Cambridge, MA and London 2011. file:///D:/Users/wzr/Downloads/coins-trade-and-the-state-economic-growth-in-early-medieval-japan-illustrated-0674060687-9780674060685_compress.pdf.

Streich, P., The Failure of the Balance of Power in Medieval Japan, 1568–1600 (2009). *APSA 2009 Toronto Meeting Paper* 2009. SSRN. https://ssrn.com/abstract=1451549.

Totman, C. D., A History of Japan. *Wiley* 2014. www.perlego.com/book/1006239/a-history-of-japan-pdf.

Wren, H. G., The Legal System of Pre-Western Japan. *Hastings Law Journal* 1968, Vol. 20, No. 1, pp. 217–244. https://repository.uchastings.edu/hastings_law_journal/vol20/iss1/5.

Yamamura, K. (ed.), The Cambridge History of Japan. In: Medieval Japan, Vol. 3. *Cambridge University Press*, Cambridge 2008.

11 Highlights of the corporate governance in the period 1338–1603

The disintegration of the Ashikaga *Shōgunate* and its consequences for corporate governance

During the Ashikaga period, the *Ritsuryō* State ceased to exist. Its governance system, based on the imperial structure set by the Taika reform, still functioned, but in an ever weaker and only nominal way. The Ashikaga system of governance was highly conservative, because the country's isolation and the reliance on tradition allowed elites to resist changes. It went full circle around during that period. Japan gradually returned to regional *kingdoms* called fiefs, headed by *daimyō*, and therefore to the pre-Taika reform clan pattern. Control of land had shifted from the emperor to great local families, shrines, and temples. The *emperors at that time reigned but did not rule*. During the Warring States period, Japan became a patchwork of decentralized units controlled through a combination of weak *shōgunal* rule (macro level) and powerful provincial lords (micro level). Personal ambition and individual aggrandizement were the ruling motives of that time.[1] Smooth operation of *bakufu* was disturbed by wars, riots, rivalry between the court and the *shōgunate*, between the nobility, temples, and shrines, leading to destruction and weakening of the country.[2] This resulted in the action of three of the most powerful warriors and leaders, who one by one consistently fought for the reunification of Japan. The Age of Warring States witnessed the gradual reassertion of central government authority, and finally at the beginning of the 17th century, Japan was reunited again under the strong *shōguns*.[3]

In the macroeconomic aspect, the multitude and depth of the changes in the Ashikaga *Bakufu* made the vertical relations very complicated, especially the relationship between the emperors (reigning and cloistered) and their regents, *shōgun* and his regent, court, later also the retired *shōgun*, government, ministers, *shugo*, *jitō*, and *samurai* in provinces. In the years preceding the Ōnin War, these relations may be considered, in the light of the Resource Dependency Theory, the Social Networks Theory, the Managerial and Class

DOI: 10.4324/9781003497936-15

Hegemony Theory, Agency Theory, and Stewardship Theory. However, during the Azuchi–Momoyama period, the Class Hegemony Theory and the Agency Theory had grown in importance. The former can be applied especially to the Age of Warring States when the three great warriors ruthlessly fought for hegemony in their class and in the state. This fight was dictated by their own great ambitions and the desire to save the country, which was weakening due to internal conflicts. The latter may be used to consider those conflicts during the Age of Warring States at the macro and micro levels. It should be noted that all the theories consider the same reality and problems but using a different point of view.

Resource Dependency Theory (RDT) can only be applied to the first decades of the Ashikaga period, when state-form organization provided synergistic benefits. As before, the emperor, and the *shōgun* formed alliances, made conquests striving to gain or hold power, improve organization in the areas of their domination or influence, and maximize their revenues. State synergies in peacetime ensured solidarity prosperity, and consolidated the country. However, the distribution of the benefits resulting from this synergy was not symmetrical. As noted earlier, Japan may be considered corporation. At first its stakeholders were happy with the revenues they received and were accepting the governance system, trying to keep it in the best form possible. For the first decades, the *shugo–jitō* system worked well. But the *shōen*, created for maximizing returns for owners by means of tax exemptions and tax optimization, got obliterated. Local nobles modified them to suit their interests. Commendation, tax exemptions, manipulation of land ownership, assessment of serfdom, and tax collection were among the instruments they used to obtain additional income and benefits which ultimately led to the destruction of the *ritsuryō* system. It led to struggle for power and benefits between the aristocrats and local landlords. The lack of compromise between them caused the court aristocracy lost its dominant position to emerging powerful *daimyō*, oriented towards creating their own domains (states) and increasing their own income. The flow of the revenues (benefits) to the highest layer of the society was disturbed by the lower, local landlords and officials. A new hierarchy of power emerged to preserve optimal for them division of revenues. As a result of turmoil and wars, the interests of the aristocracy and the local nobility were no longer compatible, the weak state did not provide synergy effects, which is why RDT began to lose its importance.

Applying the Theory of Social Networks (TSN) to the Muromachi and the Azuchi–Momoyama periods, as before, at the macro level two main networks can be identified, namely the network headed by the emperor and the network subordinated to the *shōgun*. At the micro level, two new strong networks emerged: domains consisting of castle towns and villages, and a network formed by merchants and craftsmen (business people). The latter were mostly operating under landlords, temples, or shrines. These separated social networks, and subnetworks within them, were very well organized, governed, and controlled. They had a significant impact on the governance system in the centuries to come, and established the foundations of the modern Japanese economy. Their leaders were crucial, because they connected the networks to their strategic environment – the state, direct superiors, and landlords. *Shōguns* during the Muromachi period strengthened the *shugo–jitō* system, which benefited all social networks. It not only ensured control of the country and efficient raising of revenues for the *bakufu* but also formed a solid governance structure based on loyalty and financial rewards. Stewards and constables controlled the provinces tightly and loyally, based on local custom and military House laws, rather than the centrally imposed legal codes of the *ritsuryō* system.[4] In turn, the officials were under strict control of the *bakufu* and its institutions. This system strongly protected the social hierarchy, ensuring that social networks were separated from each other, and the law ensured respect for their positions, duties, and rights. Weak network leaders were responsible for unsustainable development and crises within them. The weak *shōgun* could be blamed for the rule of two monarchs, wars, the fall of the *shōgunate*, the exploitation of peasants, and restrictions on merchants and craftsmen. The *shōgunal* network evolved into a network consisting of *daimyō* and their *samurai* retainers, which became the strongest of all networks in the Muromachi period. Each fief was similar to well-managed and efficient corporation; their *daimyo* (managers) were able to govern them well and efficiently. However, they competed fiercely with each other for obtaining more resources (wealth) or gaining more power. *Daimyo* conducted their own politics, made and broke alliances, looked for strong protectors with whom they cooperated or betrayed them. They were driven primarily by ambition or the need to defend their own interests. They also used corporate governance mechanisms, which include the creation of a *daimyo* council (macro level), as well as the governance and control hierarchy relationships within their domains (internal mechanisms). Domains can be compared to enterprises with strong managers and competing in the market for influence and position, much like clans in the early Yamato period.

Merchants and artisans created their own networks and obtained certain privileges from powerful patrons, giving them financial benefits and securing their businesses. To protect own interests, they managed to form self-governing formal institutions–guilds or (*za*), managed them professionally, and expanded them throughout the country. The development of trade and crafts was conditioned by the growing productivity of agriculture. The growing entrepreneurship of peasants led to increased agricultural efficiency, which enabled them to build local (village) and family networks. These networks (well-managed, effective, and innovative enterprises) contributed to an increase in their income and better protection of their interests. This was the only possibility for them to improve their lives (maybe with the exception of the army), because their social position did not allow them to gain political power or positions in the administration. Further development of self-governance structures resulted in greater agricultural and manufacturing production, the use of advanced technologies and the development of entrepreneurship, which ultimately strengthened and enriched the members of these networks.

Family networks, as already mentioned, can be compared to well-managed and controlled corporations whose goals, rights, and obligations, including those of their leaders (CEOs), have not changed compared to previous periods. However, due to the weakness of the government, the possibility of achieving these goals had increased. The family was still governed by a head principal, oriented towards growth of own family possessions, power, and position, who controlled and coordinated the family's policies, and initiated alliances and wars against the enemies or competitors of the family. The head of the family administrated its property, distributed income among family members, guaranteed obeying the family laws (codes), and eliminated all that could undermine the family's position and collective strength. The main aim of such a policy was to maximize the status and wealth (interests) of a family. There were fierce fights and frictions for position between and within families. For families, both internally and externally, loyalty became paramount, and any conflict of interest or insubordination was often punishable by death.

The Managerial and Class Hegemony Theory (MCHT) is probably most significant for the Azuchi–Momoyama period. The Ashikaga era was time of great struggles for power, between the emperors of the south and north dynasties (dual monarchy), and emperors and *shōguns* (Go-Daigo), and by the *daimyō* competing and fighting with the aristocracy and between themselves for fiefs and wealth. This theory is particularly appropriate for the period in which the struggle for power and centralization of the state was led successively by three great unifiers, with enormous ambitions, awareness of their own strength and fully determined in pursuing their goals.

During the Ashikaga period, the emperor was the de facto ruler and each lord swore loyalty to him, but for most of this time, the monarch was a marginalized, ceremonial, and religious figure dependent on his nominee, the *shōgun*, and powerful aristocratic families (Fujiwara, Hōjō, Ashikaga, Tokugawa). Only the emperor had the power to create these hegemons, but he was too weak to oppose the aspirations of powerful families. Personal ambition and individual aggrandizement depended much on the hegemon's personality, self-perception of power, leadership skills, and ability to gain strong allies, both on national, provincial, district, and *shōen* levels. All these features affected the behaviour and performance of the government and welfare of the state. However, the weak macro-level governance caused that managing and governing Japan shifted from the aristocrats to the powerful *daimyo*, oriented towards maximizing their benefits. The *shōen* entailed separation of ownership and control, but the lower-level nobles and warriors who gained economic strength and power in provinces created new governance structures – fiefs. For the first hundred years of rule, the Ashikaga clan maintained control of the country as stewards of emperors and were able to create a balance of power between the *shōgun* and the rising *daimyō*. The three most prominent *daimyō* families rotated as deputies to the *shōgun* at Kyōto. However, over time the *shōgunate* became too weak to protect the interests of the aristocracy, effectively losing power and hegemony. The local nobility (*daimyō*) exchanged in power the old court aristocracy. The system of governance at all levels was shaken, but not abolished. The nobility, largely new, remained at the top of the social and economic pyramid of the country. The *shugo* (managers) of the Ashikaga period, warriors and heads of powerful families, transformed into strong *daimyō* with the right to raise troops, turned the resident landowners into their vassals, expanded their power beyond military duties, took an ever-greater share of taxes from estates, and acted as civil regional rulers. They organized a strong vertical governance structure within their domains and became strong hegemons in them. The unrest and wars of the Age of the Warring States period were struggles for hegemony in a country, domain, and family. However, the war that the three great *daimyō* warriors fought for the unification of Japan was also a fight for their own power and hegemony in the country. These new powerful aristocrats became one by one hegemons of the country and its new executive leaders, crushing every enemy and obstacle on their way to success.

Another corporate governance theory that may be applied to the Ashikaga period is the Stewardship Theory. According to it, the emperor may be treated as the head of Japan considered a corporation, having its own Board of Directors in form of the Court. Courtiers–directors took actions in accordance with their interests, and ownership of land (*shōen*) and *shiki* were the basis of their position and power in the corporate state. The chief of the board was the member of the most powerful family. In the Ashikaga period, the land shifted from the imperial lease into hands of *kuge, shugo*, and managers of the *shōen*, later *daimyō*. The *shōguns* in power never rejected the authority of the Imperial House as the moral basis of their supreme political power. The emperor appointed the *shōgun* as the chief executive officer (CEO) of the company that was Japan. The *shōgun* was the steward of the emperor's property, land, and people, having the fiduciary duty towards the monarch. According to the Stewardship Theory, which has roots in psychology and organizational behaviour, managers who identified more with the company were more committed to its values, had greater intrinsic motivation, and were more willing to adopt a stewardship approach. This is how the management relationship between the *shōgun* and the emperor can be understood in a period when there were no open conflicts between them. The *shōgun* should be seen as the emperor's steward rather than an agent. Stewards are more likely to rely on personal sources of power, while agents rely on institutional sources of power. The *shōgun* was a top-level manager who served as the responsible Steward General of the country (assets) he controlled. The *shōguns*–stewards adopted collectivist goals, not individual ones as the agents did. They acted responsibly and independently, focusing on smaller profits, but always trying to take advantage of every opportunity.[5]

The relations between the principal, his board of directors, and the *shōgun* and his own management board, varied during the period under consideration. The *shōguns* elected their own board of directors in the form of government and took full responsibility for the functioning and performance of the corporation that was Japan. Inherent to this concept of corporate governance was the belief that managers (the *shōgunate*) could be trusted because they usually did their job diligently and strictly executed their rights. Therefore, the courtiers (board) entrusted the *shōgun* with providing them with a satisfactory income and easily transferred all military affairs of the state to the *bakufu*. Thus, the *shōgun* became responsible for ensuring military strength, the prosperity of the state and court, maintaining order and taking care of the interests of the nobility. Such duties could be fully fulfilled only by the strong *shōguns*. Initially, the *shōgunate* created a very effective model of governance by strengthening the *shugo–jitō* system, introducing new, rigorous rules of taxation, land management, and control. Ashikaga, although they became known as good and effective managers, did not lose the opportunity to become rich and increase their prestige, occupying the most important and profitable positions in the country and provinces. Their violation of the principle of trusteeship resulted in a significant decline in support and loyalty to the *shōgunate*, contributing to its downfall.

During the Warring States period, it was found that the *shōgunate* was unable to fulfil all its fiduciary duties towards the emperor and the state, due to the lack of resources to finance all the heavy demands and salaries of its retainers. The *shōguns* continued to lose power, along with the emperor and his court. The aristocrats were unable to compete with the growing *daimyō*, who drastically reduced their payments to the state and private individuals. The Stewardship Theory reflecting the classical ideas of corporate governance and the official ideology of management as a social service[6] finally was abandon and substituted by the Agency Theory.

Agency Theory should be used to define the relationship between the nobility, its leaders and agents in both periods considered. Their relations differed significantly in the Ashikaga and Sengoku periods, depending on the situation in the country and the personalities of the leaders of both centres of power. The interests of principals and their agents were not always consistent in the state understood as a corporation that was a *compromise of interests*. Conflicts of interest between them were resolved using diplomacy, the ability to conclude and execute contracts, the use of relationships with superiors, and finally, force. Loyalty became a very important factor in limiting the agency conflicts that existed between the court and the *shōgunate* and the internal conflicts between their members.

Formally, at the top of the governance structure was the emperor who headed the court which acted as the Board of Aristocrats (directors). The formal, nationwide, and multi-level system of governance and state control was headed by the *shōgun* and his government who were responsible for the effective *shugo–jitō* system. The *shōgun* (CEO) did not perform administrative duties personally. This was done by the *kwanryo* (manager), whose duty was to look after the provincial magnates and their affairs. The hierarchical dependences in the governance system were strictly defined and obeyed and caused the state to function like a corporation. The relationships between the stakeholders (emperor, *shōgun*, aristocrats, and *samurai*) were complicated and could not always be resolved by contracts. It was not possible to create an adequate, rational system that would satisfy all state stakeholders while maintaining traditional structures and ways of solving problems. Only a strong emperor (principal) was able to challenge the *shōgun* (CEO) and curb his executive power. The *shōen* had two lines of authority, one subject to the *jitō* and separated from the owner, and the other controlled by agents appointed by the owners. The latter were either long-time residents of the area and possibly the original commanders of some of the land that made up the *shōen*. The former were centrally dispatched professional managers,[7] who were representatives of the *shōgun* in the *shugo–jitō* system. Directors–aristocrats, with declining stakes in the state business, worked in their own interests and benefits. Their returns came from *shōen* supervised and managed by increasingly powerful and selfish agents, the provincial landowners. From an Agency Theory perspective, the purpose of a corporation is to create wealth for its stakeholders or owners. Sharing wealth with managers, which was an agency cost, was justified if managers create more wealth than they receive. Over time, the *shōen* system eroded, leaving the *shōgunate* and court nobility receiving diminishing returns, leading to conflicts of interest between them and provincial landlords.

Conflicts of interest also grew between local representatives of the central owners, who wanted to retain as much control and income as possible, and *jitō*, who were interested in increasing their share. To prevent abuse and fraud, corporations need strong boards of directors to control managers (agents), but the top two hierarchical structures, the *shōgunate* and the court, lost the ability to fulfil these duties.[8] They became selfish in their activity, causing that some powerful aristocrats and officials, managers, small landlords, and local officials turned into self-sufficient landlords ruling their own land and people. When the strong and determined *daimyō* consolidated their power in the domains, wars (conflicts) began between them for wealth, power, and hegemony. However, this situation was reversed during the Warring States era. The centralized system of governance gradually emerged as a nationwide, multi-level, rigorous system of state control, which was successively created by the three unifiers of Japan and governments closely subordinated to them. They resolved conflicts of interest through alliances and wars and demanded complete submission when exercising power. Any insubordination was punished very severely, often with the cruel death of the opponent and his entire family. Another conflict of interest occurred between the unifiers and warrior monks from Buddhist monasteries. Ultimately, it was successfully resolved as the warrior monks were defeated, and Buddhism was never again a political power threatening the country. There were also conflicts of interest at the lower levels of society. They arose because land users multiplied faster than the amount of arable land, and also because the amount of tribute that peasants and craftsmen had to provide was constantly increasing. The way to defend against the effects of the actions of local landowners and officials, as well as armed attacks, was to create unions to jointly manage forests, maintain irrigation, and defense works. Conflicts between peasants and *jitō*, in addition to the aforementioned tax collection, were also caused by the confiscation of private peasant collective funds (*tanomoshi*) created from small monthly contributions from residents of several villages. Each member of the fund could borrow money from the collected amount. Warriors who discovered such funds eagerly confiscated them.[9] Other causes of conflict included the possibility of fraud by debt collectors and imprudent borrowing, which led to conflicts between debtors and creditors. Peasant uprisings were often used to resolve conflicts of interest with landowners and warriors of sanctuaries or temples. It is also worth noting the growing conflicts of interest between the nobility and merchants. Merchants considered *social parasites* did not pay regular taxes but were obliged to pay monetary tributes to their patrons several times a year upon request. Conflicts of interest existed also within the merchant class, especially concerning the *za* and its monopoly rights. Japan's situation in the Azuchi–Momoyama period can be compared to the early Yamato, when Japan was a federation of competing, independent *uji*, but in the Sengoku period Japan was not a federation, but a country of warring states headed by *daimyō*. However, the turbulent vertical and horizontal conflicts and wars between political entities (fiefs) increasingly independent of the central authority, which led to the fall of the Ashikaga *Bakufu*, were eventually ended by the three unifiers, especially the Tokugawa Ieyasu.

The second level of governance concerns micro level. Provincial families (*daimyō*), until the first half of the 16th century, built strong economic and military bases and good corporate governance. The fiefs were managed as corporations, and they were behaving as corporations. Their domains were smaller than the lands assigned to the *shugo* but compact, easy to defend, and under very tight control. The *daimyō* turned local leaders into their retainers (loyal employees) and directly controlled the farming villages. They maintained direct control of the warrior vassals, their potential rivals, by bringing them to the castle towns of the domain. The fiefs were regulated by the *House laws* (*bunkoku-hō*) of the *daimyō* families, which defined the rights and obligations of those who served them, administered and protected their territories. These laws, based on the Joei Formulary, applied strict control over families of retainers and farmers. Inheritance by retainers got restricted to the main heir alone. The lord's permission was necessary for his vassals to inherit property or to marry. The emphasis was on a highly personal relationship between the lord and the servant, based on the loyalty. *Samurai* swore allegiance to their *daimyō* and in return were granted fiefs, in which each *samurai* had control over land and people. This created a lower level of corporations and corporate governance. Again, the similarity to Yamato *uji* may be seen as *daimyō* were self-sufficient, usually had no contacts with the capital, and favoured internalizing problems.

The Ashikaga Code (*Kemmu Shikimoku*) of 1336 was reminding the Prince Shōtoku Constitution (604) including some early corporate governance best practices and social responsibility. It stated that (7) men of special ability for government work should be chosen for the office of *shugo*; (8) a stop must be put to the practice of influential nobles and women of all sorts and Buddhist ecclesiastics making their interested recommendations (to the sovereign); (9) persons holding public posts must be liable to reprimand for negligence and idleness; (10) bribery must be firmly put down; (11) presents made from all quarters to those attached to the Palace whether of the inside or outside services must be sent back; the petitions and complaints of the poor and lowly to be heard and redress granted; the petitions of Temples and Shrines to be dealt with on their merits; certain fixed days to be appointed for the rendering of decisions and the issue of government orders. One clause stipulated a penalty against the manager, if he knew of a crime but failed to act.[10] People had chance to appeal directly to the emperor using a kind of *complaint box* which was installed in court. This document reveals that good governance practices and antifraud measures were already instituted in medieval Japan, whistle-blowers were encouraged, and some aspects of social responsibility were emphasized. Special competences were required from the *shugo* meaning that the government cared for the quality and diligence in governing land and managing people.

The *daimyō* were not the only men to emerge with greater authority as Ashikaga and *shugo* rule collapsed, and *shōen* was obliterated. In the villages around Kyōto, the status of farmers rose significantly, as agriculture became more highly developed, and commerce and small-scale manufacturing prospered. In this age of warfare, peasant farmers struggled to secure and improve their life and income. Many of them started to produce some goods for sale with the possibility to earn additional revenue, initiating and developing entrepreneurship. Villages became able to defend themselves, by forming unions to jointly manage forests and conduct irrigation works, and to defend themselves against destructive local warfare. They were headed by the elder (*otona*) who was (as previously) also an elected leader of the village government. Members regularly held assemblies at the village shrine or temple, where regulations were drawn up for the maintenance of community life. Peasant communities were blocked into groups of five families each, and these groups were held mutually responsible for the implementation of the official directives and punished for breaking law by one of its members. Agricultural villages gained self-governance, had their own authorities, managers, rules, and pursued their own goals, so they can also be compared to corporations. If a village paid its due taxes, the *daimyō* allowed it to manage its own affairs. The old tradition of internalization, that is, dealing with one's own problems, was used. During the years of lack of an effective central government, the peasants were able to organize themselves efficiently, forming a united front against the powerful military men, govern themselves, and create rules that were followed for centuries. All institutions in the country had their self-governance units that secured their own interests and ensured protection and respect for the rights of their members.

A specific model of corporate governance was developed by enterprises (*guilds*) called *za*, organized by craftsmen and merchants, which will be discussed in the next section. All institutions in the country had local government units representing them.

A general assessment of the stages of development of Japanese corporate governance until 1600 allows us to realize that the separation of ownership and control over land led to a conflict of interests and political changes, and in the long run to the devastation of the country, the growth of private property, and the stimulation of the desire to centralize the state. The analysis shows that the lack of direct and appropriate control by the owners and the introduction of managers (agents) resulted in changes in the land ownership structure (gain of wealth and power by the *daimyō*). Already centuries ago, owners who neglected their rights and responsibilities suffered losses, if they failed to resolve conflicts of interest through appropriate contracts and close supervision. This shows the importance of good governance. In periods of strong central management and strict control, order in the country was kept in macro and micro scales, the country developed well, and the entities prospered. In the periods of dispersed power, Japan plunged into bloody and devastating internal conflicts that forced significant economic, political, and social changes.

In medieval Japan, there was a well-defined model of corporate governance. At the very top of the state (corporation) were the emperor and the court. The emperor appointed his deputy or steward, a *shōgun*. The *shōgun* was the head of the *bakufu*, formed his own government, and was the true ruler of Japan. The duties and rights of all officials at all levels were well defined, and the law and the threat of severe punishment ensured compliance. The *shōgun's* control stretched to provinces governed by his military officers, *shugo* and *jitō*, who controlled all the *shōen* and self-governed peasant villages. Peasants (villages) held each other accountable for fulfilling their duties and observing the law. No aspect of their lives was left out of control. The domains were well managed by powerful *daimyō*, who after some decades of self-dependence got again under the strict *shōgunal* control. The provinces were supervised not only by governors (*shugo*) but also by auditors, who were responsible to the central authorities for the assets and achievements of the provinces they controlled.

Group decision-making promotes unanimity and a tendency to suppress public manifestations of conflict. These characteristics are a direct result of their members' respect for values such as harmony, conformism, group solidarity, consensus, belonging, and unanimity, which is consistent with the Japanese cultural tradition. Mutual investment and the pursuit of common interests in an institutional environment, in which abandonment of exchange agreements was unlikely, were a source of consensus in decision-making in rural Japan.[11] Thus, unanimity remained the principle of collective decision-making, which shaped the Japanese preference for collective responsibility and decision-making.

An analysis of the literature allows us to identify the roots of other specific features of current Japanese corporate governance. These factors, shaped by decisions made by owners and managers many centuries ago, are diligence, the ability to cooperate and organize teamwork, loyalty, respect for social and legal structures, submission to authority, conscientious fulfilment of duties, and the honour of (military) service. Confucianism has had a significant impact on the social and legal systems from early state development to the present. It promoted the importance of loyalty to the master and suppressed a decline of morals and discipline, focus on the duty of care, obedience, and respect. In the warrior state, the aspect of obedience (loyalty) was emphasized more than care. Respect for and loyalty to superiors was paramount. The lord–vassal relationship (loyalty/benevolence) was personal, of almost familial nature (lord–parent and vassal child) although at that time, family bonds were not so strong in the warrior's world. These principles are argued to be still respected in Japanese corporations, becoming one of the most important characteristics of Japanese corporate governance.

It was already noted that a very important feature of Japanese corporate governance is the use of hybridization. On the one hand, the Japanese have since ancient times shown solidarity and respect for tradition unparalleled in the history of any other modern nation. On the other hand, Japan has developed a great ability for implementing the best achievements of other nations and adapting them to their own circumstances and needs. The art of enriching their own ideas and achievements with the best of other nations is a hallmark of Japanese society, culture, politics, economy, and corporate governance. This process may be observed throughout the whole history of Japan and plays an important role today.

The rise and fall of the *za* in the pre-Tokugawa Japan

The *za*, an economic institution often compared to the medieval European guild, played a significant role in the development of the economy, especially in commerce, and governance in pre-industrial Japan. *Za* as a guild is an association of persons trading in the same product or having the same profession, and similar economic interests, which takes steps to protect and promote the commercial rights of its members.[12] Four factors, namely urbanization, political economy, human capital, and social relations, contributed to the development of guilds and their institutional diversity in the early modern period of Japan's development.[13] The guild should be seen as the commercial equivalent of the estate (*shōen*).[14]

Za began to appear in Japan during the last decades of the 11th century, at first in and around the capital, and then elsewhere.[15] A document from 1,150 states that various brotherhoods became municipal organizations registering shops or businesses.[16] However, the rapid development of za dates back to the 13th century. But they were not organized and developed enough to monopolize the production, transportation, and sale of goods, until the Muromachi period (1338–1573).[17] They were not only trade, service, and production guilds but also guilds of artists, performers, and entertainers, which survived in their original form until the end of the 16th century, when they were replaced by other forms of business organizations. Even today, performers of *kabuki* and *noh* are in associations called za.

The use of the term *za* to refer to brotherhoods began with the village shrine and temple brotherhoods (*miya za*). These were groups of villagers who took part in rituals in shrines and temples and provided various services to them. Their members, and their assistants (*yoriudo*), were subjects of temples (*jinin*), to which they provided serfdom instead of or in addition to dues paid to the temple or *shōen* (in-kind agricultural taxes and corvée in rice fields). The temple's subjects were exempt from taxes in exchange for services provided to the temple, such as cleaning, cultivating the temple fields, and clearing garbage on ceremonial occasions. The subject's helpers were peasants and artisans who belonged to a *shōen* but worked for the temples. During the ceremonies, both groups (*jinin* and *yoriudo*) occupied places designated for people providing specific services, which were called *hidari-za* (seats on the left), *yoko-za* (seats on the side), and *o-za* (main seats).[18] The roots of *za* also go back to a group that met at the sanctuary to discuss matters of worship, renovation and maintenance of the shrine, and pilgrimages. The temple (shrine) provided a place where internal conflicts and problems of the community were discussed and resolved. Members of this group acted as mediators in rural conflicts. Thus, *za* means *seat* and refers to a seat in brotherhood meetings of a village or shrine. The seat represented the right to be a member of an organization. Guilds (*za*) often called themselves *brotherhoods*, because many of them had religious institutions as their patrons.[19] The first was woodcutters' brotherhood of Yase established in 1092. It received a licence to sell firewood in Kyōto in return for cutting timber for their patron and providing members to bear palanquin. Powerful temples and court nobles sanctioned and protected a few dozen of *za*.[20] In early feudal times, merchants, manufacturers, and artisans needed protection from the lord of the manor or a religious institution due to many obstacles to doing business, including market restrictions.

Yamamura defines *za* as

> *a pre-industrial Japanese economic institution which restricted entry into, and competition within a specific product or service market in order to realize economic gains for its members (who were free to resign from it), and which also provided economic gains to the political authority that enabled it to secure those gains.*[21]

Za is also defined as a group consisting of merchants and manufacturers spontaneously formed for the common interest of the members. These were service groups subordinated to the shrines, temples, and court nobility, as well as an independent association of merchants. Trade brotherhoods were associations of people trading the same product or performing the same profession, while craft guilds were professional associations of a specific branch of industry or trade. Merchant guilds brought together merchants from a specific geographical area, including a town, village, or city engaged in trade.[22] In the 13th century, many itinerant peddlers, artisans, and merchants established *za* that paid tribute and provided various services to influential patrons in exchange for protection, trade rights, special monopoly privileges, and exemptions from customs duties.[23] According to Yamamura, the *za* consisted of people engaged in the same business activities and closely linked by common interests, mainly to increase the security and income of their members (risk reduction) and to obtain exclusive privileges. Yamamura argues that the skilled serfs (*tomobe*) of the *ritsuryō* period and the temple *za* (*miyaza*), the *sanjo* (places where skilled serfs lived), appearing in the early Heian period (794–1185), should not be considered *za* because they wanted only rights to trade in exchange for services to the powerful.[24]

The same responsibilities and privileges that defined the estate system extended to the guilds. They were used to match the mutual needs of the ruling class and suppliers of goods and services. The privileges of guilds included securing members' property rights, enforcing contractual obligations, providing an organization for the government to use in corporate rule, and managing trade.[25] They go beyond paying obligations to a patron in exchange for a market monopoly. Protection and maintenance of rights and privileges were particularly important among *za* of merchants and manufacturers. They were multifunctional, as many of them acted as wholesalers, labour brokers, retailers, producers, and processors of goods. *Za* members were highly skilled craftsmen and service providers who became very important during the Tokugawa period.[26] Despite this, these skilled craftsmen and merchants had the lowest social status in Japan. They were considered socially inferior and therefore had limited rights, which prevented them from gaining economic and political power.

Lords in metropolitan and local districts erected many barriers (*sekisho*) and collected customs duties from passing merchants. But the *za* were under the protection of powerful *daimyō*, shrines, and temples. These patrons received fees from the *za* in exchange for permission (license) to trade in various markets, preferably with a monopoly on sales in a specific market or the entire region, and for exemption from taxes and tolls, and the right to move freely.[27] The most important thing for *za* was the right to secure its monopoly. Officially recognized *za* received monopoly rights for their goods in exchange for regular deliveries and serf labour.[28] A characteristic feature of the early *za* was the strict control of these entities by their patrons (lords). The patron protected his *za* from other lords or brotherhoods, helped settle disputes with outsiders, promoted their business interests, and sometimes sponsored them. A patron's ability to provide this protection depended on his political power and status. Disputes were resolved in courts, where patrons of brotherhoods competed to protect and expand the rights of their *za*.

Merchants competed for membership in various brotherhoods, while brotherhoods competed for the use or control of roads, for the right to trade in monopoly controlled markets, and for monopsonic control of certain resources necessary to produce the goods they traded. They tried to manipulate input and output markets to their own advantage. Although there were *za* already in the Yamato period (there were over 56 of them of various sizes), it was only in the 11th century that they began to play an important role in the economy. They usually consisted of 10 members, but some had more than 60 members, while others had only one or two members. *Za* members were under the protection of lords or temples and were therefore exempt from business tax, market tax, and customs duties and enjoyed the freedom to conduct business. They could leave their *za* and create a new one separately. The condition for joining the *za*, which was an established organizational structure, was subordination to the lord.[29] Belonging to the *za* was conditioned more by having a common patron than by staying in the same place, because the brotherhood could unite representatives of one profession in different places. The protection of the lord was one of the most important privileges for the *za* of merchants and manufacturers. As the 13th century progressed, the development of *za* became more and more dynamic and the factors behind this development became more obvious. The nobility ruling agricultural estates realized that an effective way to increase their income was to use their political power to provide patronage over non-agricultural activities, especially trade associations of merchants and craftsmen.[30] This helped the nobility not only increase their income but also obtain much needed and desired goods and services. This was also in line with the central government's desire to maintain the supply of important goods and ensure the development of skilled crafts.[31]

Since the rise of the *samurai*, the *shōen* owners had experienced a constant decline in their tax revenues so they needed income from their *za*. The number of *za* therefore increased, providing an institutional way to compensate their promoters for falling land returns, encouraging further specialization of producers.[32] The nobility's income depended on the ability to provide *za* with legal and political protection, access to the market and prestige, which caused other brotherhoods to choose them as their patrons. The latter made *za* patrons very competitive with each other.[33] The *samurai* allowed the court and temple nobility to share profits from *za* in exchange for imperial support for the *bakufu*.[34] Political instability under the Kamakura and Ashikaga *Shōgunates* allowed the court nobles and the temples to increase the *za* under their protection with a minimum of interference from the *samurai* class preoccupied with the wars. The development of the *za* entered a new phase during the politically turbulent last decades of the 14th century (Kemmu Restoration) which showed that the increase of the *samurai* power was irreversible and that the income from *shōen* for court nobility and powerful temples would continue to decline.[35]

At this time, an increasing number of peasants were producing goods for sale in the market, so they began to form *za* and ally themselves with the political power that suited them. Because they realized that their profits would increase, if they became full-time traders, so they wanted to be sure that their rights would not be infringed upon by competitors.[36] Individual members or groups of merchants from certain villages began to cooperate to expand their rights to mutual protection and profits. They joined different brotherhoods, because each product had its own *za*, and access to a given market was controlled by the political authorities, who granted privileges to different brotherhoods. Access to markets depended on the influence and power of *za* patrons, which extended over many regions through their branch temples or scattered *shōen*. All relevant matters were clearly stated in an agreement about the sphere of influence. Some *za* obtained the right to hold a monopoly in several districts, only *za* members were authorized to trade certain goods in specific markets, and outsiders could only sell their goods, after paying some form of tax to enter these exclusive markets.[37]

As already mentioned, *za* were independent, self-governing organizations whose members had the same or similar professions and whose purpose was to promote common interests in the economic, political, social, cultural, and religious fields. Literate and skilled craftsmen and merchants formed *za* in order to pursue their own interests. Membership in *za* was voluntary. Members of *za* were able to govern a formal organization and properly use their human capital, as well as develop clear rules for electing officials and making collective decisions.[38] *Za* were a bridge between the countryside and the urban centres. According to Yamamura, they were involved in various fields of trade and production and enjoyed certain privileges; however, their activities as independent organizations were not as pronounced due to their insufficient development as formally structured industry associations. Limited effective demand, free access to the brotherhood, and the resulting competition hampered the specialization of most *za* in the 13th century. Most of the benefits of *za* specialization, accrued to sponsors, *za* members, and consumers of the products, as the *za* monopoly had not yet been securely established during this period.

The increasing use of coins in exchange helped generate profits from trade and encouraged *za* patrons to acquire more of these institutions. They realized that receiving patronage payments in cash rather than in kind reduced the transaction costs associated with acquiring desired goods. Thus, trading became profitable over longer distances and in larger quantities, making *za* increasingly profitable and desirable. The monetization of the economy made it easier for *za* patrons to share the monopoly's profits because a percentage of total sales could be more easily measured and collected in cash than in goods or services. Yamamura writes that despite restrictions which the *za* imposed on trade, the effects of these institutions on commerce were positive. *Za*'s ability to specialize and reduce the costs of acquiring information about new market opportunities provided greater benefits to society than the costs it imposed. The monopoly profits were limited by the high costs of enforcing the monopoly. The demand for most goods was elastic due to the general level of income of the population and the possibility of using home-made substitutes.[39] Generally, guilds performed many important functions in the local economy. They established monopolies in their territory or in a particular industry or trade, set and maintained standards of quality for goods, ensured the integrity of trade practices in their industries, sought to maintain stable prices for their goods and services, and promoted the interests of guild members so that they could achieve their economic goals.[40]

In the 14th century, *za* split into *hon-za* (old *za*) and *shin-za* (new *za*) systems.[41] In the former, taxes were imposed on a whole *za*, and its members had a duty of labour services, while each member of the new *za* was taxed individually and paid his obligations either in money or in the goods he traded. The new *za* was more independent of the patron's power. Thus, development of the new *za* threatened the monopoly rights of the old *za* causing conflicts of interests between them. Although the new *za* did not directly challenge the privileges of the old, more established *za*, the latter wanted to enforce their monopoly rights against newly created individual competitors and potential groups of rivals.[42] The interests of these za, which possessed monopoly rights, conflicted with those of the newly emerging merchants in the surrounding villages, as well as with the interests of the proprietary lords. However, the old *za* were prohibited from taking any action that limited the activities of their younger rivals. All *za* begun to concentrate their efforts on securing their monopoly rights rather than on expanding their markets, as they had been doing during the preceding century. Some *za* located in rural districts (*inaka-za* or *sato-za*) were established on the basis of the bargain market. In such cases, the village was separated from professional *za*. Only those who paid a certain amount of taxes could form a *za*, through which they handled their goods. The members of such a *za* were wealthy farmers who sold the goods they produced on the market, as well as a few intermediaries from other areas.[43]

As far as the governance structures of the *za* are concerned, *zato* was the head of it, the *konokõbe* managed its divisions and was the leader of the workers, there were also *otona* (alderman) and assistants called *satanin*. They were elected by *za* members and took responsibility for running it. This system was derived from the ancient *be* corporations. *Za* usually had (presumable) four divisions, each led by a *konokõbe* accompanied by his assistants (*satanin*). *Zato* and *otona* had the same social status as landowners (*myoshu)*, although in the villages it was not as high. Aldermen (*otona*) had the right to collect annual customs, to control the members, and to expel from the business those who were not obedient. A *satanin* (assistant) played an important role among the members of the *za*. The *za's* policy was decided at the meeting of *za* members called *yoriai* (kind of an annual meeting of shareholders). *Yoriai* meetings also provided residents of neighbouring villages with the opportunity to meet each other. Hideyoshi banned them as well as collaboration (*moshiawase*) of merchant groups, and the *za*.[44]

In towns, rich people, especially factors, started to accumulate capital by becoming wholesalers, and influential members of *za*. They obtained the right to elect the town elders (*otona*), who were to exercise local authority through assemblies. The use of the same titles as those of village leaders, such as *otona* and *toshiyori* (headmen representing the common residents to higher political authority), indicated that *za* were not under external control but self-supporting organizations operating in their own interests.

Corporate responsibility encompassed the entire guild system, from granting rights, assessing guilt, to imposing fees. In the 14th century, there were many cases where members of *za* punished monopoly breakers, for example, their production facilities were destroyed for selling without permission. When the situation was beyond the *za* control, it appealed to its lord (patron) for intervention.[45] The organization to which the law-breaker belonged could be held responsible and punished for his actions. There was intense competition between the brotherhoods on markets, most of which were merchant guilds or craft guilds. Merchants from the *za* located in the rural area gradually moved into urban districts, where local merchants imposed a tax on them to enter the city and allowed them to sell goods only through established channels.[46] *Za* were formed in almost all the castle towns and prosperous districts. As Japan's decentralization reached its peak and political competition intensified, the number of professional brotherhoods increased from a few dozen in 1200 to several thousand. The accelerated growth of *za* encouraged them to increase their activities, especially efforts to enforce their monopoly rights.

The guild should be seen as the commercial equivalent of the estate (*shōen*): a tool of social regulation for both client and patron.[47] Urban trade guilds originated in the formation of cooperative associations among merchants and artisans who earned their livelihood exclusively from commerce and the production of goods for the market.[48] The increase in the number of *za* in the 14th century resulted from a combination of political and economic circumstances, especially the development of trade, the increase in its profitability, and agricultural productivity. By contrast, the number of economically self-sufficient *shōen* decreased as more of them became dependent on external markets on which they sold their surpluses and purchased more and more goods from more specialized and therefore more efficient producers.[49] Markets offered new venues for transactions outside the government-controlled payment system and gave agricultural estates the freedom to expand the range of goods that brought the greatest returns.[50]

Goldsmith argues that the enforcement of rights and privileges of the *za* was left to the guildsmen themselves. Much of the guild's policing power came from the right and ability to govern its own members through collective responsibility supported by a shared identity and shared jurisdiction. They were established according to principles that all members exercised equal rights in the election of *za* officials, received an equal distribution of profits on shared capital ventures, and were equally subject to the rules adopted by the za and the equality of all members who collectively possessed monopolistic rights; the non-recognition of the rights of any individuals who were not za members; and a specific ranking system among the various *za*.[51] Their members were aware of their corporate responsibilities and actively used them as a mechanism of social control both on the road and at home. The guild by-laws were designed to limit corporate responsibility and to protect its reputation. Its merchants were prohibited from extending credit and engaging in bad business practices. According to some guilds' statutes members could undertake major contracts only after consulting with the entire guild and jointly signing it. Any violation of the *za* regulations or agreement (contract) resulted in the person's expulsion from the guild. Members of *za* valued tradition and often made reference to their old lineage, usually associated with the royal household. However, during the Sengoku period, class distinctions among *za* members and a breakdown of the cohesion of these guilds began to appear. Rights to *za* membership began to be traded, and za came under the domination of a few members whose positions of leadership were secure. Some *za* tried to change it and strengthened the principle of equality among members, but the growth of output and commerce during this period caused that merchants who were not *za* members were able to engage in commerce, especially those protected by a military lord. These problems caused weakening of *za*. They were soon replaced by wholesalers (*ton'ya*) who began to control commerce, gradually absorbing the rights once enjoyed by the *za*.[52]

Members of the *za* were not able to accumulate wealth sufficient for investments because of the relatively slow development of the Japanese commerce and limited number of rich and politically potent merchants. The lack of a sufficient number of wealthy merchants with strong political and economic power meant that they were unable to buy freedom of action. The skilled and educated craftsmen and merchants of medieval Japan were considered social inferiors (below peasants) and were not allowed to hold any government offices.[53]

The emerging Sengoku *daimyō* (lords of warring provinces), preoccupied with military and political crises, were pressed for cash needed for their battles. Most of them wanted the development of *za* because they were a reliable source of income for them. Therefore, certain ad hoc arrangements were made, which depended on the strength of the regional *samurai* class, the degree of feeling of power of the *bakufu*, the court nobility, and the temples. However, when they gained sufficient military power to protect their land, they started to implement measures which in effect abolished the *za*. According to Yamamura, although the need for funding from *za* continued to grow, supplementing declining *shōen* revenues, but court and temple aristocrats, losing their high positions and political power, were increasingly unable to protect their *za*. It soon became clear to the *za* that, to maintain their privileges, they had to rely on the regional *samurai* and *bakufu*.

The fighting d*aimyō* appointed official merchants (*goyoshonin*), usually from their own *samurai* or *za* leaders, who became the main purchasing agents for their armies and retainers, collected taxes on trade and supervised it. Some *goyoshonin* were dispatched to Kyōto to purchase the needed goods, but most of them remained in the domains, to carry out their tasks. It is worth noting that Hideyoshi and his powerful allies continued to make a limited use of *goyoshanin* (official merchants appointed by the *sengoku daimyō*) to acquire necessary military commodities (rice and oil) or to deal in lucrative Chinese imports. Neither the *daimyō* nor their agents were interested in generating income for the court aristocracy and temples; therefore, their receivables, including those from *za*, began to decline rapidly. This caused serious problems for *za* monopolies at the turn of the 15th and 16th centuries. Since their patrons could no longer provide them with support, they turned to the *bakufu* or regional *daimyō* (lords of warring provinces).[54] However, in the mid-16th century, *daimyō* with large and secure domains adopted a new policy called *rakuichi-rakuza*, advocating free markets and free *za*, the implementation of which required the abolition of all forms of trade restrictions. The development of free economic activity was more advantageous for them because they could directly collect all the taxes they imposed without having to share them with the *za*. Thus, the old rules that strongly protected *za* began to fade because they were no longer compatible with the growing free local trade and industry, causing the destruction of *za* monopolies. Control of trade became an economic and military necessity for *daimyō* fighting for strong control over their domains. Neither the emperor nor *shōgun* had enough power to influence events outside the capital, so the *daimyō* could develop economic activities within their domains and reap the benefits.[55] Secure and strong *daimyō* were able to collect any taxes and all indirect profits from increased economic activity.[56]

The great unifiers, Nobunaga, Hideyoshi, and Ieyasu, had differing views on encouraging free trade. Oda Nobunaga, promoting a new economic policy, effectively liquidated the market privileges (monopoly) of the guilds and all tolls on the roads. In this way, he significantly reduced the income of the local *daimyō*. Oda introduced the mentioned earlier new trade policy called *rakuichi-rakuza*, which guaranteed that anyone could set up a business without any fees or taxes, and removed the restrictions to the free flow of goods and people from one area to another (free market, open *za*, no trade restrictions). Following it, Sengoku *daimyō* had to abolish both monopoly guilds (*za*) and the obligation to trade in certain privately controlled markets. This policy enabled merchants and artisans to free themselves of their subjugation and allowed them to form new commercial relations that broke the monopoly power of *za*.[57] Although *daimyō* applied the *rakuichi-rakuza* policy, granted merchants the right to freely conduct business in their castle towns, abolished market taxes and monopolization of markets, Oda Nobunaga did not implement these policies in Kyōto and Nara. The *za* remained there active, existing merchant guilds were protected, and their special rights were recognized. *Za* under the patronage of court nobility and religious institutions continued to trade throughout Japan. Thus, without disturbing their activities, Oda managed to retain both the dominant economic role of the capital and access to provincial goods. According to Leen, the most important factors that contributed to the abolition of *za* and ensuring Oda Nobunoga's hegemony were the creation of a free trade market (Oda established the first free trade market in Gifu in 1567), the monetary system (*erizeni-rei*), military power, and elites.[58] A decree issued by Oda Nobunaga in 1568 stated that

> *No one shall in any way hinder merchants coming to trade at the Kano market; no merchants shall be required to pay debts at the market; taxes on structures and land on which residences of merchants are erected shall be exempted; no monopoly by any za and no privileges of any members of a former za shall be recognized; and all trading shall be unrestrained.*[59]

The greatest threat to Nobunaga was the Buddhist sect Ikko-Ikki, which strongly opposed the rule of the *samurai*, and therefore in 1570, Oda began an invasion of the Ikki temples. He conquered one by one and took over their estates and *za*. Although Nobunoga questioned the existence of *za* under the control of the court aristocracy, it was Hideyoshi Toyotomi who ended the process of their destruction in order to stimulate free trade.[60] He dissolved all *za* belonging to the court nobility, shrines, and temples, and abolished all restrictions on the flow of goods throughout the country. The liquidation of *za* resulted in lower prices of most of goods in the years 1570–1590 (no monopoly profits).[61]

Along with the successful national unification, an increasing number of *sengoku daimyō* supported the policy of the *rakuichi-rakuza*. An important indirect benefit for them from the abolition of *za* was the improvement of the financial situation of peasants in their domains. This was the result of the free realization of profits from trade and the cessation of exploitation of peasants by *za*, thanks to which wealthier farmers were able to bear a greater tax burden. The increase in trade resulting from the abolition of *za* and tariffs, and the unification of measurement standards, caused the profits made by the inhabitants of the domains and their *daimyō* to exceed the benefits they had previously received from the *za*.[62] The weakness of the *za* reflected the relative slowness of the growth of the economic power of the merchant class. The unifiers established the economic importance of castle towns as free markets. They removed non-agricultural means of economic support for the old nobility and limited the political and economic power of religious institutions, which made it possible, to establish the central political and economic authority of a unified Japan.[63] When Japan was finally reunified, merchants began to run businesses independent of local authorities. It should be noted that the *be* and *za* corporations were the predecessors of the Japanese corporations, which gradually developed and improved over the following centuries.

Notes

1 K. Asakawa, Japan: From the Japanese Government History. In: H. C. Lodge (ed.), The History of Nations. Vol. 7. *John D. Morris and Company. The Collier Press,* New York 1906, p. 95. www.gutenberg.org/ebooks/45645.
2 J. Murdoch, History of Japan, from the Origins to the Arrival of the Portuguese in 1542 A.D., Vol. I. *The Asiatic Society of Japan,* London 1910, p. 590. file:///D:/Users/wzr/Documents/Japonia%20Ks1/Ksi%C4%85%C5%BCki%20Hist/A%20history%20of%20Japan%20Volume%201%20(1903).pdf.
3 E. I. Segal, Coins, Trade, and the State Economic Growth in Early Medieval Japan. Harvard East Asian Monographs. *Harvard University Press*, Cambridge, MA and London 2011, p. 22.
4 J. R. Goodwin, J. N. Piggott (eds.), Land, Power, and the Sacred: The Estate System in Medieval Japan. *University of Hawaii Press*, Honolulu 2018, p. xxvii.
5 H. K. Baker, R. Anderson (eds.), Corporate Governance: A Synthesis of Theory, Research, and Practice. *John Wiley& Sons, Inc*., New York 2010, p. 180.
6 B. Tricker, Corporate Governance: Principles, Policies, and Practices. *Oxford University Press*, Oxford 2015, p. 65.
7 J. P. Mass, The Kamakura *bakufu*. In: The Cambridge History of Japan: Medieval Japan. Vol. 3. *Cambridge University Press*, Cambridge 2008, p. 84.
8 H. K. Baker, R. Anderson, Corporate Governance: A Synthesis of Theory, Research, and Practice . . . op. cit., p. 178.
9 E. I. Segal, Coins, Trade, and the State Economic Growth in Early Medieval Japan . . . op. cit., p. 98.
10 Ibidem.
11 R. C. Marshall, Collective Decision Making in Rural Japan. Vol. 11. *University of Michigan, Centre for Japanese Studies* 1984, p. 4. https://expeditiorepositorio.utadeo.edu.co/bitstream/handle/20.500.12010/18289/9780472901999.pdf?sequence=1.
12 M. L. Nagata, Brotherhoods and Stock Societies: Guilds in Pre-Modern Japan. *International Review of Social History* 2008, Vol. 53, pp. 121–142.
13 J. Lucassen, T. De Moor, J. L. van Zanden, The Return of the Guilds: Towards a Global History of the Guilds in Pre-Industrial Times. *International Review of Social History* 2008, Vol. 53, pp. 5–18, *Cambridge University Press.*
14 B. Goldsmith, Amassing Economies: The Medieval Origins of Early Modern Japan, 1450–1700. A Dissertation Submitted to *The Department of History and The Committee of Graduate Studies of Stanford University* July 2008, p. 95. file:///C:/Users/WZR/Documents/WErsja%20ostateczna/out.pdf.
15 K. Yamamura, The Development of Za in Medieval Japan. *Business History Review* December 1973, Vol. 47, No. 4, pp. 438–465.
16 M. L. Nagata, Brotherhoods and Stock Societies . . . op. cit.
17 www.britannica.com/topic/za.
18 K. Yamamura, The Development of Za in Medieval Japan . . . op. cit.
19 M. L. Nagata, Brotherhoods and Stock Societies . . . op. cit.
20 K. Yamamura, The Development of Za in Medieval Japan . . . op. cit.
21 Ibidem.
22 F. J. Gamba, Business Associations as Tools for Promoting Efficient Business Performance: The Historical Perspectives and Evolving Roles. *African Journal of Management Research (AJMR)* 2020, Vol. 26, pp. 22–38.
23 Ibidem.
24 K. Yamamura, The Development of Za in Medieval Japan . . . op. cit.
25 B. Goldsmith, B. Goldsmith, Amassing Economies: The Medieval Origins of Early Modern Japan, 1450–1700 . . . op. cit., p. 96.

26 K. Yamamura, The Development of Za in Medieval Japan . . . op. cit.
27 M. L. Nagata, Brotherhoods and Stock Societies . . . op. cit.
28 T. Toyoda, Japanese Guilds. *The Annals of the Hitotsubashi Academy* 1954, Vol. 5, No. 1, pp. 72–85.
29 Ibidem.
30 J. W. Hall, K. Nagahara, K. Yamamura (eds.), Japan Before Tokugawa: Political Consolidation and Economic Growth, 1500 to 1650. *Princeton University Press*, Princeton 1984, pp. 308–309.
31 M. L. Nagata, Brotherhoods and Stock Societies . . . op. cit.
32 T. Toyoda, Japanese Guilds . . . op. cit., pp. 72–85.
33 M. L. Nagata, Brotherhoods and Stock Societies . . . op. cit.
34 K. Yamamura, The Development of Za in Medieval Japan . . . op. cit.
35 M. L. Nagata, Brotherhoods and Stock Societies . . . op. cit.
36 K. Yamamura, The Development of Za in Medieval Japan . . . op. cit.
37 T. Toyoda, Japanese Guilds . . . op. cit.
38 J. Lucassen, T. De Moor, J. L. van Zanden, The Return of the Guilds . . . op. cit.
39 K. Yamamura, The Development of Za in Medieval Japan . . . op. cit.
40 www.britannica.com/topic/guild-trade-association.
41 T. Toyoda, Japanese Guilds . . . op. cit.
42 J. W. Hall, K. Nagahara, K. Yamamura, Japan Before Tokugawa: Political Consolidation and Economic Growth . . . op. cit., p. 309.
43 T. Toyoda, Japanese Guilds . . . op. cit.
44 Ibidem.
45 B. Goldsmith, Amassing Economies: The Medieval Origins of Early . . . op. cit., pp. 98–101.
46 T. Toyoda, Japanese Guilds . . . op. cit.
47 B. Goldsmith, Amassing Economies: The Medieval Origins of Early . . . op. cit., p. 95.
48 J. W. Hall, K. Nagahara, K. Yamamura, Japan Before Tokugawa: Political Consolidation and Economic Growth . . . op. cit., p. 309.
49 K. Yamamura, The Development of Za in Medieval Japan . . . op. cit.
50 E. I. Segal, Coins, Trade, and the State Economic Growth in Early Medieval Japan . . . op. cit., p. 10.
51 J. W. Hall, K. Nagahara, K. Yamamura, Japan Before Tokugawa: Political Consolidation and Economic Growth . . . op. cit., p. 310.
52 Ibidem, p. 310.
53 K. Yamamura, The Development of Za in Medieval Japan . . . op. cit.
54 Ibidem.
55 A. R. Leen, M. C. Huang, How a Free Market System Resulted in Hegemony and a Magnificent Era: The Case of Nobunga Oda, 16th Century, Japan. *Archives of Economic History* 2008, Vol. XIX, No. 1, pp. 5–16, ISSN 1108-7005.
56 M. L. Nagata, Brotherhoods and Stock Societies . . . op. cit.
57 K. Yamamura, The Development of Za in Medieval Japan . . . op. cit.
58 A. R. Leen, M. C. Huang, How a Free Market System Resulted in Hegemony . . . op. cit.
59 K. Yamamura, The Development of Za in Medieval Japan . . . op. cit.
60 M. L. Nagata, Brotherhoods and Stock Societies . . . op. cit.
61 T. Toyoda, Japanese Guilds . . . op. cit.
62 K. Yamamura, The Development of Za in Medieval Japan . . . op. cit.
63 M. L. Nagata, Brotherhoods and Stock Societies . . . op. cit.

Bibliography

Asakawa, K., Japan: From the Japanese Government History. In: H. C. Lodge (ed.), The History of Nations, Vol. 7. *The Collier Press*, New York 1906. www.gutenberg.org/ebooks/45645.

Baker, H. K., Anderson, R. (eds.), Corporate Governance: A Synthesis of Theory, Research, and Practice. *John Wiley & Sons, Inc.*, New York 2010.

www.britannica.com/topic/za.

www.britannica.com/topic/guild-trade-association.

Gamba, F. J., Business Associations as Tools for Promoting Efficient Business Performance: The Historical Perspectives and Evolving Roles. *African Journal of Management Research (AJMR)* 2020, Vol. 26, pp. 22–38.

Goldsmith, B., Amassing Economies: The Medieval Origins of Early Modern Japan, 1450–1700. A Dissertation Submitted to *The Department of History and The Committee of Graduate Studies of Stanford University* July 2008. file:///C:/Users/WZR/Documents/WErsja%20ostateczna/out.pdf.

Goodwin, J. R., Piggott, J. N. (eds.), Land, Power, and the Sacred: The Estate System in Medieval Japan. *University of Hawaii Press*, Honolulu 2018.

Hall, J. W., Nagahara, K., Yamamura, K. (eds.), Japan Before Tokugawa: Political Consolidation and Economic Growth, 1500 to 1650. *Princeton University Press*, Princeton 1984.

Leen, A. R., Huang, M. C., How a Free Market System Resulted in Hegemony and a Magnificent Era: The Case of Nobunga Oda, 16th Century, Japan. *Archives of Economic History* 2008, Vol. XIX, No. 1, pp. 5–16, ISSN 1108-7005.

Lucassen, J., De Moor, T., van Zanden, J. L., The Return of the Guilds: Towards a Global History of the Guilds in Pre-Industrial Times. *International Review of Social History* 2008, Vol. 53, pp. 5–18. *Cambridge University Press*. www.jstor.org/stable/26405465.

Murdoch, J., History of Japan, from the Origins to the Arrival of the Portuguese in 1542 A.D., Vol. I. *The Asiatic Society of Japan* 1910. file:///D:/Users/wzr/Documents/Japonia%20Ks1/Ksi%C4%85%C5%BCki%20Hist/A%20history%20of%20Japan%20Volume%201%20(1903).pdf.

Nagata, M. L., Brotherhoods and Stock Societies: Guilds in Pre-Modern Japan. *International Review of Social History* 2008, Vol. 53, pp. 121–142. *JSTOR*. www.jstor.org/stable/26405470.

Segal, E. I., Coins, Trade, and the State Economic Growth in Early Medieval Japan. Harvard East Asian Monographs. *Harvard University Press*, Cambridge, MA and London 2011. file:///D:/Users/wzr/Downloads/coins-trade-and-the-state-economic-growth-in-early-medieval-japan-illustrated-0674060687-9780674060685_compress.pdf.

Toyoda, T., Japanese Guilds. *The Annals of the Hitotsubashi Academy* 1954, Vol. 5, No. 1, pp. 72–85. *JSTOR*. www.jstor.org/stable/43751448.

Tricker, B., Corporate Governance: Principles, Policies, and Practices. *Oxford University Press*, Oxford 2015.

Yamamura, K., The Development of Za in Medieval Japan. *Business History Review* December 1973, Vol. 47, No. 4, pp. 438–465. www.jstor.org/stable/3113366?seq=1&cid=pdf-reference#references_tab_contents.

Yamamura, K. (ed.), The Cambridge History of Japan. In: Medieval Japan, Vol. 3. *Cambridge University Press*, Cambridge 2008.

12 Japanese corporate governance

A conclusion

As already mentioned, the analysis presented in this book covers a period of over 16 centuries, therefore, due to the length of this period and the number of important changes that have occurred in it, they only allow for a very general analysis of corporate governance. The analysis presented in this book covers over 16 centuries. During this period, four phases of state development can be distinguished. The first is the period covering the centralization of the state, the second is the process of creating the *Ritsuryō* State, the third concerns the breakdown of the *ritsuryō* system and the decentralization of state power, and the fourth includes the decades in which Oda Nobunoga, Hideyoshi Toyotomi, and Tokugawa Ieyasu took turns fighting for the reunification of Japan, and when the Tokugawa *Shōgunate* was established by Ieyasu. In terms of state organization, five models may be associated with these periods: a decentralized model, a decentralized model becoming centralized, a centralized model, a centralized model becoming decentralized, and a decentralized model becoming centralized again. During a period of time corresponding to a millennium, that is, from the proclamation of the Taika reform introducing the state ruled by the emperor in 645, until the building of solid foundations by the Tokugawa *shōgunate* in 1615, the changing and turbulent system came full circle. Japan again became a strictly centralized state under despotic rule, but this time by the *shōgun*. However, unlike the Taika reforms of 645, this centralization process was very long, costly, and bloody. The waste of lives and the misery experienced by many in the country resulted from political disruption, but despite this, the economy developed, thanks to new technologies, such as improved irrigation in agriculture, modern equipment, and new, sophisticated goods production. Good management, the creation of a tax system that motivates people to increase production and introduce innovations, acquire new skills and improve work organization, allowed to increase production productivity and profitability. The state created conditions and opportunities for the development of entrepreneurship and enrichment.

Since the dawn of Japan, it has been possible to track the effective use of production factors, the implementation of which has been constantly improved over time. However, the role of capital in Japan was played mainly by rice, in which the country's economy was based for centuries. During the period under consideration

DOI: 10.4324/9781003497936-16

(till the end of the 16th century), land was the primary source of revenue for the state and its citizens, and so the main basis for the economy. To acquire new land and to increase its productivity were the most important concerns of those who ruled Japan and governed agriculture. The main economic problems were related to land ownership, the rights to the taxes levied on it, and methods for measurement and division of land. For the recipients of tax revenues, the main issue was tax optimization, that is, maintaining and expanding the tax base and striving to increase the revenue generated from it. Over the centuries, agricultural policy was changing but it was always aimed to maximize revenues for aristocracy (highest class), who created the *rules of the game*. However, serious problems emerging in this area showed the aristocrats, and later the *samurai*, that maximizing their own interests required providing appropriate incentives to rice producers (peasants), that is, enabling them to achieve and retain a certain surplus. This conclusion became the principle of an extensive management system oriented towards maximizing the interests of aristocrats, which became the basis for creating a corporate governance system.

It can be argued that it is justified to use the term *corporate governance* in relation to Japan since the very beginning of its history. As already noted, the use of the term *corporate governance* in ancient times may be justified by treating Japan as a business group consisting, depending on the period under consideration, of such subgroups as *uji*, provinces, districts, domains, villages, and townships, and by the existence of enterprises such as *be* corporations, *shōen* (closed and independent entities that existed within the framework of the national political authority), and *za* corporations. The joint-stock companies discussed in the study were understood as having stock in trade not to be sold or partnerships whereof the capital is divided or agreed to be divided into the transferable shares of interest. The central government created a rational and good system of governing the state and its components, headed by the monarch and/or *shōgun*. Corporations operating in the country had also developed a specific corporate governance model, tailored to their own needs. They included company bodies that may be compared to the board of directors and the general meeting, and the internal audit and external audit. It can therefore be concluded that internal and external corporate governance mechanisms were used.

The first stage of the process of creating the Yamato governance is concerned with the *uji*, the autonomous, self-governing organizations, struggling to continue their existence and to gain wealth and power. After strengthening their position, the *uji* had begun to compete for hegemony which was finally gained by the Yamato clan. Around the 3rd century, this leader of the federation formed the Yamato kingdom. It was a political union of the *uji* of favoured lineages and *be* corporations (occupational groups), headed by the Daio *uji* (the imperial clan). Its king, striving to create a centralized state, managed to transform the *uji* federation into a hierarchical structure, later into a state. The then-existing Clan Federation may be compared to a family or today's enterprises competing to maintain or increase their position in a competitive market. These clans (*uji*) meet the mentioned earlier characteristics of a corporation. They had the right of formation by registration or rather acceptation by the monarch, limited liability towards the federation and the king, perpetual succession, the right to sue and be sued or complain to the monarch or to solve the problem by force, to purchase (capture) and hold real property, to have a common seal, and to govern by enacting private clan's by-laws and statutes (laws). The clan corporations fulfilled the most important characteristics, being the essence of corporateness, so *immortality* (a perpetual succession of many persons) and *individuality* (acting as a single individual). The definitions provided by Jensen and Meckling (1976) that corporation is *a nexus of contracts* or *a compromise of interests* may be applied to them as well. These definitions fully correspond to the characteristics of Japanese corporations developing in the period from the dawn of Japan till the end of the 16th century. The centralization of power led to the creation of Japan, which was compared to a business group (corporation), or a large family (*ie* or *uji*), consisting of subordinated subgroups more or less closely connected with the centre of power.

The executive rulers the emperor (rarely) or *shōgun*, their courts, and officials of different ranks were able to build a good governance system – centralized or decentralized in some centuries. The effectiveness of the state changed depending on the level of its development, its financial strength, the degree of centralization of power, the land ownership structure, and the degree of state control over both land and people. The systems discussed evolved under the influence of hybridization, a process by which Japan took the best achievements of other countries and adapted them to its own reality. The evolution of the country resulted not only from historical and economic realities but also, above all, from the ambitions of the elites and their desire to obtain privileges (position and status) and financial benefits. Less prominent clan members and local officials followed their example, and this enabled them to strengthen their position and, over time, to seize power and create the *samurai* state. *Shōguns* were able to create excellent governance and supervision structures, which, for a long time, were good enough to satisfy the interests of all the state's stakeholders.

Throughout most of the period under review, three levels of rivalry in the fierce struggles for power and privileges may be distinguished – high or state (the court nobles, descendants of the former powerful *uji* and the highest-ranking officials in central government), medium – concerning provinces and their lower structures (local lords with some military strength and position in provincial government), and essential – the farmers' and artisans' level. At each of these levels, due to the powers held, the optimization of interests took place, to varying degrees and with different effects.

The first level comprises the most powerful and influential aristocrats and court officials, that is, those who had the power to shape the state's policy to their needs. The aristocracy was always at the head of the state (ruling class), forming a kind of board of directors. The *directors* competed strongly and fiercely with each other, which led to changes in the groups and factions in power, namely the position of hegemon held by the emperor, *shōgun*, or great civil or military aristocratic families. They were oriented towards increasing their power, and extending their ownership of land and the tax revenue base. To fulfil this aim, they had to establish a proper governance system. Thanks to their power, they were able to obtain lucrative titles and land grants, and then, owing to their court position or connections, took steps to acquire various privileges, especially tax exemptions. They could plan, establish, and control policy concerning governance structures, and the law relating to land, commerce, and taxes, and make them compatible with their expectations and needs. The desire to increase income by the highest court and state dignitaries led to creation of *shōen*, large land estates, operating on the basis of corporation. *Shōen* owners employed professional managers to manage their estates and to ensure proper relations with the political and business environment. *Shōen* were the result of cooperation on three aspects: national policy concerning ownership and taxes, especially tax credits, the effectiveness of tax measurement and collection, and the production base. The latter concerned free farmers paying taxes on their produce. The *be* corporations, *shōen*, and *za* were revenue-oriented organizations which required advanced governance, management, assessment, and control. They contributed much to the creation of an effective Japanese corporate governance system.

Initially, ownership and control of land were not separated (*uji*), but the situation changed in the *Ritsuryō* State when land was leased from the emperor by free farmers. During the Heian period, ownership and control of land (*shōen*) became increasingly combined. In Heian era, the landlords preferred to enjoy life in the capital and, if they earned the expected income, they did not interfere in the management of the land belonging to them. Systemic changes, such as nationalization of land, centralization of the country, hegemony of the emperor, introduced by the *ritsuryō* system, enriched the highest elites but significantly decreased their responsibility, involvement, and supervision over land that was the source of their income. Landowners attached much more importance to increasing their wealth than to the fiscal situation of the state. The deteriorating financial situation of the state had finally a serious impact on their finances and power, so they concentrated on adapting policies to their needs, using various methods, even war, as tools of policy enforcement.

As noted earlier, *be* corporations, *shōen*, and *za* were managed by professional managers whose main task was to meet the financial expectations of landowners and other stakeholders – the state, provincial officials, and farmers. When the state was weak, local magnates and officials, in order to meet the expectations of their superiors, and at the same time increase their own wealth, dared to impose on peasants more and more burdens, such as *suiko*, additional serfdom, unreliable crops measurements, or falsified crop and population records. These methods were very effective and contributed to an increase in the wealth and importance of local notables. They used loopholes in the law, and other methods to maximize their wealth within the existing rules. In time, the weak financial situation of the state, its inability to keep order, class-oriented policies, and struggles for power between the most powerful aristocratic families, led to the emergence of *samurai*.

The third, and most important level of revenue generation, was from peasants. Paying taxes due became the responsibility of the entire village, the *community of five* (households), and the family (orders from above). Shared responsibility not only resulted in cooperation but also ensured strict mutual control. Peasants had to follow the obligations inflicted on them and had no right to discuss or minimize them. However, farmers could reduce their burden (depending on their financial situation) by land commendation, abandoning farms, or armed rebellions. These forms of resistance, summarized in the book, were often used and made the elite realize that farmers could not be burdened with duties beyond the level that would ensure them a modest existence and at least a minimal profit. As already mentioned, peasants had to get a small return on their hard work, or else they would lose interest in farming the land and rebel or run away, causing losses to their superiors and threatening the existence of the entire economy (system). Since then, conscious elites had created structures that allowed farmers to make modest profits, which created incentives to work and increase land productivity and innovations. However, at the same time, most of the rewards from agricultural production efforts went to the members of the higher levels of the tax system.

Examples of the application of good corporate governance were guilds and merchant houses that developed and implemented not only their own effective governance (management) structures but also codes of good practice (conduct). They were able to protect not only their business interests but also the ownership structures and high position of their families. They functioned as well-organized and governed companies, strongly controlled and supervised. These early enterprises, which met the aforementioned criteria of corporation, were the roots of future large Japanese corporations. They were also the seed of the development of capitalism, which, thanks to the internal system, regulations, management and supervision methods, and the implementation of new technologies, was able to flourish quickly in the Meiji period. It would not be an exaggeration to say that they were the seeds of the development of the modern Japanese economy.

As noted earlier, some practices developed in ancient Japan have survived to this day, influencing the uniqueness of Japanese corporations, as well as their management and supervision. Despite exceptional respect for their own traditions, the Japanese have shown great skill in implementing the best achievements of other nations and adapting them to their own conditions and needs. It should be stressed that since the Yamato era (or even earlier) the use of ideas from elsewhere, mainly from China (hybridization), has been used to modernize Japan, its economy, and its governance. The Yamato corporate governance system laid the foundations for the specific nature of the Japanese model of corporate governance. Subsequent epochs contributed to the strengthening of this specificity.

The authority of power holders in Japanese society is derived directly from the influence of Confucianism and Shintoism, which for more than 1,500 years played a major role in shaping Japan's history. They stabilized Japanese society, emphasizing the need for good governance, supervision, ethics, social hierarchy, harmony, duty, and respect for authority. Confucianism became an important tool for strengthening the power of the central government, creating consent for the social order, and promoting social responsibility. Since ancient times, principles of social responsibility have been applied in Japan. They were already reflected in the reforms undertaken by Prince Shōtoku. His Twelve Level Rank and Cap System (603) created a new organization and court etiquette, and emphasized the importance of the Confucian moral virtues: wisdom, righteousness, justice, loyalty, temperance, frugality, and modesty in the exercise of authority, personal values, and relationships. Confucianism promoted the principles of *ren* (humanity) and *junzi* (the nobleman). Humanity, the chief virtue and basic duty of a nobleman, is based on kindness and love for people and includes good conduct, compassion, and kindness. These principles should characterize the authority of the emperor, the head of the family, and any commander or official who, for the good of their subordinates, should not give orders contrary to their good.

Prince Shōtoku created a fair (responsible) system of state administration, taking into account promotions based on education, ability, competence, merit, and individual achievements, and he advocated the appointment of educated, talented, and experienced people to government positions, regardless of clan or title. Such skills were guaranteed by strict state examinations and apprenticeships that candidates for positions in the state administration had to take. Social responsibility was therefore promoted, encouraging the development of humanistic values, respect for the rights of individual members of society and its institutions, as well as just action compatible with the law in force, and education. In addition, the Law (Constitution) of the Seventeen Articles (604), the first set of legal recommendations for public officials, included moral and political principles reflecting social responsibility. It established the ideals of the state and the rules of human conduct. It created a system of supervision over the state, its institutions, and officials in power, and thus a socially responsible system of governance. The principles are also a great example of hybridization. It should be emphasized that most of them have not lost their relevance to this day and can be a guide for any community, of all ages. The respect for superiors, knowledge, and education – a distinguishing feature of Japanese people and corporate governance today – comes from ancient times.

Another manifestation of hybridization, or the transplant effect, is the *Ritsuryō* State. As previously stated, the state of codified law (*Ritsuryō*) can be seen as a hybrid of two organizational principles: Japanese *uji* society (clan) and Chinese historical civilization. The Taika reforms of Emperor Kōtoku in the year 645 initiated revolutionary changes in the politics and administration of the country, and introduced or confirmed elements of social responsibility. The reforms defined a number of responsibilities of provincial governors, who were obliged to keep population records and accounting books, allocate land, act as a father to the people, support agriculture, right wrongs, listen to complaints, maintain irrigation systems, public buildings and pastures, and ensure the defense of the province. No aspect of life of the population could escape their attention. At the heart of the Taika reforms was the idea of social responsibility. On a macro scale, responsibility to the aristocracy was dominant, and it was through this prism that the responsibility of the rulers towards peasants, craftsmen, and merchants lower down the social order was shaped. This led to a situation in which the separation of ownership and control was formalized. As a result of legislative, organizational, and economic changes that occurred due to the Taika reforms, Japan became a highly centralized and unified state in the 9th century. Aristocratic Japan continued to borrow concepts from China, shaping them to suit domestic needs. The Heian court adopted the Chinese code of decency, decorum, restraint, and self-control, alongside the flourishing of Japanese culture and thought. History started to play a major role in Japanese culture – Japan's emperors had found legitimacy in tradition, both mythic and historic, and scholars studied national morality and the value systems of their country's past. The homogeneity of Japanese culture was ensured primarily by the family functioning as a corporation, respect for knowledge, power, superiors, and higher-ranking people. Law had emphasized social hierarchy, obedience and responsibility since the 7th century. The hierarchical social system *warrior-peasant-artisan-merchant* (called *shi-nō-kō-shō*) was arranged in a hierarchy of moral virtues and secular authority in descending order of status (from top to bottom). The basis for this highly hierarchical social order was a very complex system of codified rules and regulations. This was a manifestation of respect for Confucian values, which were grounded in the mentality of the Japanese. An important feature of Japanese corporate governance is respect for family and tradition which may be traced back to ancient times (*uji*). Family was always very important in Japan. The old ancestral ruling structures (e.g. Yoritomo, Tokugawa) served as models for governing the state, families, and merchants' and craftsmen's houses, and corporations. Family codes not only created the corporate culture, and governance structures of today, but, as noted earlier, also were the predecessors of modern corporate governance codes.

Individual rights were not important, or rather non-existent. The suppression of individual interests for the good of the group became distinguishing feature of Japanese culture and governance. Behaviour incompatible with social norms brought shame upon a family. The *samurai* code sees it as lack of respect for their *daimyō* (commander). In turn, the *samurai* ensured the conformity of the peasant class by example or, when necessary, by fear. According to literature, the specific features of the current Japanese corporate governance system include also a strong group identity – with the family (clan), the corporation (*be*) and the community; and the ability to cooperate, organize teams and engage in self-sacrifice, stemming from agriculture and legal requirements. These age-old rules have not lost their relevance and are arguably still evident in Japan today. A focus on the duty of care, loyalty, submissiveness, responsibility, obedience, and respect between superiors and inferiors belongs to them as well. The reciprocal obligation became an established pattern, promoting morality and discipline. It may be concluded that these Confucian values have influenced the Japanese social system since the dawn of the state, and are arguably the most important features of Japanese corporate governance. Other important characteristics are internalization of problems, unity against outsiders, respect for law, and recognition of social differences, stemming from a highly developed sense of responsibility in the Japanese character as well as by the age-old practice of severely punishing offenders, their families and the communities to which they belonged. Two further characteristic features of the Japanese corporate governance are diligence and consensus. The focus on diligence is manifested in directing corporate governance (supervision) towards stimulating efficiency, competitiveness, and development by relying on recording and auditing business transactions, exercising control, and if necessary, levying penalties. Consensus was strongly emphasized during the Kamakura period, when complex administrative laws were developed. Through consensus, all boards arrive at unanimous decisions, a process that expresses the Japanese predilection for collective responsibility and for collective decision-making. Unanimity continues to be the rule for arriving at decisions as the Japanese became skilled at reaching collective decisions. It may be said that many of the social practices identified with modern Japan have their origins in all the historical eras discussed in this book.

Thus, the past shaped Japan and made it a strong state, forming specific features of the Japanese people, their culture, and corporate governance. Historically conditioned nationalism (starting with the Mongol invasions) was developed extensively and intensively during the *bakufu* rule, strengthening the nation's unity, its readiness for self-improvement, the notion of sacrifice for the good of the country (or community), and the ides of social usefulness. It can therefore be concluded that the most important features of the modern Japanese model of corporate governance have their roots in ancient Japan, especially in the Yamato era and then in Nara, Heian, Kamakura, Muromachi, and Azuchi–Momoyama periods. The following centuries only confirmed or strengthened them.

Index